MARY J. MACLEOD was born in Somerset, educated in Bath and qualified as a state registered nurse in Bristol. Now retired, she worked as a nurse in Bristol, London, Bedfordshire and the Hebrides. She has four children, five grandchildren and five great-grandchildren and lives in Cornwall with her husband and two dogs.

D1152825

More Tales from the Island Nurse

MARY J MacLEOD

Luath Press Limited
EDINBURGH
www.luath.co.uk

First published 2014

ISBN: 978-1-910021-17-0

The paper used in this book is recyclable. It is made from
low chlorine pulps produced in a low energy, low emissions manner
from renewable forests.

Printed and bound by
MBM Print SCS Ltd., Glasgow

Typeset in 10.5 point Sabon
by 3btype.com

*This book is dedicated to Elizabeth
– a dear friend.*

*I thank all those members of my family
and my friends who have encouraged me.
I thank 'Andy' my 'techno wizard' and the people
in the book for just being themselves.*

Contents

Prologue

AGAIN AND AGAIN my thoughts return to that happy time spent among the beauty and peace of the islands of the Hebrides.

I remember the warm, unquestioning welcome of the people; the stoicism with which they met the hardships of lives lived in that remote place and the laughter and banter of the ceilidhs in crowded croft house kitchens on cold winter evenings.

I recall the island's unsophisticated children who delighted in the simple things of life: the sheepdog trials, the arrival and departure of the little island plane, the comings and goings at the steamer pier and a school outing to a castle on an adjacent isle.

I knew old folk who had tales to tell of an earlier era; of a time before radio, electricity, planes and cars. Tales of war and the cruelty of the sea, of family and loyalty and stories with no beginning and no ending.

Papavray – I need to revisit you in my memories, write once more of the splendour of your mountains and seas and enter again into the lives of your gentle people. I want to revel in the remembered smell of peat smoke curling into the frosty air from tiny white chimneys, to feel the soft rain on my face or to hurry through a storm, head down to the cosy shelter of our home among the hills and glens of that beloved isle.

I shall remember and dream again as I look back over the years.

Introduction

IT IS THE EARLY 1970s and the Macleod family have been on Papavray, a small island off the west coast of Scotland, for over two years now. The island is only twenty miles long and five miles wide with the mighty bulk of Ben Criel keeping watch over the little villages, the glens, the harbour and the rugged coast.

We see again the beauty of this little world with its wild weather and glorious sunsets, its tumultuous seas and snowy mountains and we feel the warmth of the close-knit community.

The nurse's duties continue, her husband pursues overseas contracts and the boys grow and enjoy the freedom of this remote location.

Once more, we meet crofters: Archie, Mary and Fergie H; Big Craig, the roadman; Doctor Mac, the island GP; Duncan, the Laird; Elizabeth, the teacher; John, the policeman; Rhuari, our island giant; and Father Peter, who visits again. The nurse's first grandchild is born and her parents come for a holiday, strangers turn up on Papavray and crofters tell spooky tales.

But then, quite suddenly, the nurse's life changes dramatically and the family leaves the island for new adventures in far-off California and Nevada with their sunshine and their different lifestyles. Spiders, speedboats and silver mines now figure among the mountains and lakes, oceans and swimming pools in those far lands.

From old Sarah to wee Murdo, from a cow in a kitchen to MI6, tears and laughter rub shoulders as life continues on Papavray.

I

Down in a Ditch

GEORGE AND I sat looking out of the window at the rain lashing down and dreamed of a holiday in the sun. It was about the sixth weary week of almost persistent rain and we were yearning for the warmth of the Mediterranean or the Canaries, where we had been accustomed to holiday before our great escape to the North. These thoughts only surfaced briefly in midwinter, when the days were short and dark and the nights long and even darker and the storms seemingly unending – as now – and we would experience a sort of 'cabin fever' and long for a holiday.

But then, suddenly, a silver sun would break through Stygian clouds to bathe the sparkling slopes of purple mountains, and touch the sea to create restless pathways of golden water. The wind would drop and we would stand in awe of the sensational and enduring beauty in which we were privileged to live. We would wonder just why we had fancied the six or seven hundred mile journey to Heathrow or Gatwick, a wait of x-number of hours in a crowded, stuffy airport, the cramped and uncomfortable flight with the very real possibility of the loss of our luggage and the press of dozens of angry, pushing, perspiring folk (perhaps also minus luggage) in blistering heat. Why would we do this?

Why? Here, we could wander unhurriedly in the clear air, and watch the shafts of sunlight weave between the peaks of the mountains until a golden day faded into a shining evening. Then pink and orange streaks would appear in a silver-blue sky and soft mist would begin to obscure the hills so that only their tops showed, seeming to float in the heavens. Then we were content, once more, only to leave our hallowed isle for the briefest of times. After all, we had a warm, welcoming home in a superb location with incredible views, in a friendly village on a glorious island! What more could we want?

The boys were happy in the island culture, with outdoor pursuits and the freedom to learn the lessons of life as well as more academic ones. They knew folk of all ages: the differences did not seem important. Nick was now old enough to join the sailing club and was accepted by 'the young lads' *and* the older men. He fitted in wherever he went. But he was not a good scholar: I think, perhaps, he loved the outdoor life and the freedom *too much* and gave little thought to the future. Papavray only had work of the manual kind, and no apprenticeships. School leavers with high grades usually got into college or university but further education did not look as though it would be an option for Nick. But he loved the sea and had met a deep-sea diver who was prepared to take him on at weekends and possibly train him for a job on leaving school. I was alternately horrified and relieved! It was undoubtedly dangerous, but at least he had found a very real interest which might prove useful later – I hoped.

At Andy's age, there were no such worries. He was happy at school, with his friends and with Nick. They still fished and climbed and 'messed about in boats'. In Andy's case, the worries of the wide world were still a long way into the future.

I enjoyed my work as the district nurse. I liked caring for the elderly, tending children, advising mothers, dealing with injuries, illnesses, emergencies and generally being part of the fabric of the island. Consequently, I was welcomed into the homes and lives of the islanders in an affectionate and, perhaps, unique way.

George, the only true Scot among us, was the one who was not entirely content. He was happy to be on his mother-isle, of course, but found the pull of the exciting overseas jobs, that he was called upon to do from time to time, irresistible. Our original intentions had not included such things, but had centred on local or semi-local work and there was plenty of that. But he enjoyed the challenge of the more sophisticated work abroad. And, inevitably, the weather just now was adding to his impatience to get away on the next contract and I, too, was so fed up that I almost envied him.

So here we were, gazing at the rain and dreaming of holidays and sun and exciting jobs – all the things we had left behind!

At that moment, Andy came bursting in from school, bringing us back to reality with a bump.

'Hi Mum, Dad. Murdo is here. He's going to stay for a bit. His dad is working in Coiravaig and he's picking him up later. Can we have something to eat, please? We are starving.'

Having eaten enough for an army, they departed over the croft to play some complicated game involving a lot of rolling about in the wet grass. They did not even seem to notice the rain. A few minutes later, they were back.

'Mum! Mary told us to tell you that Archie said that Murdo's dad is in a ditch in Coiravaig.' Andy paused for breath.

'Slow down, slow down. What has happened?' I was already collecting my first aid box and my nursing bag.

Taking a deep breath, Murdo took over. 'Archie was passing where Dad was working and saw him in the ditch, somewhere on the track to the witches' house. Mary was with Archie. Archie stayed with Dad, but Mary got a lift back and saw us on the croft. His truck is stuck.' As an afterthought, he added, 'He's bleeding.'

I was horrified. How long had he been there? How bad was he?

'Let's go,' said George. 'Everyone into the Land Rover!'

At that moment, Nick appeared from the shore, heard this and said, 'Mum's Mini is behind it.'

'Well. Move it!' I said.

Everyone stopped quite still, looking at me. Nick was only thirteen! Pulling on my wellies, I said, 'For heaven's sake, Nick! I know you have been driving it up and down our track for months.'

As we set out, Murdo said, 'Archie might get his tractor and pull Dad out.'

I was thinking rather more of the bleeding and how severe it might be and wondering how long Murdoch had been there before Archie had discovered him. Amazingly, the rain had stopped but the high wind might hamper any rescue.

There was a horseshoe-shaped marshy area at Coiravaig which was covered by the sea in exceptionally high tides. There were large peaty holes surrounded by spongy grass so the narrow track across it had been built up by about four or five feet. It led to the house that the boys called the 'witches' house' and on up to good grazing on the hill behind it. That was where Murdoch, senior, had been working.

We swung round the last bend in the road and could see the truck lying at a crazy angle, virtually hanging off the edge of the track with the driver's side only just above the marshy ground. It was so far onto its side that we could see the underneath. Archie had climbed up to pull the passenger door open and was leaning in and down to where Murdoch, still sat in the driving seat.

'Hurry!' Archie shouted, 'She's slipping all the time. I can't get him out. He's stuck!'

Murdoch's voice came to us. 'I can't get my foot out; I think it's stuck under the pedal. And my leg's bleedin'.'

'Archie, I must get in to see to the bleeding,' I called as I approached.

'No, no. The movement might make her slide right in.'

George came nearer, 'Not if you, (meaning Archie) Nick and I haul on this side, (indicating the passenger side which was almost vertically above the driver's side). Our combined strength would be enough to stabilise it and Mary J could go round the other side and see to Murdoch.'

George, Archie and Nick grabbed parts of the passenger side of the truck to pull it and to use their weight to counterbalance the slithering vehicle. This seemed to work, and I was able to squelch my way round to the driver's side, in the cold, sucking marsh. Murdoch's door was broken and hanging off. I could just get my head and arms in to the cab.

'Where does it hurt, Murdoch?'

'Foot mainly. Can't get it out.'

'Did you hit your head at all?'

'No. No, I didn't. But there's a lot of blood down here.' He indicated the other leg.

I could see a deep gash which was certainly bleeding heavily but not so much as to be life-threatening, so I turned my attention to the foot.

'Can you feel that?' I asked, pressing his welly.

'Yes.'

'Can you move the foot at all?'

He wiggled his foot, saying, 'Yes, but it's mighty sore.'

'I'm going to bind the cut on that leg and then I'll cut your welly off this one, so that we can get your foot out.' I hoped that I sounded confident: there was no guarantee here.

Calling to Andy to bring the first aid box, I eased myself into the cab.

'Whoa! Whoa! You're shifting her!' George warned. 'Be as quick as you can.'

'Pass me a lump of cotton wool and a bandage and I'll just bind it roughly for now.'

The boys took me at my word and an enormous piece of cotton wool was tossed down in to the cab, followed by a bandage some four inches wide! It would have to do.

'Buck up, Nurse. We can only hold this for so long.' Archie was sounding worried. 'This wind's not helping us any.'

I began to cut away Murdoch's welly around the accelerator pedal. Surgical scissors are hardly meant for thick rubber, but eventually I was able to pull some of it away. With every movement, Murdoch winced in pain.

'Murdoch, I'm going to try to lift the pedal a bit. Now the boot is almost gone, can you try to pull your foot out when I say? It will hurt a lot – but I think it will work.'

'Aye – that I'll do, Nurse.'

The pedal was old and battered and quite loose, so I was able to move it fairly easily, while Murdoch pulled on his lower leg with his hands to help to free the foot. He was a canny countryman and a tough crofter and he would realise the dangers that he and I were in should the men be unable to hold the truck and prevent it from sliding. It would probably topple into the marshy ground trapping us beneath it. So, he pulled and wriggled and finally out came the foot! His sock had gone and we could see that there was a deep wound on the instep.

'He's free!' I shouted. 'Now, we have to get out.' There was no way that he could climb up to the passenger door, so we would both have to slither out of the broken driver's door into the wet, black soggy ground.

'Hurry, hurry you,' shouted Archie. They were pulling and holding with all their strength, but we knew that by struggling to get out we would be shaking the vehicle, causing more strain, and the truck would slither ever nearer the edge of the track.

I grabbed Murdoch's arm and began to heave him out. He was determined to help himself.

'Go you, Nurse – out of the way – round past the bonnet. They'll no' hold her with me jaunterin' about tryin' to get out o' here.'

He was breathless with pain and effort but he seemed more concerned for me.

'Come on.' Ignoring his advice, I caught hold of his jacket and dragged him out of the door. I probably caused him even more pain but the men were grunting and gasping now and I could feel the vehicle shuddering and slipping with every gust of wind.

Then we were out! Murdoch could not put any weight on his foot, but we both half crawled, half waded through the smelly, wet mud.

'Mum! It's going! Quick! Get out of the way past the bonnet. Quick!' Nick shouted frantically.

Archie was peering across the bonnet. 'They are free of it and comin' round the front,' he reported to the rest, who could not see our progress. 'They are out of the way now to the side. We can leave it go now!' And they did!

The old truck reared up and slid gracefully down into the mire with creaks and gurgles as it all but disappeared, only the underside of the engine remaining visible.

Everyone helped Murdoch and me up onto the track. We were completely covered in disgusting, green and brown, slimy, smelly, peaty mud and shivering with cold. Shows of emotion were not in the male crofting culture, but Murdoch gripped my hand briefly.

I swilled my filthy hands in a puddle and inspected the foot. The remains of the boot had long gone. An angry bruise was developing and the whole foot was swelling as we watched. The grazes that *we* had probably caused trying to release him were not as deep as I had feared, and he could wag his toes and his ankle. It seemed unlikely that he – or perhaps *we* – had broken any bones.

'We need to get him to the hospital to get this stitched soon and to have his foot X-rayed.' I looked around. Everyone was rubbing screaming muscles and stretching aching backs. There would be some stiff people tomorrow!

Murdo went over to his father, 'You alright, Dad? I'll milk the cow tonight for you. Andy will help.'

Andy looked a little startled at this. Milking was not high on his list of achievements.

Murdoch, senior, grinned, 'Thanks, lads. So I can retire now, can I?'

George and Archie made a 'fireman's chair' and carried him to the Land Rover, Andy and Murdo holding a leg each.

'Nick, sit beside him and maintain pressure on the leg. My dressing does not seem to be doing the job.'

Suddenly, Nick and I looked at each other and grinned. 'What does this remind you of, Mum?'

'That plane crash last year!'

On that occasion, too, Nick had been told to 'maintain pressure on the wound'.

'Thank goodness, there are lots of us around – I remember it being a pretty lonely and worrying time, then,' I said, thinking of the unconscious pilot, the twisted aircraft, the darkness and the feeling of helplessness. No – this was nothing like that awful day.

I climbed into the rear of the vehicle as I was so dirty. Murdoch must have been in pain, but he still managed to joke with the boys, telling them that the hospital staff would hose him down outside before they would let him in, because of the smell of the disgusting, slimy mess that covered him. Being in the same state, I let the others take him in: I felt that one person with half a marsh was enough for any hospital.

Murdoch recovered quickly. There were no bones broken, but he needed eight stitches in his leg. He was back at the site four days later with his tractor, as were Archie and Fergie with theirs. It took the combined efforts of all three to release the truck from the suction of the marshy ground. Murdoch maintained that the engine started at the first pull but we all felt that this was another of his jokes!

The patient seemed to recover rather better than the nurse and the helpers on this occasion. George, Archie and Nick were stiff for a week. I just seemed to be sore everywhere.

Oh! And the cow did get milked that night – but not by Andy!

2

Grey Shadows

THE CROFT HOUSE was not particularly remote, but the little row of fishermen's cottages built in front of it and facing the harbour obscured it from the road: one could go to and from the cottages themselves without noticing the old place – it was so tucked away. But from the tiny back gardens of the cottages, the near derelict building could just be seen beyond the scrubby, overgrown bushes that surrounded it. Arthur and Aggie MacGilvery's cottage was the nearest and they had the best view of the ramshackle place.

I was calling twice daily to clean and dress a deep hole in Arthur's foot caused by his garden fork. He had refused a tetanus immunisation in spite of considerable pressure from Doctor Mac.

'I've stabbed myself often enough in my eighty years and I've never had any bother. I'm no' havin' this tetynus now!'

He had been lucky, but the lengthy healing process needed constant monitoring as he insisted on earthing up his tatties wearing only his slippers (pulling boots on was too painful), so the dressings were often full of soil by the time I arrived to change them.

'Is it no right yet, Nurse?' asked Aggie.

'Not yet, Aggie. If this stubborn old husband of yours would just rest, it would heal much faster.'

'Ach. The bodach! He's that cantankerous!'

Arthur bridled. 'Well, I've been stopping and sitting on the wall to rest sometimes. But, you know, Nurse, I've been seein' some weird goings-on at yon house.' Nodding his head, he indicated the old croft house behind his garden.

'Who lives there?' I asked.

'Ach, 'tis in such a state that no-one comes now but it's supposed to be for holidays. This funny body from down in England used to come.'

'Ach, you're haverin'.' Aggie seemed uncomfortable and was trying to stop Arthur's tale. This was odd, as all islanders love a bit of gossip.

'I'm tellin' you,' resumed Arthur, taking no notice. 'There is something goin' on!'

'What sort of something? And, would you please stay still so that I can dress this foot?'

On this occasion, I got no further as there was no more talk of unusual things. Presumably, Aggie had persuaded him to be quiet by a wink or a nod.

But the next morning, when I arrived, Arthur was sitting on the garden wall in the sunshine, staring at the old croft house.

'See, Nurse. I told you!'

I looked where he indicated, but could see nothing unusual – just the bleak-looking old house with the sheep-nibbled grass growing right up to the door, which was almost obscured by a solitary rocky outcrop.

'I can't see anything, Arthur.'

'Wait you – there!' Arthur pointed.

I looked again and gradually I seemed to be able to pick out a grey figure standing in front of the rocky outcrop. Had she (he?) been there all the time? He or she was the same colour as the granite and the area was in a deep shadow, so perhaps I had just not seen him or her at first.

'Who is that?' I asked.

'Who indeed?' replied Arthur in sepulchral tones. 'No-one that *you* have ever seen.'

I glanced at him. He shrugged.

I looked back at the figure. He or she had gone!

'Where has she gone? Into the house?'

'Doubt it.' He shook his head.

'So where…?' I began.

'Where indeed?' This was all that Arthur would say.

I sensed something unnatural – one might say *super*natural – about the incident, but perhaps it was just a trick of the light. Maybe there had not been a figure at all. There was a deep shadow by the rock and I had only glanced for an instant.

Arthur and Aggie seemed to be disturbed and had obviously been aware of something odd for some time but, as I tended the grubby foot, they seemed to put the whole thing out of their minds and I was pressed to have the usual cuppie and dumpling. We talked about the weather, the price of sheep at the last sale and all the usual things.

'You are getting fey,' scoffed George, when I told the family about it all. 'You have been with these crofters too long.'

When I went to do the next dressing, it was as though the whole subject was now taboo. Nothing was said at all! So, apart from the usual discussion about the weather and the price of sheep and so on, we were silent. But Arthur and Aggie were not their usual selves. They were staunch Free Kirkers, and anything smacking of the unnatural or psychic was severely frowned on by that denomination. Had the minister been to see them, I wondered? They would not have dared to *tell* him of the weird things but they might be feeling guilty or confused. Perhaps because of their simple lifestyle, crofters seemed to have some sort of connection with an extra dimension not experienced by the average person, so the stern doctrines of the Free Kirk must be difficult to reconcile with their intuitive acceptance of the unexplainable. So, apart from the inevitable discussion about the weather and the price of sheep (again), nothing was said.

Then I discovered that the infection in Arthur's foot had worsened in spite of all my efforts. His temperature was up and there was an angry red line travelling up his leg.

He looked flushed.

'Have you been taking the antibiotics?'

'No, Nurse, he hasnae,' burst out an exasperated Aggie. 'I told you, Arthur, that it would go bad ways.'

'Why, Arthur, why? It could have been healed up by now.' Oh, these people, I thought. So stubborn, so aggravating and yet so likeable and so genuine.

'Ach. All these pills and potions! 'Tis not natural.' Arthur was not convinced even now.

I glanced at my watch. 'I'll take you to see Doctor Mac now, Arthur. He needs to see this. His morning surgery will not be finished yet.'

It was not far to the surgery but I knew that if I left them to organise a lift with a neighbour, it would never get done.

Arthur was bundled into his coat by an anxious Aggie and hopped to the car. I helped him into the seat and as I went round to the driver's side, Aggie touched my arm and, nodding towards the weird old cottage, whispered, 'Don't let him get worked up about yon, Nurse. 'Tis not in the Lord's plan, you know.'

But Arthur was not easily put off and brought the subject up right away. 'Aggie worries that it's no right. The Kirk will no like it at all. But we can't help what we are seein', can we, Nurse?'

'What *have* we seen, Arthur?' I wondered.

'Ach, 'Tis the old biddy as owns the house. She was that fond of the place at one time. I'll get Ally [his son] to ring them down in England there and find out. But I know why she's here – aye, I reckon I know why!' He paused (for dramatic effect?). 'She's gone, you know, Nurse. That's what it is. She's gone.'

'Gone?'

'Aye. Gone. Passed on. Passed over. Gone!'

'Oh.'

'I'm thinkin' 'tis her: come back.'

'Come back?'

'Aye.'

'You mean as a... a...?'

'Aye – as one of them. The minister would no like to hear me sayin' that, but I can't help what I am seeing.' He glanced at me. 'You don't believe a word of it, do you, Nurse?'

'Well...' I floundered a bit. 'We don't actually know that the old lady has died, do we? But I have had one or two odd experiences since I have been here on Papavray, so I'm not dead against it all. But I'm just not sure and I find it difficult.'

Having lived on the island for over two years now, I was not only getting used to the crofter's beliefs in such things, but I felt myself becoming more open to possibilities that I would have rejected out of hand when I was living in the more sophisticated South. Scepticism and sophistication seem to go hand-in-hand but now, living 'closer to the soil', I felt the freedom to consider the possibilities and, perhaps, the humility to realise that we do not know everything yet. Not by a long way!

'Aye. Aggie gets feart. She's too churchified, y'see.'

We were at the surgery by now. Doctor Mac was concerned and, after severely reprimanding Arthur for gardening in that state, he prescribed antibiotics by injection twice daily, in addition to the antiseptic dressings. He insisted that Arthur must rest the foot. Privately, I thought I knew *where* he would rest it – on the garden wall, watching the old croft house. It was also pretty clear that I would be visiting these two quite a lot, so I braced myself for more about the 'old biddy'.

The following day, Ally popped in to say that, sure enough, the old lady had died just over a week ago.

'Told you, didn't I, Nurse?' claimed Arthur in triumph.

But Aggie was frightened. She couldn't eat and wasn't sleeping well.

'I wish the silly old bodach would stay inside. It's doing no good to keep staring at that place, watchin' for her. It will all stop in a whiley – when she's laid to rest.'

'How can you be so certain, Aggie?' I asked, intrigued.

''Tis obvious, Nurse. She's betwixt and between just now. When the minister – whoever they have in England – has asked for peace for her blessed soul; then she'll be at rest.' She sighed. 'But that will no be too soon as her sons are both in Canada and have to get all the way back for the funeral.'

'Why do you think she is hanging around *here* instead of her home in England?' I asked.

Arthur spoke up. 'I'm thinkin' there's something in there that she wants. She keeps going to the door – maybe through it, I can't see – but there's something in there. Aye.'

He had a faraway look in his eyes which I regarded with suspicion. He was planning something!

'What are you up to, Arthur?' I asked as I pumped antibiotics into his thigh.

'Ouch! I felt that…' He looked at me. 'I know, Nurse – if I had taken the pills, I wouldn't need the jabs…'

I smiled at his pretended discomfort. He was a tough old seaman: it would take more than a needle to upset him.

'What *are* you up to?' I repeated.

'Well, it's like this – Aggie knows this too.' Aggie nodded. 'She, old Martha, lived there with her parents when she was a wee girl. I knew her when we were young. She grew into a bonny lass indeed, but she took up with a tinker. Her parents didna like that. He moved on and she went off to the mainland for work. Well, that's what we were told, but the truth came out eventually: she left to have a bairn.'

Aggie nodded sadly. 'The wee soul was put out for adoption and we didn't see aught of Martha for years as her parents would have nothing to do with her. When they passed on, she came sometimes with her husband and her two sons. We had a talk one day and she told me that her husband was a hard, cruel man and she hadn't dared to tell him about the bairn that she had had. She said that she had traced her wee daughter, 'Trudy' – about thirty by then – and she was disabled and almost destitute. She used to save some of her housekeeping money secretly, to send to her, but no-one knew about her – not the husband or the sons.'

'We might be about the only ones still alive who remember all about it,' Arthur took over. 'I wonder if she's no at peace because she wants her sons to know about the wee girl. They are two good lads who know only too well what their old father is like. If they knew that they had a half-sister and that the girl needed money or care or something, they could see that she got it. And they would, I'm sure. So, *I* think there is a letter in there – maybe a solicitor's or a will – and she wants it.' He slapped his thigh to emphasise his point.

'That is a lot of supposition. Guess work really, Arthur. And how is she to get it? I don't think ghosts or… um… whatever can change things – like picking a letter up and posting it…' I was getting into ridiculous realms here.

'Ha, that's where I come in…'

'No, Arthur. You canna go breaking in.' Aggie was nearly in tears.

'Breaking in? I'm not needin' to, there's plenty gaps in the walls and windows.' He paused and gave a theatrical sigh. 'But with this foot…' He was staring at me. I couldn't believe this!

'No, Arthur. No, no, no. I can't go breaking and entering.'

'No breaking; just entering, Nurse. T'would be doin' the right thing for the poor lass. Aye, the poor wee soul that she is. And we'd be free of old Martha.'

I refused. I protested. We drank tea and I protested some more.

I was still protesting as I pulled on one of Arthur's old boiler suits over my uniform and began to push my way through the bushes towards the old house. The house that I was definitely *not* going to enter. Ha!

Arthur was right: there were plenty of gaps; the place was far from secure. I was able to wriggle through with ease, still wondering how on earth I had let myself be persuaded into this crazy stunt.

Inside, it was gloomy: the tiny windows shed very little light but my eyes gradually adjusted and I was able to see what had been a surprisingly comfortable room with some good quality furniture, pretty china and various ornaments, all now covered in layers of dust and mouse droppings. I looked around, trying to imagine where 'the old biddy' might have hidden a letter or a will. I discounted the roll top desk as being too obvious a place. (After all, her husband had visited occasionally.) The usual ladder-like staircase led up to the only bedroom and the toilet was in a 'wee hoosie' outside. Where to begin?

I searched in kitchen drawers, under the bed, behind cushions on the old settee, inside the jugs on the mantelpiece, behind and in the bookcase – no books – just a lot of rubber bands, old shopping lists and some coppers, saved for a long forgotten purpose, no doubt. But no letter.

I was on my knees, peering beneath a chest of drawers, when I felt that I was being watched. I looked guiltily towards the window, thinking that I had been observed entering the house. There was no-one there! But I felt a 'presence' of some sort. I was not convinced by Arthur's theories, but I was not entirely sceptical either and I had not relished being a part of this spooky adventure. There *was* something there. The net curtain was moving, perhaps in the draught from the door? But as I looked, I realised that there was no curtain there at all – just a grey shadow that I could actually see through.

There was no sound either (except my heart, hammering on my ribs), but the shadow, almost formless, seemed to move across the room and gradually evaporate as it reached the dresser with all its cups and plates still waiting for the diners who would never use them.

What had I seen? Perhaps the changing light as the sun went in? Maybe the swaying of the bushes outside the window? I don't know, even now, if I saw anything at all. But, suddenly, I wanted to get out of that house. I was mad to have come in the first place!

I turned to go, but my eye fell on a sewing box on the bottom shelf of the dresser. A memory flitted through my mind. Biddy! Chreileh! Her mother had hidden a letter in a sewing box, knowing that men are unlikely to use a sewing box. Perhaps…? Just perhaps 'the old biddy' had done the same so that her husband would not find it.

I scrabbled among the buttons, pins, needles and bits of ribbon. Nothing! Then something in the chintz lining crackled. I ripped the stitching away. There was a chunky letter. It was too dark to read anything but it looked official. I stuffed it in my pocket and went!

Back in the cottage, Arthur was ecstatic (if a little smug) as he and Aggie peered at the envelope. It had been opened and resealed and was obviously a document of some sort.

'Should we read it, Nurse, do you think?'

'After all this effort, I think you should. To be sure that it is what you imagine it to be.'

I was struggling out of the boiler suit. 'Then you could get Ally to ring the sons in Canada and hope that they will help the girl. That way the husband won't know anything until it is too late… hopefully.'

It was all getting too complicated for me – I had done my part. I needed to get on with my interrupted visits.

I left them to pore over the legal jargon, mull things over and tell Ally, who lost no time in phoning the 'old biddy's sons'. I hoped that a wrong would be righted. I like happy endings.

And, of course, when I went to visit the next day, Arthur couldn't wait to tell me that the grey figure by the rock had gone. I didn't tell them about the shadow I had seen in the old house. That was just between me and... what?

3

Clannan Beg

THE ROAD (scarcely more than a track but roughly tarmacked) leading out of our tiny village of Dhubaig, followed the coast for a mile or two and then started the steep climb up to Loch Annan and Ben Criel. Over thousands of years the waters flowing out of Loch Annan had carved a deep gorge in the granite rocks. The road now perched on one side of this gorge with the hillside rising above, while on the other side a deep dark chasm dropped to the waters of the burn many feet below. Gnarled and stunted trees grew in this ravine. Others waved their heads above the road to give dappled shade in the sunshine of a summer day or to rattle weirdly in the wind when covered with icicles in winter. Because of the tumbling burn, the air in the deep glen was always damp so that the trees and the rocks which rose up on all sides were blanketed with mosses and lichens.

Altogether, it was a steep, beautiful, rather eerie place, dangerous in winter and gentle in summer.

This stretch of the road figured highly in Dhubaig's life as it had to be traversed before tackling the far more challenging Loch Annan hill and the slopes of Ben Criel in order to get to 'the other side': Dalhavaig, Cill Donnan, the school, the hospital and so on.

When we first arrived on Papavray, I thought of Clachan Beg as just one more hill among so many, but, gradually, I became aware of a sort of hush in the voices of the crofters when talking of this particular hill. It seemed that it had a story to tell but no-one wished to tell it. Many things had happened on that hill and only some could be explained.

Two or three hundred years ago, when this road had been nothing more than a track negotiable only by pony or on foot, a traveller came across the hills to Dhubaig. He was an itinerant preacher determined to save a few Hebridean souls.

The man was welcomed and invited to stay with one of the crofters. He was fed and listened to with politeness as he preached fire and brimstone – exhorting them all to penitence. After a day or two, he went round the croft houses asking for donations so that he could go to 'darkest Africa' and preach to the 'heathen natives'. The people had very little – not enough for themselves – but they gave what they could.

However, one of the crofters became suspicious of the preacher and, while he was asleep, rifled the sack which he carried everywhere with him. In it he found gold coins such as he had never seen before, some jewellery and hundreds of coppers which the man must have collected from other villages such as Dhubaig.

The crofter told five of the men. They came back to the house to challenge the preacher but he had gone; he must have heard them talking. They went after him and caught him up in Clannan Beg. They attacked him with sticks so that he dropped the bag and ran. In their estimation, justice had been done; they had retrieved more than they had lost. But one hot-headed crofter pursued the man, struck him with a stone and killed him. The others – decent men – were horrified, but clan or family loyalty persuaded them to cover up the whole incident by burying the body and the jewellery. They would keep the dark deeds a secret.

But after that night, whenever the six walked in Clannan Beg, they heard footsteps behind them, getting closer and closer, but when they turned round there was never anyone there. They became scared – demented – and began to scream and babble so that the whole village soon knew their terrible secret.

The six decided to secretly exhume the body and burn it, hoping that this might destroy the ghost. So the grisly remains were dug up, but they were found to be so decomposed and wet that nothing would burn so they were reburied. The phantom footsteps continued. So they took the remaining money to a high cliff and threw it into the sea. This too failed, as the unremitting tide kept returning coins to the shore and the ghostly footsteps continued.

When Archie told me this tale (not at a ceilidh in the usual way, but privately) he said that, as many of the present villagers were descended from these six men, no-one admitted to hearing the footsteps. But they *were* still heard sometimes, he assured me. Did Archie hear them? If not, how did he know that it still happened? I didn't ask.

Oddly, a year or so after Archie's story, I found an old coin on the shore. I said nothing. I did not want to open that particular 'can of worms' again. The coin is still in a drawer in the house somewhere.

I'm fairly sure that George cannot possibly be descended from any of those doubtful characters but even so Clannan Beg has not been very kind to the Macleod family. This was the hill where I had a burst tyre and a broken steering column when on duty one day but our problems in Clannan Beg started long before that – just a few weeks after arriving on Papavray.

Andy had started at the little primary school situated near the hospital at Rachadal. The four children from Dhubaig were driven the ten miles or so in the 'school car', Mungo's ancient estate car (the crofters still called such vehicles 'shooting brakes'). Sometimes a crofter would beg a lift so all the children had to be packed onto the back seat – there were no seat belts then. A bit of pushing and shoving went on but at least they were warm. Mungo's heater had never been known to work or, said some, he did not know how to turn it on!

One winter day, the snow had begun to fall as Mungo picked the children up from the school. It was quite deep and slippery by the time he started to descend Clannan Beg. All the children were in the back as Jacko had claimed a lift.

Suddenly, on a steep bend, the car slid sideways, hit the rocks bordering the road and turned onto its side. Another foot or so and it would have hurtled down into the burn.

The first I knew of all this, having only just returned from a local call, was when Andy came in, blue with cold and shaking uncontrollably. His feet, clad in ordinary shoes, were so cold and wet that he could scarcely do more than shuffle. Lots of rubbing with warm towels, some dry clothes, hot cocoa and a seat beside the Rayburn restored him and he was able to tell me the whole story.

'I was on the bottom of the pile, Mum. We were all squashed in the back and wee Murdo-John was on my lap. We were playing 'I Spy' but it was boring because we couldn't really spy anything; the windows were all steamed up.'

'How did it happen?' I asked, still rubbing his feet.

'The car skidded on the ice or the snow and Mungo said some bad words… Mum, what does "bugger" mean?'

I ducked that one. 'Please, just *tell* me what happened.'

'Mungo waggled the steering wheel but the car just kept on sliding. Then there was a big bump and a bang. Wee Murdo-John fell off my lap and the car turned onto its side and still went on sliding. Then there was another bump and Mungo said that we'd hit the rocks. Then the car stopped, but I was on that side and everybody landed on top of me. I couldn't breathe properly because Roddie was on my face so I pushed him off and then I could breathe, but I was squashed against the door and the handle was sticking in my back and it hurt.'

For the first time since arriving home, Andy began to cry.

He sniffed and continued, 'I was on the bottom of the pile, under all the others. Jacko got us all up and out, but we had to wait in the snow for Mungo. He was stuck behind the steering wheel and there were a lot more bad words, but he got out and we all walked home in the snow. It was *so* cold, Mum. Mum, what *does* "bugger" mean, 'cos Mungo said it again?'

I just was not in the right frame of mind to go into explanations or anatomical definitions – I would need notice and a rather less stressed atmosphere to do that one justice!

'I think a hot bath might be better than all this chat,' I said. Cowardly? Maybe.

Later, I heard the story again from Jacko. It seemed that all the children, some bigger than Andy, had been thrown to one side and Andy was, indeed, 'on the bottom of the pile' of children. He was very lucky not to have any broken bones but he was very sore and bruised from the weight of so many sturdy youngsters pressing him against the door handle. I thanked Jacko for what he had done in getting them all out and bringing them home.

'Aye. Mungo and me, we felt like the Pied Piper of Hambelline,' said Jacko.

Clannan Beg was particularly difficult to negotiate in early morning icy conditions. On such days, no-one wanted to have to follow old Dougall (he was a notoriously bad driver) up the two bad stretches of road; the Clannan Beg hill and even worse – Loch Annan hill. Usually, I got away before him as everyone tried to do, but one day I was late.

On this incredibly beautiful but searingly icy morning, I slewed and slid towards Clannan Beg, getting ready to engage second gear and give the accelerator plenty of punch, the only tried, tested and usually successful way to keep the wheels turning and the car moving forwards and upwards. My heart sank as I saw the back of 'Daft Dougall's' car ahead of me, making its ponderous way towards the dreaded hill.

I had just begun the ascent, hoping forlornly that *he* might make the top and so leave me the chance to do the same when, to my horror, I realised that, not only had he stopped going forwards, he was actually sliding *backwards* down the hill towards me. There was nowhere to go, nowhere to pass or pull over: the ground rose on the right straight from the edge of the narrow road while on the left was the deep, gaping, rock-filled chasm. With no time to think, I gently pressed my brake and stopped just before his car hit me. I kept my foot down hard on the pedal and my brakes held us both, to a degree, so that we slid about on the road rather than one or other or both plunging into the burn far below. We gradually came to a stop. Silently thanking the Good Lord for both of us, I was amazed when Dougall exploded from his car and stalked towards me, clearly very angry.

'Could you not have got out of my way, Nurse? Or backed down the hill to let me by at yon passing place?'

I couldn't believe my ears.

'Dougall! My brakes saved us *both* from going over the edge. You are lucky that I *couldn't* back down the hill. As if I had time anyway, with you sliding back into me!'

'What about my car? I'll not get going again. What are you going to do about that?' he ranted on.

'Me? My car is damaged at the front and so likely to be more serious than yours. Anyway, Dougall, neither of us is likely to get going. We shall just have to wait for someone to come with a tractor.' I knew that Archie patrolled the road on such days making sure that folk got 'off' in the mornings and earning himself a little pocket money towing them out of trouble if they were stuck.

'Well, I'll no be payin' for that! That's your job, Nurse.'

'Dougall, I think we had better leave all this to our insurance companies. I don't think you quite understand.' I fetched my insurance company's address from the car and handed it to him. He looked puzzled.

'I havenae one of these to me.'

'I'll call round this evening and get it from you then.' But I was already guessing that he was uninsured.

'Oh. Aye. Och, 'twas not my fault.' He drew himself up. 'I'm not feeling like acceptin' responsibility for this, Nurse. So I'll want you to pay for my damage.'

I stared at him. Was he living on another planet? He obviously had no idea about the procedures to be followed after an accident.

Luckily, at that moment, I heard the unmistakable sound of Archie's tractor. With the usual puff of black smoke, he rumbled to a slightly uncertain halt.

Taking in the situation, he said, 'Ha. I see that Dougall has been drivin' backwards again. Do you not think you'd get there faster, Dougall, if you tried forward gear.'

Dougall scowled, ''Tis Nurse's fault. She should a' got out my way.'

'Ho,' said Archie, 'it's that one again is it? Doesn't want to give his insurance number, Nurse, is that right?'

'Well, yes, Archie. He doesn't seem to understand…'

'Oh, he understands alright. He isn't insured at all. He is hopin' you'll just get fed up and pay up.'

'No, Archie, I won't. If he had not been so rude and aggressive, I might have done, but now I'll have to get the police…'

'No. No. There's no need, Nurse. I'll pay *my* part.' Dougall was suddenly full of co-operation.

'You'll pay *all* of it – yours *and* Nurses, ye daft bodach.' Archie was grinning. 'I'll make sure he pays. He doesna want the police – what with no insurance y'understand.'

'He doesn't seem to realise that if my brakes had not held, we could both be down there,' I said, pointing down into the abyss.

'Aye. He's hopeless. Shouldna be on the road.'

But next winter, he was still on the road – and off it – and we still had to try to get away from the village before he did.

A few nights later we braved the wind and rain, which had replaced the snow, to struggle over the croft to Archie and Mary's house to a ceilidh, where the chatter and singing was going full swing.

'Where's Roderick? He said he'd be here,' wondered Archie.

'Ach, he has a sick beast. He's doubtless in the byre with her.' Callum-the-hill lived near Roderick.

We waited, chatting, for a while then Murdo began to grin. 'Do you mind one time when he'd no turned up at a ceilidh. He'd been struck by lightning?'

George and I pricked up our ears. We felt a story coming on.

'What happened?' I asked.

''Twas a long time ago – maybe thirty year or so. Roderick used to sell much more stuff in his wee shop back then includin' meat. He'd walk for miles, deliverin'. Very few had cars then, y'see. Well, he was on his way up Clannan Beg to old Mrs Mactickle…'

I interrupted, '"MacTickle"?' I've never heard that name before.'

'Ach, no. Y'wont. The old soul had something wrong with her mouth and she couldna say "MacDougall". It came out "MacTickle" so we always called her that.'

'Aye,' said Fergie. 'But I don't think old Mr MacDougall did much ticklin'. She was a sour old besom, to be sure.'

'Fergie!' Mary pretended to be shocked.

Murdo continued. 'She lived up in Clannan Beg…' He noticed our puzzled looks. There were no houses in or near the Clannan Beg now.

'Aye.' He shook his head. ''Tis not there now. 'Twas washed away during the big flood in '60. But she'd been dead a long time by then.'

'Good thing, too. She'd have died in the flood anyway.' Archie sounded lugubrious.

Poor Murdo must have wondered if he would ever get to tell his story. He had a slurp of tea and started again.

'Well, he was on his way up there when there was an almighty storm. Came from nowhere. Thunder, lightnin' and hailstones. He'd have been about under all those old trees by then.

Well, when it got to seven o'clock, old Mary, Roderick's mother, began to worry. Then when eight and nine came and still no Roderick, some of us men set off on tractors to see would we find him. The storm and the lightning was something terrible. We were just gettin' to yon hill, when we saw him comin' towards us. He was walkin' like a drunken man but we knew fine that Roderick never took a dram. We called him to climb up to take him home but he didna seem to hear us and when we looked at him, we could see that he still had the meat.

'What are y' comin back for? Ye havena taken the old caillach the meat yet.' He said nothing and just stood starin' ahead and his eyes looked funny.

'Well, we took the meat to old Tickle, but when we handed it to her, she screamed and yelled that it was all muddy and soggy and she'd not have that and she'd no pay for it and so on. Ach! The woman!

'We left and took the meat. It did look a bit muddy but it was dark, y'understand. We took Roderick to his house and when his mother saw the meat, she screeched, sayin' that it was cooked and burnt and who had done that? We looked and sure enough, it was all charred up. So we looked at Roderick's hands and they were all red and sore. Then we could see that his coat was burnt in front. His hair, too, was standing on end and he was still starin' at nothing. He'd been struck by lightning, alright!

'Next day, we took him to the doctor. *He* said that the lightning had struck the meat and not Roderick and that he was very lucky because the lightning had cooked the *meat,* not Roderick. Imagine that! Just a split second of lightning cooked that meat!'

'Was Roderick alright?' I asked.

'Aye. It took a day or two for his hands to heal and he was a bit dazed for a whiley, but he was soon as right as rain.'

Just then Roderick himself pushed open the door and stood looking round. We were all staring at him.

'You've no bin struck by lightning this time, then?' said Archie, grinning.

'Ah. That's what it is then. Which time were you telling them?'

I was puzzled. 'Was there more than one time then?' I asked.

'Oh, aye,' said Roderick, as though being struck *more than once* by lightning was the most normal thing in the world.

'Only about a month after the first time, I was gettin' the cow in across the croft in another awful storm. I just remember lookin' round at the cow and she was lyin' on the ground, not moving; and the rope round her neck was smokin' and I could smell the smell of meat cookin'. She was dead. Aye, 'twas a blow, indeed. She was a good milker.'

Roderick seemed more concerned at the loss of the milk cow than the danger that he had been in.

'What about you, Roderick? Were you alright?'

'Oh, aye. The rope had burnt ma hand, but that's all. Oh, and ma coat sleeve was all burnt, too. Aye. Two coats burnt in the one month.' He shook his head. '*And* the cow.' He brightened, 'But we used the carcass.'

'How do you mean?' asked young Janet.

'We chopped her up and everyone had a bit.'

'Ugh,' said Janet.

Archie laughed. 'Who had the bit that was already cooked – the neck?'

Roderick grinned. 'I did. Ma Mother said it tasted grand.'

Everyone laughed, tea and dumpling were passed around and Janet was asked to play her bagpipes. To these folk, lightning striking the same person twice within a month was just part of life – and a good story for the ceilidhs.

I was thinking how such an incident would have been dealt with in the towns and cities of the South. The papers would have had a field day with scientists, meteorologists, statisticians, storm-chasers and fanatics all clamouring for print space. Roderick would have been subjected to medical tests and long term monitoring, his coats examined and calculations made about the amount of heat, while erudite professors reported their conclusions in the *Lancet*. And so on.

What was it on Papavray? Just a story for the ceilidhs!

4

A Cow in the Kitchen

BUMP! BANG! Shake! Bang! The house was shaking: the dogs exploded into hysterical barking.

It was early in the morning. I *had* been asleep.

I jumped up, totally disorientated. Something was shaking the house.

Dragging on a dressing gown, I rushed onto the landing. Nick was there before me and was just about to run down the stairs, when there was a terrific crash and broken glass cascaded into the kitchen.

'Wow!' Nick stood stock still.

'Shoes!' I shouted.

'What?'

'Get some shoes on!'

Flinging on whatever came to hand and telling a sleepy Andy to stay back, Nick and I started down the stairs just as there were more thumps and bumps.

Then, to our utter amazement, a large, brown, bovine head appeared through the broken door and two black eyes gazed at us. Dollach! Mary's spoilt and pampered house cow, who must have, somehow, broken into the utility room through the back door and now wanted to complete her journey into the kitchen.

'Oh boy,' gasped Nick. 'What now, Mum? She'll cut herself to ribbons if she tries to come on through that hole.'

Between the kitchen and the utility room, we had a completely glazed door in order to let in more light. Dollach had barged into the glass, making a large hole, but there were many lethal shards of glass sticking out round the edge. She was now standing in the utility room, eyeing the kitchen as though about to continue her adventure.

'We'll have to try to push her backwards. Mind the glass, Nick.'

Together we approached the cow, who gazed at us as though to say, 'Okay, So this is what *your* byre looks like.'

With one each side and pushing her head and slapping and pushing her shoulders, we shoved her until we were breathless.

She would not move. She just stood there staring ahead, not to be thwarted.

'You stupid, stubborn old cow...'

I knew that the dogs would move her, but they would rip their feet on the glass so I had kept them back.

'We'll just have to persevere, I think.'

We did. Push, push, slap, slap.

Finally, she began to move, but once going, she did not stop and crashed bottom first into the washing machine. But the back door was at the side so we had to try to turn her round.

'Not enough room,' said Nick. 'She will have to go out bum first.'

So now we had to steer the back end of her towards the back door, through which we hoped to push her, while preventing the front end from demolishing the broom cupboard. I reflected that cows were *very* big creatures.

'How did she manage to get in? Her bottom doesn't look as though it will go through that doorway.'

Although we had her straight onto the door, it did not seem that we were going to be able to push her enormous rear through it.

'But she got in...' Nick frowned.

I had a sudden, hysterical urge to laugh.

'Well, it's like babies. You can get them out but you'd not get them in again.'

Nick looked at me in a slightly worried way.

'It's okay, Nick. I haven't lost it altogether.'

'If the door frame wasn't there, we might...' he muttered.

'I suppose we'll have to get the entire frame out,' I said with a resigned sigh. 'Archie... or Roddy?'

Nick thought for a moment. 'I can do it with a sledge hammer.'

Thinking of my poor house and Nick's inexperience with sledge hammers, I hesitated.

'Mum?'

'Alright, but don't knock the entire house down.'

I received a pained look from Nick, but then we both realised that one of us would have to keep the cow where she was while the other went for the hammer.

'Wheisht you!' came a well-known voice.

I was never so glad to hear Archie's Celtic tones as he appeared on the other side of the shattered back door.

The trouble was that Dollach heard it too and, associating it with milking time, started to thresh about, knocking two coat hangers and an anorak off the wall.

'Whoa! Whoa! Aye. We have a wee problem here, I'm thinking.'

Archie scratched his head: he was pondering. I became aware that I was in a fluffy dressing gown, but decided that this was no time for modesty. Nick looked expectantly at Archie, who seemed still to be pondering. Then he eased past Dollach, stepped over the glass and stood looking at the broken glass door. Then he calmly walked across the living room to the porch door and stood looking at it.

'Ha,' said he. 'It won't work.'

Suddenly realising what he had been contemplating, I was horrified and *more* than glad that 'it' *wouldn't* work. He had been thinking of taking that wretched cow through the kitchen, through the living room and into the porch, if only those doorways had been wider!

I was speechless. I think he guessed my thoughts.

'I'll be having to take the back door frame out then, just now.'

Nick looked at me.

'Yes,' I said. 'We thought of that.'

'Or I can get Fergie and we'll see if we can squeeze her together a wee bit. She came in so she should be able to go out.'

Nick looked at me again. He was afraid I was going to start on about 'not getting babies in again' and rightly guessed that Archie would not understand the doubtful humour.

A small voice from the stairs suggested, 'Pull her tail.'

'Aye, indeed, and we could do that too. I'll be away for Fergie, I'm thinking.'

Archie could feel the tension in the atmosphere. He was always so helpful that I was usually prepared to forgive any mischief that his animals got up to but to think of taking a cow through a living room... well.

But our troubles were not over. Just then the call of nature overcame her and Nick had to jump back as a stream of dung was aimed at the deep freeze (blessedly, tightly shut).

Nick appeared to know a few words that were decidedly suspect but in the circumstances, I let it pass. One of them however was most apt!

So we stood one at the head and one again at the tail of a cow in a utility room with one broken back door on one side, a shattered glass door on the other, a dented washing machine, a broken wall mirror, coat hooks on the floor and a huge, smelly puddle of cow manure with Andy's anorak floating in it!

Could things get any worse? Yes, they could!

Dollach suddenly became bored and threw her head up with force, burying one horn so deeply into the plaster on the wall that, as she panicked and tried to free herself, a section of plasterboard about three feet in diameter came away, pinioned on the horn. This frightened her so much that she started to fling her head around in a panic.

'Leave her, Nick. Get back. You are going to get hurt.'

Nick leaped into the doorway of the little shower room, while I retreated behind the remains of the glass door.

'She's going to completely wreck the place, Mum.'

'I know,' I said glumly, almost past caring by this time.

She threshed about, knocking down everything on window sills and shelves until she had almost rid herself of the plasterboard. Just a few ragged bits were left hanging from her horns, but she was still flinging her head around and drumming the floor with her front feet, while swaying her rear end back and forth with some force. Suddenly, she managed to turn right round in the small space and, spying the outside world through the open doorway, she lowered her head and charged for it.

There was no need 'to squeeze her in a bit' or 'take the door frame out'. With a triumphant bellow, she threw herself at the opening, was through and, almost without a pause, on her way to freedom, taking with her most of the door surround, two hinges, a small piece of door and several bits of plasterboard.

We just gaped! What utter havoc!

'What's happened? I can't see.' Andy was still on the stairs.

I went to him and picked him up as he had no shoes on, and carried him into the utility room. He gazed around. 'That's two doors, a washing machine, part of the wall, all the coat hangers, the mirror and my best anorak. Will we be able to use the freezer again?'

He had put it well, I thought.

I could hear shouting and Archie rushed past the back door (or where it had been) yelling at Dollach, who was making for the hills.

Fergie panted in and then stopped, aghast.

'Wheisht you! What a beast is that one!'

He looked at the dung now spattered everywhere.

'I'll be clearin' this,' he said, and added with meaning, 'and so will Archie.' He shook his head. 'That is a gey weird beast, just.'

He cleared the dung and general mess while we collected the broken glass from the floor and removed the sharp pieces of the smashed pane.

He said, 'I'll do the plaster and the hooks and things, but we'll have to be tryin' to get a cupla new doors. 'Twill not be easy, foreby.'

No, I knew that it would take weeks ordering from the mainland, then many weeks more to persuade the timber yard to deliver them.

'George and I will take the measurements in the Land Rover when he gets back,' I said. 'Then we'll fetch the new doors when they are ready. That way, it will be a bit faster than waiting for collection and delivery.'

Two round trips of two hundred and fifty to three hundred road miles and eight sea crossings! And I still didn't know if the washing machine would work.

Archie finally returned with Dollach, holding her tail.

'Mary J... I'm *so* sorry... I'll... um...'

'Archie. No – not now! Take her away! And find me a door or wood or something to fill that hole!'

'Yes, Nurse, yes... yes... ah. Yes, I will indeed, just. Yes, I'll do that.'

He was more subdued than I had ever seen him – I had been *very* firm.

So for three months, we lived with a boarded hole instead of a back door, no door at all between the kitchen and the utility room, a wall that looked like a jigsaw puzzle, a washing machine that leaked – and we had to buy Andy a new anorak. All because a stupid cow had fancied a look at our kitchen!

5

A Quiet Bay?

NEAR OUR LITTLE harbour town of Dalhavaig, a tiny lane led off the road down between rocky outcrops towards the sea, where it ended at a pebbly shore with the neighbouring island of Eilean Mor visible in the distance. At one end of this small beach was a smart modern bungalow and at the other a traditional croft house, much extended and altered. Both were in idyllic positions: facing south to the sea and protected from the north by low cliffs and trees. The sea lapped at the steep beach just a few yards away while the blue hills of Eilean Mor, across four or five miles of water, formed a perfect backdrop to the huffing waves and murmuring sea. It could be wild here in bad weather but there was still a sense of grandeur and time-lessness to this little place – tucked away in its own quiet world.

The croft house was owned by a lady from Edinburgh, who brought her disabled young son here for long holidays. He was a bright thirteen-year-old who had his sights already set on university, but was so disabled physically that he needed complete care. Whenever they were on Papavray, I visited twice daily to help Audrey to wash and dress Harry in the morning and put him to bed at night. Various medication and treatments were administered by this dedicated mother, but I sometimes felt that she must lead a very isolated life devoted entirely to her son.

I spent many hours with them over the years, but I still have no idea what happened to the husband and father. Had he died, I felt that he would have been mentioned so I concluded that either Audrey had not been married or that the husband had left her to cope on her own. Sadly, I have come across this scenario all too often – a husband and father who cannot cope emotionally and physically with a badly disabled child and abandons the mother, sometimes providing for them in absentia but often not even that.

Harry's health was precarious and so Audrey had home-schooled him from infancy and the lessons went on while on Papavray too. He was a studious boy with heavy, horn-rimmed spectacles, a quiet voice and a sense of humour which, in the circumstances, I found humbling. The croft house had been altered and adapted to accommodate all the paraphernalia necessary for his care and comfort, with a special shower, hospital-type bed and a wheel-chair which Audrey would push to the front of the house in good weather so that Harry could watch the birds and the sea.

While visiting them, I became aware for the first time of the owner of the smart bungalow at the other end of the beach. We had heard that Sandra Wainscott and her husband had had it built fairly recently for holidays. They had lived in London and scarcely used the house, but now they were divorced and Sandra had decided to live on Papavray permanently. She seemed a strangely reclusive person for one who had lived in the hustle and bustle of London. She shopped on the mainland, not locally; she was never seen walking and did not attend any island function. She drove to and from the mainland with never a wave to anyone. Of course, this behaviour was quickly noted by the crofters.

I consulted Mary – the fount of all local gossip.

'I'm not knowing at all,' she said in a disgruntled fashion – she liked to *know* these things.

'She doesna speak to folk, she doesna shop on the island, nor, use the garage. But I'm hearin' that there is a daughter that might be comin here...'

'How do you know that, Mary?'

Mary moved her milk pail from one hand to the other. 'Well... ah. It's like this y'see: the woman doesna get much mail, so when a card came for her, Postie couldna help but see...'

I smiled. Postie would have devoured every word on that card and faithfully broadcast the content to all and sundry.

Mary prepared to move on. 'This Sandra is a posh sort of person I'm told but her daughter canna write her letters well or spell right.' And with this severe comment, she disappeared into the byre.

'Odd,' I thought, but without much interest. However, within a week, Sandra and her problems were very *much* of interest.

It all began when Sandra rang me from the Dalhavaig post office to ask me to visit her daughter the following day. She (the daughter) had moved into one of the small row of cottages by the harbour.

'I'll have to be there too,' Sandra added, giving no explanation.

But it did not work out like that at all.

It was a bright, crisp morning with white, fluffy clouds playing hide and seek with the sun. I had just finished helping Audrey with Harry and we had tucked him up in his wheelchair, which Audrey pushed to the front of the house.

Suddenly, a woman's piercing scream shattered the peace and a man began to shout hysterically.

I turned, startled, and there was a young woman striding into the sea, fully dressed. Sandra was screaming at her to come back as she rushed after her while a young man stood ineffectually nearby, shouting and crying.

As I looked again at the young woman, I was horrified to see that she carried a bundle of shawls. It was a baby! And it was in great danger!

I was rushing along the beach, tumbling over the pebbles and Sandra was now following her into the sea.

'Valerie... stop... come back... the baby...' She was gasping as she struggled through the cold water.

The girl turned. 'Don't care... don't care. Don't want her or *him*.' She looked venomously towards the young man, who still had not moved.

'No, no. Come back. We will sort everything...' Sandra had now reached her daughter and tried to grab her arm. The girl struggled and pulled away, then she hit her mother on the side of the head. I heard the thud as I, too, rushed into the water. I needed to get the baby before the girl should drop it, or even try to drown it.

Sandra had fallen into the water head-first, while the girl waded on deeper and deeper.

I had a split second to decide. Do I rescue Sandra, who might be unconscious and in danger of drowning, or pursue the girl to try to rescue the baby from a similar fate?

I waded on towards the girl – was this the right decision? Was it a decision at all? It was probably instinctive. A helpless baby, a deranged mother... I did not have time to think logically.

'I'll get Sandra,' shouted a voice behind me as Audrey waded past towards the now spluttering woman.

'Valerie, come back! I am here to help you,' I called.

She stopped and turned so quickly that I thought for a moment that I was about to get the same treatment as Sandra. But she just stared blankly at me.

'Who are you?'

'I am the district nurse and I am here to help you and the baby.'

'Wha' for?'

'It's what I do. We help young mothers to cope with new babies. Looking after a baby isn't easy, is it?'

'No… I… I don't know what to do. And she cries *all* the time.' She paused and glowered across to the young man. 'And *he's* no help.' (I can well imagine, I thought.)

'If you give me the baby, I will look after her so that you can get some rest, Valerie… and I am sure your mother will help you to cope. Come now, give me the baby, Valerie, then you don't need to worry about her.'

I was speaking through chattering teeth and my legs were beginning to go numb. Valerie looked undecided, but I could see that, in spite of her stated indifference to the child, she was holding her clear of the water. She stopped for a moment and I thought I had got through to her, but then she started off again into deeper and deeper water. No matter how she held her, the baby would soon be submerged.

I was right beside her now and held out my arms for the child. If I tried to grab her, I might make Valerie stumble… I might stumble myself and fail in my attempt… or I might provoke her to toss the baby aside. Anything was possible. But I might *have* to make a grab for her if all my entreaties failed.

'Valerie, we are all very cold. You are shivering. Shall we go back to the shore? I will look after baby, I promise and you can get dry…'

She stood still.

I continued, 'We'll make some tea and have a nice warm up.'

(The thought flitted through my mind: Here am I in deep, cold water with a deranged mother and a baby in danger – and I am talking about making tea?)

But it worked! Valerie turned towards me, silently handed the baby to me, and strode off towards the shore and the young man.

As I had been entreating the girl to give up the baby, I had been aware, out of the corner of my eye, of Audrey dragging a spluttering Sandra out of the sea and sitting her on the pebbles where she coughed up a lot of sea water and looked around fearfully. She tried to stand.

'No, no,' cautioned Audrey, 'stay a moment to get your senses back. I can see that Nurse has the baby and your daughter is alright. Look! She is walking up the beach now.

Valerie was, indeed, marching purposefully towards the man. He cowered as she stood before him. With a mighty swing, she whacked him so hard that he fell onto the pebbles where he crouched, whimpering.

I was wading back to the shore carrying the damp little bundle which was so quiet that I had the sick feeling that we might be too late. I hadn't even seen the child among all the shawls, but I knew she must be very young. Reaching the pebbles, I ran as fast as my stiff legs would allow towards Audrey's house. I knew it to be warm and clean, and that it had a telephone.

I smiled at Harry as I passed. He had seen it all but, of course, could do nothing. How terribly frustrating that must have been, I thought somewhere at the back of all the other thoughts running through my mind.

Once in the warm kitchen, I unwrapped the little bundle. The child was alive, but cold and sleepy, her limbs floppy. She was unresponsive, her eyes open but unfocused. At this young age she would not focus well anyway, but this was bad. I took all the damp clothes off and, finding a folded sheet warming by the Rayburn, I wrapped her in it, trying to hold her away from my own wet, dripping clothes. Running into Harry's room, I laid her on his bed, where I knew Audrey always kept an electric blanket ready to warm his bed. I switched it on.

Audrey and Sandra appeared. Taking in the situation with the baby, Audrey said, 'Upstairs, Nurse. Out of those wet things. There is a dressing gown on the door of my room.'

Off I went while Audrey and Sandra took off the outer layers of their wet things and Audrey fetched a couple of pairs of pyjamas as being easy to get on to limbs stiff and blue with cold.

Now dry, I could tend the baby without making her wet again. I wished she would cry, but she just gazed at the world with dull eyes.

'Audrey, can you phone Doctor? Tell him it is urgent. I think baby is very dehydrated. And can you boil some water, meantime, and I will try to spoon it into her. Sandra, does Valerie breastfeed her?'

'No. She won't have anything to do with her. But I got milk powder and bottles when the baby was born. It is all in my house, but could we get it? What do you think is going on over there? I wonder if she – or perhaps Alf – will attack us if we try to go in.'

Audrey spoke. 'I think we should get the police as well as the doctor.' She glanced apologetically at Sandra. 'Your daughter is distraught and as for the young man...'

Sandra dropped wearily into a chair. 'Yes. Do that. I have tried but...' She sounded defeated.

While I spooned the warm water into the baby's mouth, holding her closely to my own now warm, dry body, Audrey rang Doctor Mac and then John, our policeman. She gave them both an abbreviated account of the morning's events and Valerie's aggressive behaviour.

'Bring someone with you,' was her parting shot to John. Wise woman! He would probably bring our island giant – Rhuari.

I suddenly thought, Has baby a name?

Sandra sighed, 'Valerie wants to call her Marilyn and he wants Fredericka.' She looked at us. 'They are both subnormal,' she continued. 'I have yet to learn how they met but neither has any idea how to look after themselves let alone a baby. They had a huge row about the name: Alf's father was 'Frederick', Valerie is crazy about Marilyn Monroe. Alf hates me; Valerie sides with him but sometimes attacks him. He has not even touched the baby – he's afraid of her, in fact – thinks she is some sort of alien or something... I just don't know where to turn. Valerie was in a home near Malcolm – my ex – but turned up here. He got her the cottage and then Alf arrived... it just goes on and on.'

'Let's call her "Bonny", in the hope that she becomes "bonny".' Audrey was decisive and as it seemed ridiculous to discuss names at a time like this, we all agreed.

Just then, there was a crunching on the pebbles as Doctor Mac drew up. I gave him a brief account of all the happenings so far and he briefly examined Bonny.

'Are you three ladies alright after your ducking?' he asked.

We all agreed that, although shaken, we were alright, but very aware of our strange outfits.

He gave a quick laugh at this.

'Well, I shall take the baby to the hospital. She needs rehydration and nourishment and then a thorough assessment.' He looked doubtfully at me in Audrey's dressing gown. 'Ahh. Can you come with me?'

'Come,' said Audrey, making for the stairs. A moment or two later, I reappeared clad in a pair of trousers several sizes too big and a voluminous jumper. Audrey was a big lady. Poor Doctor Mac was hard pressed not to laugh.

Wrapping little Bonny in an eiderdown, the doctor and I left for the hospital just as John arrived with, yes, Rhuari.

'We have to go,' called Doctor Mac. 'I'll see you later, John. There has been violence so I suppose... the cells. Keep those two apart or we will have murder on our hands.'

John's police station – his house – had only two cells. It seemed that both would be in use for a few hours at least.

Once we had handed over our little burden and Doctor Mac had thoroughly examined her, the hospital staff took over. A drip was put up and warmth applied. They would begin feeding in an hour or two, and then every three hours, as Bonny was only two weeks old and less than six pounds in weight.

'She will be alright,' Doctor Mac assured me. 'Now we have to decide what to do with her when she is well.'

'I don't think the parents are fit to look after her. Perhaps Sandra, the grandmother...' I wondered.

'I get the impression that she is not very stable either. Or perhaps she is just tired and shocked – I only saw her for a moment.' Doctor Mac was usually a good judge of people and I was surprised at his assessment of Sandra's character and capabilities.

Doctor took me back to Audrey's house, where she and Sandra were drinking tea and Harry was back inside as the weather had turned cold. He was as excited about the events as any thirteen-year-old would be, and professed Alf to be 'an idiot' and Valerie to be 'scary'.

Audrey told me that John had had no trouble with Alf, who snivelled his way to the car; but that Valerie had had to be restrained as she was kicking and screaming. Rhuari was just the man for this as he combined great strength and determination with gentleness and compassion. John had 'used his services' on many occasions.

I was happy to collect my wet clothes, go home, get into another uniform and set off to finish the day's work.

I was back at Audrey's house in the evening to help with Harry.

'Sandra is back in the bungalow but Doctor decided to send Valerie straight back to the maternity hospital on the mainland as she has some heavy bleeding,' reported Audrey. 'I don't suppose her ducking helped.'

'What about that young fellow?' I asked.

'He's banged up,' put in Harry in a satisfied tone.

Audrey smiled. 'He is staying in a cell for the night. Just to have somewhere to put him, I think,' she said. 'Sandra is going to have much to deal with, it seems.'

I remembered Doctor Mac's opinion and wondered how she would cope.

'I'll go to see her tomorrow,' I said. Sufficient unto the day, I thought, as I thankfully drove home to family and fireside.

When I went to help Audrey in the morning, there was a shining Daimler parked beside the bungalow.

'Malcolm, Sandra's ex, arrived late last night. She had phoned him. I'd asked her in for a drink, I felt sorry for all her troubles... you know, Nurse, I don't think she's up to coping with the baby; the daughter, perhaps, that hopeless young man, not at all – so I hope this Malcolm can sort everything out.'

We were getting Harry installed in his chair when a very large man emerged from the bungalow and drove off.

'That's a super car,' said Harry. 'One day, when I am old enough, they are going to get an adapted car for me. Then, when I'm in it, I'll be like everybody else.' This was obviously a dream cherished by Harry – 'to be like everybody else'. I was deeply affected by his cheerful acceptance of his condition and his simple ambitions.

That evening, the news from the island hospital was devastating.

Harry was near to tears. 'The baby, Nurse. It died. Isn't that awful? Was it the water, or the cold?'

In fact, it was probably both because the child was warmed and rehydrated but did not respond and developed breathing problems. I was shocked and upset, as we had held high hopes for little Bonny's recovery.

'Malcolm seems a very caring and capable man and is going to deal with all that the baby's death entails. He has packed Alf off to his parents in Aberdeen and Valerie is to go to a psychiatric unit when she is released from the maternity hospital.'

'What about Sandra?' I asked. 'She must be so upset about the baby and her daughter.'

Audrey shuddered. 'No. In fact she said that it was a good thing that the baby died as she did not want to have to look after her *or* Valerie.'

'Oh, my!'

Harry was listening to every word. 'That's horrible,' he said. 'Suppose Mum had felt like that about me!'

We were both quite astonished at his understanding of the attitude of Sandra as opposed to his mother's.

Audrey was near to tears as she hugged him. 'I love you, Harry. How could I not care for you?'

But he was still distressed. 'But the poor little baby...'

As I left, I whispered to Audrey, 'You have a super boy there, Audrey. You have brought him up beautifully and you care for him so well.'

She smiled. 'Oh no, Nurse, we look after each other.'

It seemed that Sandra had had a nervous breakdown some months ago. She had turned against Malcolm, attempting to harm him but he did not want to bring it all into the public arena, so they had agreed to part quietly.

He had done his best for Sandra and Valerie and was now trying to arrange some sort of future for them both.

Next morning, John's car and another police vehicle were by the bungalow. Audrey met me on the beach.

'Sandra has disappeared. They have been searching all night. Malcolm is distraught.'

They searched the island, moved to other islands and the mainland – nothing! Weeks went by and then Malcolm received a letter from New Zealand. Sandra had met up with an old lover and was living in Christchurch. She was not at all concerned on hearing from Malcolm that everyone had been worried about her safety, and did not ask about her daughter at all. Doctor Mac's instincts had been right – yet again.

* * *

About two years later, Malcolm and Audrey were married. He proved a great father for Harry, who eventually became a research scientist.

6

Josh

SON JOHN AND girlfriend Joanna seemed at last to be settling into the life on Papavray. It was not easy for them as they were young and had lived in the centre of London with all its traffic and noise, excitement and interests. London was a very 'now' place, Joanna said. Places such as Papavray had appealed to John from childhood as holiday or camping destinations, so he appreciated the quietness, the empty roads of the island and the freedom to roam anywhere the fancy took him. But he missed the 'buzz' of city life: the nights out, the pop concerts, the bright lights and his many friends. Joanna missed all these things too and added to that list was – shopping. 'Proper' shopping – as in Oxford Street or the Portobello Road. Papavray was a decided shock to a shopaholic, as we were more than one hundred road miles and two sea crossings from shops (other than the small island ones). Even in Inverness, the range of goods and the styles of clothing were very limited, running to good tweeds, woolly jumpers and sturdy footwear. None of these things were to Joanna's liking as she favoured flowing skirts, colourful beads and bandana-type headgear: all very attractive on such a lovely young girl. John could not get enthusiastic about shops, as he hated shopping with a passion. He still does!

I think we did not fully understand the difficulties of the transition for them and should have expected a more prolonged settling-in period. We had made the move for very different reasons and were now becoming established in the community.

But, gradually, they made friends: some being incomers like themselves. They revised their ideas of what constituted a good night out and got used to at least some of the island limitations. They went to ceilidhs, met friends in the pub and walked a lot. An added change for Joanna was being without a job: she had always worked in a variety of retail-related jobs and now she found time hanging on her hands. She eventually made friends with a girl who started a business making heavy jumpers, so was able to work with her and enjoy her company.

At about this time, they went off to London and were married there. At least that is what they *said* they had done. Who were we to argue?

Meantime, Joanna's pregnancy was progressing. She kept very well and the usual arrangements were made for her to go to the mainland hospital about two weeks before her due date. All island births were expected to take place there. But, in this case, the baby seemed to have a sense of humour. Joanna would have pains off and on from seven months onwards. Everybody would be mobilised, John's rather elderly car being kept filled and ready, bags packed, phone calls made... and then the pains would subside and the little joker would settle down again in the warmth of the womb. Well, it *was* cold outside!

Eventually, the inevitable happened and no-one really believed that the pains, on that dark, windy night, were the real thing. But, of course, this time the labour progressed far more quickly than is normal for a first baby and we had to rush Joanna to the *island* hospital, as there was no time for the long journey to the mainland. We used my car as John's was not over reliable and we completed the twenty-two tortuous miles in twenty minutes and arrived with only minutes to spare.

A bonny boy entered the world at two in the morning, weighing eight pounds. My first grandchild! Mother and baby were well. Joanna gazed at the child as though surprised that he was there (which she might well have been after all the false alarms) and she seemed rather scared at the thought of being responsible for this vocal, but helpless, scrap of humanity. She had beautiful, blue eyes which were now wide with apprehension.

A few days later, George and I brought her and the baby home – to our home, so that I could look after them. They stayed for a week, while Joanna got used to the baby's demands; and John, looking slightly dazed, immediately became the proud father and took to the many baby chores with a will, appearing to enjoy every aspect of parenthood.

Many names had been bandied about, predictably none of them were traditional, but the little chap was eventually called 'Josiah', or 'Josh' for short. I liked the diminutive more than the full name.

None of our crofter friends could understand why they should have chosen this name, as *they* all named their children after a relative – or, as they said, *for* a relative. The result of this habit was the degree of confusion which so often reigned when several people had the same name within the same family. I was frequently asked if we had a Josiah in *our* family. Sometimes, it was assumed that the baby was named after the biblical character, and this seemed to these Free Kirk stalwarts to smack of Papism. Josh himself, however, was goo-ed over and admired: all crofter women seem to adore babies.

John was now working for the Laird, restoring old estate buildings for holiday accommodation or for agricultural use. He enjoyed the outdoor life and the regular hours, while Joanna was happy to have him at home at night to help with the new baby.

Nick was delighted with the little chap and often nursed him to sleep, while Andy was rather overwhelmed at the idea that he was an *uncle* at eight or nine years old, but was happy to boast about this amazing fact to the children at school. I think he was probably disappointed in their reactions for they would be completely unimpressed. The generations among the crofters often overlapped, as couples married at a very young age and had babies almost immediately, while many a forty-year-old grandma was astonished to find that she was pregnant, long after she thought her family to be complete. Apart from the financial aspect (which did not seem to bother anyone) this rather haphazard attitude towards family planning made little difference to the fairly modest expectations of most islanders.

Very few young people had 'careers' on the island. Careers were only achieved by leaving Papavray for university or other training, and then the resulting employment, for which so much time had been invested, would almost always be in a mainland town; perhaps even overseas. The ordinary island jobs in hotels, at the harbour or on the croft could be managed easily with babies or young children in the family, because there was always a mother, aunt, sister or cousin who would be delighted to take a turn at 'minding' the child. So children grew up surrounded by members of the extended family and were usually well-adjusted and relaxed. This is something which has almost been lost in the busier South and I wonder how long the islands will be able to hold on to this culture of close-knit family care and loyalty?

Josh grew into a sturdy, chubby baby and Joanna's circle of friends grew to include many young mums and their children. They were fascinated by her clothes and the fact that she had lived and worked in London. Most of them had never been farther than Inverness. So Joanna, if not exactly a celebrity, was certainly 'different'.

Although everything seemed fine on the surface, I could not rid myself of the feeling that Papavray, to John and Joanna, was only a short-term stepping stone to something else. What that was, I had no idea and did not wish to ask, because I liked having them on the island and was a little afraid of what they might tell me. But before anything could be decided, an opportunity to make a lot of money presented itself.

Another oil rig was to be built in one of the sea lochs. Workers of all sorts were needed, from highly trained engineers to totally untrained construction crews. John decided that this was an opportunity not to be missed. Being a young, strong, willing lad, he was taken on immediately and, within a few short weeks was commuting by helicopter from the island to the mainland camp, which had been hastily built on the coast near the rig, to house the workers who came in from all over the UK. The men (and they *were* all men) worked three weeks on the rig (being ferried the short distance to and from the camp each day) and two weeks off, when they were airlifted to their homes; or in the case of island dwellers, the nearest island with an airstrip or landing place for the helicopter.

Although this was a huge boost to their security, it meant that John would be away again for some of the time and Joanna would be by herself. She spent quite a lot of time at our house for baths, washing and drying of baby things and clothes, and some meals, but lived most of her time in their caravan, which was now quite homely with a little wood-burning stove and bright walls. John's absences were a disappointment, but she now had plenty of friends who often kept her company.

For the young men who were prepared to work on the rig, there were undreamed-of wage packets. But, strangely, many able-bodied men, who probably needed a boost to their income, were not willing to stay away from home to 'be stuck in the middle of the sea' as they put it, and have to sleep in a camp. The whole idea of leaving home and croft seemed abhorrent to these men and they were loud in their condemnation of the young-sters who were so happy to do just that. Was this a fear of new technology? Of change, in such a dynamic way? Or was it an unwillingness to forsake, for even a short time, the culture of crofting and fishing, on which the islands had relied for generations? Whatever their reasons, they were adamant that nothing was going to persuade them to leave home and hearth. I could not make sense of this attitude because there were no contracts or agreements and these men could have tried the life for a week or two, and left whenever they wished, if it did not suit them. But that was the 'way of it' as they said.

There were certainly dangers as the whole operation was new and untried. Hard hats were supplied but many would not wear them. There were no life jackets or steel toe-capped boots and the only protective cloth-ing was a waterproof jacket. The seas were rough and the work involved huge pieces of heavy equipment, which had to be winched hither and yon with cold, wet hands and stiff muscles on a heaving, plunging platform. It was not surprising that there were far more accidents than there would have been in a properly run enterprise.

John and Joanna quickly accrued some considerable savings. The only place on Papavray to spend money was the pub, and with a new baby to look after, their visits to the hostelry were few and far between. They now lived some ten or eleven steep and tortuous miles from us, so babysitting for an evening was rarely an option, particularly if I was 'on call'. But occasion-ally, with a lot of organisation, I would look after Josh while they went to the mainland for shopping. Even this was awkward because Joanna was breastfeeding him. And very successfully. He gained weight at a prodigious rate, slept well and was bright and alert.

But, as I suspected, the money was being saved to fund an 'escape', as

Joanna deemed their plans. They were going to move back to the south for John to find work and for a lifestyle more familiar to them both.

So one bright day, when Josh was about eight months old, they packed everything they possessed into John's new (well, *newish*) van and set off on the long journey south. John looked slightly wistful as he stood in front of our house, saying his 'goodbyes' and gazing at the blue, sun-soaked mountains, the white, fluffy clouds dancing in a turquoise sky and the green patchwork of crofts scattered throughout the valley below us.

I was dejected: downcast to be saying goodbye to our first grandchild after knowing and loving him for so short a time, but I supposed they were doing the right thing. John's work on the rig was coming to an end as the structure entered another phase and Joanna certainly found life on Papavray very dull. We were all miserable while waving to the retreating van as, with a cheery 'toot-toot', they rounded the bend on the road above our house and disappeared.

7

Tears and Twisters

ONE VERY EARLY morning, before it was properly light, I walked dejectedly along the shore at Dhubaig, kicking the pebbles and occasionally hurling one into the sea. I was engrossed in sad thoughts, and angry at what I felt was the injustice of fate. We were such a small community that it was impossible not to get emotionally involved sometimes.

I had just lost a patient; a dear, sweet, uncomplaining lady called Minnie, whom I had been attending daily since my arrival on Papavray. I knew that I was being irrational; she was nearing eighty, but she was so much more than a patient; more like a grandmother. Her death was not even really unexpected: she had been deteriorating for some time, having suffered yet another stroke.

The phone had rung at three in the morning; I dressed hurriedly and contacted my long-suffering neighbour to say that Andy would be on his own for an unspecified time. (Of course, George was away – again.) Leaving lights blazing and the door unlocked for Janey to get in, I drove off at speed. She would spend the rest of the night (or however long it took) on the sofa.

I stumbled up the slope to Mary-Anne's house. Lights were on and the door was open. Mary-Anne, usually the soul of good cheer, stood in the hall with tears streaming down her face.

'Oh, Nurse, Nurse. She's gone! She's gone, and I didna know. I never said goodbye.'

A storm of weeping followed and she hid her face in my coat. I was shocked! I should not have been surprised, but I think I had persuaded myself that Minnie would rally once more and *her* life and *my* visits would go on as before. With a very heavy heart, I attempted to soothe the distraught woman.

I went into the bedroom. Minnie looked so peaceful and natural! I had often found her asleep when I visited and now she looked no different. Lying amongst the snowy pillows, with the flowered eiderdown pulled up to her chin, she had almost certainly died in her sleep. I hoped so. The room was littered with all the paraphernalia of the long-term sick or disabled – a commode, a walking frame, a pile of extra pillows, crutches and specially-made shoes. It all represented the last ten years of a life that had previously been lived entirely for others: a childless life; a life of hard croft work and caring for her family; a devout Free Kirk life.

Over the years, I had heard the story as we chatted, while I bathed her, combed or washed her hair, dressed her and tidied the bedroom. Then I would help her to the chair by the fire in the kitchen and Mary-Anne would bustle about, insisting on making me a 'strupak'. So the conversation would become more general, and Mary-Anne's opinion of Minnie's self-sacrificing ways would tell me all that this modest lady would not have done.

Minnie had been the oldest of six children and the only girl, born to a brutal father and his cowed, ineffectual wife. Angus Mor, a big man as his name implies, frequently beat his wife and thrashed the children. The boys had to help with the croft work and the fishing from the age of about eight, while Minnie looked after the latest baby and did most of the housework and washing. As soon as they could, the boys left and ran off to sea or found work elsewhere. Minnie's mother complained constantly about everything and Angus took to the drink in a big way, becoming ever more violent.

By now, Minnie was in her twenties and had a 'young man'. He could not have been a very strong character, said Mary-Anne, because Angus frightened him away. So the miserable situation continued, until Angus got in a fight one night, killed a man and was jailed for manslaughter. Relief at the freedom from his tempers was short-lived, however, as Rory, the oldest brother, came home, having been dismissed from his job for drunkenness.

So the years passed: Minnie looking after an increasingly cantankerous mother, (Mary-Anne maintained that she was not ill at all, but just liked being waited on) while Rory was in the pub every night, drinking away his unemployment benefit. He did nothing on the croft, and expected Minnie to look after him, the house, the animals and their mother, and to clean for the Laird to earn some much-needed money. All this, Minnie did with stoicism, upheld, she said, by her faith.

I once said to her, 'You have not had much of a life, Minnie – with all the drudgery and no thanks for it.'

'Ach, it was no too bad. I had my faith y'see, so my life was not joyless.'

I had to accept this, as the Free Kirk had obviously sustained Minnie, but I always felt that particular denomination to be, in itself, oppressive and joyless.

Time went on. The mother died (Angus had died in prison many years before) and, following tradition, the croft went to the brother, who promptly turned Minnie out. So Mary-Anne, a widow of many years, happily took Minnie in and it must have seemed that, at last, she would have an easier life. But the fates were against her: she had a massive stroke just two months later. How unkind life can be!

In the ten years since then, her brother had not visited her once. Now she had gone! I hoped that the faith which had sustained her to the end would grant her the rest she believed would be hers after death.

And here I was on the shore, trying to throw off the depression I felt, before going home. Dawn was beginning to break and Andy would be waking. Janey would have guessed that Minnie had 'passed on', and would be ready to scuttle away to spread the news, and offer Mary-Anne help and support. I sat on a rather damp rock in the early morning gloom and gazed unseeingly out across the ocean towards the distant isles – and wept. After a while, I pulled myself together and turned for home.

A sudden strong gust of wind blew my hair over my face and I realised that the early morning had been unnaturally calm and quiet. The sea, usually pounding on the shore where I had been walking, was glassy, lapping gently on the pebbles. Before that sudden gust, there had been a quiet stillness. Sunk in my thoughts, I had not been aware of the unusual weather.

As I returned to my car, I could see an area of water, about ten or twelve feet in diameter, ruffle and churn, and a moment later a foaming wave broke noisily on the shore and rattled among the pebbles. Just one – no more! As I drove the short distance home, leaves on the road began to dance and swirl, lifting and shivering before disappearing skywards. Gravelly dust formed mini tornados, rising and falling in small circles several feet or more from the ground. The glen and the village, however, seemed to be quiet and I was just dismissing the small episodes from my mind, when I saw Fergie's flat, corrugated iron byre roof lift, fall back into place, lift again and rise several feet into the air before settling back once more onto the stout stone walls of the building. Something very odd was happening!

I stopped the car at the top of the track leading down to our home, and watched, puzzled and fascinated, as the weird flurries of wind struck randomly in the village. Some washing on a line hanging limp and motionless one minute, leapt into the air, was ripped from the line and flapped off towards the sea. *Towards* the sea? Our weather usually came *from* the sea – the Atlantic – but this strange wind was from the east.

Looking towards the mountains on the islands to the north, I saw blue-black clouds finding their way between the peaks, while swirling, grey-white ones raced round and round below them, leaving trails of mist. I had not seen anything quite so odd, even here in the Hebrides where we seemed prone to all manner of strange phenomena. Last November, for instance, we had had a week of unnaturally icy, Arctic conditions with no wind at all. This time it was the *wind* that was unnatural.

I looked down towards our home. We had some small, scrubby trees beside the byre and, as I watched, the two on the east side of the little copse suddenly bent over, broke and were blown along the ground, while nearby, some late flowering dahlias remained standing tall and undisturbed.

I descended the track. Andy was up. 'Mum. The chimney rattled just now and Janey's fire went whoomph!'

'I dinna know what happened foreby, Nurse. I was lighting it as I always do when this wind roared down the chimney. Just look at everything!'

'Don't worry, Janey, I'll see to this.' I looked at her. 'You need to clean up, though.'

Janey departed, but was back immediately.

'Nurse, your window's gone.'

'What?'

'The window in the shower room. It's gone.'

Unable to believe my ears, I hastened to the shower room. The window really had gone – not just broken or loosened, but gone completely – and was lying on the ground outside, some feet away.

'Well! Whatever is happening is beyond me. But I think you had better hurry off home, Janey. All this must be the forerunner of some *very* wild weather. Many, many thanks, as always.'

Janey departed, tutting over the news about Minnie, and I rang Doctor Mac.

'I think you should stay put for a while, Nurse. The weather is so very strange and I feel that there is worse to come. There is no wind at all here but it is raining stair-rods. Most unusual.' Doctor Mac was not perturbed. He never was, no matter what the elements threw at us.

As I put the phone down, the house gave a sudden shudder: doors rattled, window catches loosened and a window flew open. In an instant, small ornaments, towels and a sliced loaf of bread seemed to be flying about the room. The fire, which had started to 'draw', blew out of the fireplace, sparks and glowing peats landing on the carpet and nearby chairs. I beat at the sparks with a cushion, and then lifted the smouldering peat from the singed carpet back onto the hearth.

'Andy, sit on the floor behind the sofa.' It seemed the safest place – away from the windows and the fireplace. The dogs began to bark as more small objects and bits of food were hurled to the floor. I crouched beside Andy and the dogs, but then I wondered if the cats were outside, so I peeped out of the open window. I was just in time to see two chickens fly past. But they were not flying! Not of their own volition, anyway: they were being hurled through the air by the wind. Then the chicken coop followed, breaking up as it flew past. There was nothing I could do for the chickens so I ducked in, out of the fury. But not in time! Just at that moment, a gust of wind threw the window against my head. Andy screamed as he saw blood rushing from my scalp, and had the presence of mind to fetch a towel, which I held tightly to my head. I explained that it looked much worse than it really was as scalps bleed profusely for 'any little thing'.

'Little thing! Mum, you are covered in blood!'

The towel was now wet and I was feeling a bit shaky so I sat on the floor and leaned against the sofa. After a while, the bleeding began to lessen, so I wrapped another towel round my head like a turban. Somehow, a nurse in uniform with a blood-soaked turban round her head seemed so ridiculous that we were able to laugh.

'Mum, it's stopped!'

Everything was suddenly still: the window stopped swinging, the door ceased to rattle. Slices of bread, pieces of paper and other odds and ends gradually fell to the floor, while the fire sulked quietly in the hearth. It was eerily calm, although I could still hear a roaring in the distance. We peeped out (very cautiously, this time). We could see a funnel of black cloud and dust swirling round and round as it hurried over the crofts to the sea. It was picking up bits of tin, animal feed bags, feathers, hay and bits of plants. A tornado? Here, in Scotland? But what else?

We started to move around picking things up, shutting windows (those that *would* shut) closing doors and preventing the dogs from gorging themselves on all the bits of food lying on the floor. A lump of marmalade had been thrown against the hot Rayburn and was sizzling happily as it burned and solidified – I would never get that off! – pictures were askew, some clothes, stacked ready for ironing, were on the floor and a plant pot, complete with plant, was upside down on the dining table.

I cautiously opened the back door to look for the cats. The byre door had disappeared and there was a big dent in the side of my car, presumably where the door had been thrown against it on its way to freedom. (We found the door the next day in the burn, some fifty yards from the house.) The cats appeared from the hay shed and rushed indoors, heads down but unhurt. Upstairs, we found windows broken but the hinges had held. Dressing-table accoutrements were scattered everywhere. In the bathroom, there was similar mayhem, including two toothbrushes down the toilet! Andy guffawed at this, his schoolboy humour to the fore. The muddle was severe, but the actual damage was minimal, even outside. The copse and much of the 'garden' had been flattened, but our sturdy house seemed intact.

'What's that thing over there, Mum?'

A piece of blackened and twisted metal lay in the burn. The chimney cowl! No wonder the fire had 'blown down' and 'whoomphed'!

Everywhere was still and quiet, but gradually I began to hear voices as people ventured out to inspect the damage and exclaim to each other. I felt it was now safe to send Andy round the village, to see if anyone was injured and might need help.

Surprisingly, I seemed to have been the only casualty and my cuts were not serious.

On Sunday, I took the dogs for a walk on the shore. It was only two days ago that I had been here, walking and thinking; but the beach had changed dramatically. Where there had been pebbles, there was now black sand, like the beaches on volcanic islands. The sea, too, appeared dirty and all manner of flotsam was floating in the shallows. But the vertiginous hills looked clean, bright and rain-washed, and a silvery sun shone between the peaks of the distant mountains in a deep blue sky.

I sat on the same rock and felt the return of peace in my soul. The burn, widened by the storm, chattered nearby, finding its new route to the sea; oyster catchers skimmed the waves, while gannets performed their skilful dives, emerging with shining fish. A small boat rocked gently in the bay as two figures cast their lines. I could smell peat smoke from some of the croft houses and the musty aroma of warm seaweed. Sea pinks nonchalantly waved their heads, and a robin perched on the grassy bank and eyed me speculatively.

Nature is resilient, unperturbed by its own recent outburst. The hills, the sea, the glen were all at peace in the sunlight on this – the day that we call 'Sunday'.

At peace. Minnie, too, was now at peace, and I was able to be more rational about her death. Maybe, she would not have wanted to go on living the half-life with which she had been left by the strokes. Now, her spirit, at least, was whole and happy, resting in God's arms, as she had believed that it would.

The island would mourn Minnie, but with great respect for the way that she had lived her life. However, no-one would ever forget the day she died.

'The day that Minnie died? 'Twas the day of the tornado.'

8

A Light in the Night

'I DID *SEE* A LIGHT in the church!' Andy was trying to convince Nick.

'You're just imagining it,' said Nick. He was in no mood for ghostly lights in old buildings – his mind ran more on the lines of girlish smiles and pretty faces.

'I'm not! I was on the shore with Thomas and we *both* saw it. It wasn't bright enough for a torch – more like…'

Nick interrupted, 'More like a candle, held by a lady in flowing white robes, gliding through the church in the darkness, wailing pitifully…' Nick grinned at his own imagination.

Andy was getting *very* annoyed, 'I was *going* to say, "a cigarette lighter".'

The wrangle continued with Andy insisting that he and his great friend, Thomas, the factor's son, had indeed seen a dim light in the once splendid old church on the shore.

I began to listen. It became obvious that Andy really was serious. He was referring to the large, near-derelict church built many hundreds of years ago on Dhubaig's shore. The bay was shaped like a flattened horse-shoe with an arc of steep cliffs at one end, where there was just enough room between the high tide line and the folded and tortured rock face for the mighty bulk of the church to be located.

I think that the sea must have encroached since its building, for the old grey stones were now washed by every spring tide and lashed mercilessly by the winter storms. A heap of pebbles blocked the entrance where the sturdy, but now decayed door once welcomed worshippers.

As with all derelict buildings on the island, most articles considered to be of any use had been 'rescued' for the repair of a byre or as a croft gate, or just as firewood.

The fallen slates, too, had been broken up and scattered to cover byre floors or croft pathways. 'Recycling' may only now be gaining popularity in the cities of the south, but it has always been the norm among the people of the Hebridean islands. The garnering of anything that might be useful is instinctive for those who live in remote places, far from timber yards and DIY stores. So, apart from some sea pinks and scrubby grass, together with a thistle or two, there was little of interest *inside* the old church.

But the *outside* must once have been quite impressive. Unlike the austere and often ugly churches much beloved of the Free Kirk of Scotland, this place had once had ornate embellishments including a short spire. The sad remains of that now lay scattered on the shingle, while snarling faces of gargoyles on broken pinnacles leered down at all the sinners who passed beneath. The once elegant, mullioned windows looked out at the sea, sometimes framing a sparkling blue vista, but more often taking the full force of the gales that swept across the bay.

It was rumoured to have been a Roman Catholic Church, but I found this hard to believe, as all but a few of the Outer Hebridean islands are fiercely Protestant. No-one seemed to know its history, or when it closed its doors forever. From time to time, some ill-advised enthusiast from a southern town would try to buy it with some idea of converting it into a holiday home. These plans usually suffered a quick reversal when the first high tide was seen to batter its way into what would have been made into a tastefully appointed sitting room. In any case, the Laird would not, or *could* not sell it, as he was unable to establish whether it belonged to his estate or to the church – Roman Catholic or otherwise. Such confusion was not uncommon in the islands. So it stood on the shore, slowly breaking up, slowly returning to earth and sea; the rocks of which it was built gradually regaining their freedom from the hand of man.

None of this concerned Andy, of course. To him, it was a magical place to play; to imagine all kinds of sinister goings-on and to fight endless battles with his friend Thomas.

'Mum! Mum, you are not listening. I really did see a light, although we were making a noise and it went out. I wish Dad was here and we could go and investigate.'

'Dad is on the mainland getting electrical stuff for the castle; I don't know if he will get home tonight. In any case, it's too late.'

Andy was crestfallen. 'Well, couldn't you…'

'No!' I said firmly. I was not inclined to poke about in a dark old church at nine o'clock at night, in the pouring rain.

'I'll go if Fergie or Archie could come too.' Suddenly Nick's love-life paled in the face of adventure. Not surprising, perhaps, as he was only fourteen.

Just then, as though on cue, Fergie's voice was heard in the porch as he removed his boots. This was a courtesy that he always extended and, whilst I appreciated the consideration shown in respect of my carpets, there was sometimes a price to be paid if the boots had been on his feet all day!

'Fergie,' babbled Andy, 'will you come down to the church on the shore. I saw a light there…'

'So did I,' said Fergie, to Andy's great satisfaction. 'On my way here. Now what was it that I was wanting, I wonder? And where is George?' Fergie gazed around as though expecting George to be hiding somewhere.

Nick's lively imagination had been stirred at last. 'Never mind that. Let's go and find out what's going on at the church.' In spite of an age gap of some fifty years, Nick and Fergie were great friends.

Fergie looked at me. I knew when I was beaten, so the boys pulled on their waterproofs and boots while Fergie resignedly donned his again, picked up his torch and off they went into the night.

Half an hour went by. Then another.

I sat by the fire, listening unhappily to the tumult of the storm, which seemed to intensify by the minute. Hailstones rattled at the window and fizzed on the hot peats in the fireplace, while the wind roared in the chimney. 'Never Silent' is the name given to the north wind in myths and legends. How right that is!

I pulled on a coat and went outside to stand at the front of the house. In daylight, this vantage point commanded a truly breath-taking view of mountain, glen and sea. And even at night, I might have had the welcome sight of bobbing torches wending their way over the crofts. But as I gazed into the night, trying to keep my eyes open in the wind and driving rain, I could see nothing but darkness in the glen: even the mountains were lost in the rain. Only the sea glittered and foamed in the bays as it roared and sucked at the fragile land, as though to devour it.

I was just turning to get my wellies to go and look for them, when I heard a shout above the fury of the storm. Gradually four figures emerged from the darkness into the light spilling from the windows. Four? Who had joined them? I stared, but did not recognise the outline of the fourth. Andy was gabbling something, but it was lost in the clamour. As they drew nearer, I saw that the fourth figure was that of a drenched, ragged man. Was he a tramp? He was certainly a stranger to the island.

'Mary J,' bellowed Fergie, trying to make himself heard above the tumult. 'This is Steve. We found him sheltering in the church. He needs some food. By! He's gey wet, foreby.' And wet he was!

'In!' I ordered, opening the door. Steve glanced at me, but did not reply. We were all blown into the house by the force of the wind. I went to put the kettle on, urged the boys out of their wet things and had a quick look at Steve, now that we were in the light. He was haggard, dirty; half-starved and had a haunted look about him.

Fergie was showing an unexpectedly sympathetic side as he spoke quietly.

'You'll be fine the now, Steve. Mary J will find you some dry clothes. And perhaps you want a wash.' Steve was sitting awkwardly on the edge of a kitchen chair and seemed not to hear Fergie at all.

I pulled myself together and showed Steve to the ground-floor bathroom indicating the shower. I gave him a towel and went to get some trousers and a pullover belonging to George. Back in the kitchen, I looked enquiringly at the three.

'Who is he and what's the story?'

'We found him in the church, trying to pull together the remains of a tatty tent,' replied Fergie. 'There was nothing left of it and all his food and bedding was soaked. If we hadn't gone down there, I don't know what would have happened to him.'

'What do you make of him, Fergie? Has he spoken to you?'

'He's muttered things, but I'm not knowing what to make of him at all. I think he's been in some sort of trouble and been living rough for some time. Maybe a death. Or divorce or something.' Fergie warmed to his subject. 'He might be a criminal on the run.'

Andy looked rather scared. 'Do you think so, Fergie? Maybe he's murdered somebody.'

'That I have not!' Steve stood in the doorway. We had not heard him come back into the room. He looked shocked and angry. 'It was not my fault.'

None of us could think what to say, but then we variously brought out that trite remark – so inadequate for such times – 'Sorry.'

As always, practicalities were a blessing in awkward situations and I busied myself making tea and cutting sandwiches. As an afterthought, I opened some cans of Scotch broth and put them to heat on the Rayburn. Steve resumed his seat on the kitchen chair and watched silently.

I became aware of the barking of the dogs and remembered that they were in the porch. I let them in. They stood for a second and then bounded towards Steve. He showed no sign of surprise at their precipitous approach, but immediately knelt on the floor and took them both in his arms, crooning to them. As he fussed and cuddled the two delighted animals, he seemed to change. He looked up at me with a smile.

'I had dogs. My... my wife and I had dogs.'

With a sigh of relief, I felt that normality was being restored. We all sat round the Rayburn for warmth, and drank soup from mugs and munched sandwiches. It was obvious that Steve had had little, or nothing, to eat for some time. As the heat warmed him, he began to look less pinched, but his eyes were dull, his skin grey and his figure emaciated. I tried to guess his age. He could have been anywhere between thirty and fifty.

We all chatted about nothing in particular, just trying to put Steve at ease and then, quite suddenly, he began to talk. It was as though the pent-up floodwaters of suppressed emotions had been released.

'It was about this time last year,' he said, staring straight ahead. 'Sylvia, my wife, was expecting our first child. She had begun labour early – about eight months. I rang the GP, who said to take her straight to the hospital; not wait for the ambulance. It was weather rather like this and I was driving fast. I was almost there...'

Steve took a shaky breath. 'I was just turning into the hospital emergency entrance, when an ambulance, going very fast, came the opposite way. I swerved and hit the wall of the hospital. I was knocked out and came round in the A&E department. I remember looking for Sylvia and they said that she was in the maternity ward. They wouldn't let me go to her as they insisted on stitching me up first.' He pulled up a sleeve and we saw a huge scar running up his forearm.

'Eventually, I went through. She was there alright, but the baby had been born dead and Sylvia was in a bad way. She had lost a lot of blood, due more to the birth than the accident, they said.' Here he paused for so long that I began to think that he was regretting his confidences. But with a huge sigh, he continued his sad tale.

'She lived for another two days; she had developed septicaemia and the antibiotics didn't work. She remained unconscious until she died so she didn't know about the baby.' He nodded slightly. 'I'm glad of that, at least.'

Fergie and I murmured our sympathy. The boys didn't know what to say, so wisely kept quiet. The tale was harrowing enough, but there was another cruel twist to come.

Steve continued, 'I was arrested. It seemed that I had been going into the Exit instead of the Entrance. The ambulance was coming out at speed; going to a car crash. Also, earlier in the evening, long before Sylvia started labour, we had had a bottle of wine with our dinner. Because of the baby, Sylvia had very little, so I finished it off. When her pains started and things were not right, and the GP said to take her straight to the hospital, I had completely forgotten about that wine! I just didn't give it a thought.' He looked around at us, obviously wondering if we believed him.

'Well, of course, with that and going into the hospital the wrong way, they accused me of manslaughter.'

'Manslaughter?' Fergie was incredulous.

'I was so upset at losing Sylvia and the baby that I didn't argue. And I blamed myself for everything. Still do. So I went to prison. Eventually, my solicitor insisted that I appeal and they decided that it was "dangerous driving" instead. I did six months and then they let me go. I didn't *want* to be free. I didn't want to *live*!' He sighed. 'Sylvia's family, all our friends, everyone has turned against me. I don't blame them. My job went when I was convicted. I've been roaming about in the Highlands, living rough, not eating… not caring.'

'You sound as though you were hoping to die, perhaps?' I asked gently.

His eyes were full of misery, as he nodded. 'But it doesn't work like that does it?'

I shook my head. 'Don't you know *anyone* you could go to? Where do you – or *did* – you live?'

'Dundee. Yes, I have a sister. She was living abroad at the time, but she's back now and living in Inverness. She wrote to me in prison and wanted to come to visit, but I wouldn't let her. I didn't want to see anyone.' He paused. 'We used to be close, though.'

'I think you know that you can't go on like this, Steve. You need help to deal with the guilt. It's destroying you. It was an accident! A dreadful one, I know, but not really your fault. Would you let me talk to our island GP in the morning? I think he might be able to get you some appropriate help, and perhaps we could get in touch with your sister. She'll probably know that you have been released. She might even have been looking for you.'

Before Steve could answer, Fergie said, 'He could stay with me the night, and get things going in the morning.'

'Good idea,' I said. I was relieved that the problem of a bed for Steve for the night had been solved so easily. I looked at him, 'Can I ring Doctor, Steve?'

His shoulders sagged but he heaved a sigh and nodded. Perhaps he felt that it *was* time to try to forgive himself.

I heard from him some weeks later. He was visiting a counsellor regularly and his widowed sister had taken him to live with her. He had found a job in a rehoming centre for dogs and cats and had adopted a collie himself. Remembering the interaction between him and our two dogs, I could see that this would help *him* – as well as the dog. He seemed hopeful, if not happy. It would take a long, long time.

9

The Calm *and* the Storm

I WONDER WHAT could be more relaxing and rewarding than sitting alone on the shore on a warm, sunny morning? No work (day off) no boys (out for the day) no George (away on a contract)… just me and the two dogs, Pip and Squeak.

The advancing army of the white-topped waves was sparkling in the silvery sunshine of a spring day. The ruined castle on the headland, brilliant against a blue sky, appeared to grow out of the rocks rather than having been built among them, while cattle nosed between the old walls searching for the longer grass which grew in the sheltered corners.

I sat on a grassy stump, where the pebbles gave way to the scrubby vegetation, and leaned back so that I could watch the clouds as they scudded past. Although there was a serene calm where I sat, the wind must have been strong at higher levels as these grey and white, woolly clouds were hurrying across the sky, appearing to nudge each other out of the way. I watched, as they formed and re-formed, changing shape, changing colour as the sun caught them, climbing and falling until they became amorphous as they hid behind the distant mountains.

In our wild location, we needed to make the most of any calm, warm weather with which we were only occasionally blessed. We were more used to apocalyptic storms, snow, icy roads, heavy rain and the rattle in the wind of the bare, brittle, winter branches of our few trees, rather than gentle breezes and dry, sunny days. But all this buffeting by nature's forces is what had fashioned our mountains, burns, shores and the islands themselves: had formed the torrents that rushed down the hillsides, the lochs, dark under grey skies but glistening in sunlight, or restless with huffing wavelets in the wind. Even while we grumbled about getting wet every day for, it seemed, weeks on end; even when we battled to keep the car on the narrow, rutted road in ice or snow; even when I was called out, yet again, at three in the morning on a cold, dark, winter night – yes, even then – we loved this beautiful place with its unique culture and homely people, its sense of timelessness, its history and its folklore. I often felt that the whole spectrum of life was played out in miniature around us.

Animals and birds were very much a part of all this and as I sat now in salty air redolent of warm seaweed and drifting peat smoke, I could see the oyster catchers with their sad call skimming the waves, while seagulls and buzzards patrolled the skies in competition for the meagre pickings of sea, land and sky.

My work was all about the *people*, of course, and I found endless interest in their lives: their opinions, struggles and beliefs as well as their ailments. Old ladies with leg ulcers would tell me about their families in far-flung countries as I dressed the sores; old men with chest infections would wheezily recount stories from their wartime service. Elderly folk with arthritis, due to the damp air of the islands (there were too many such sufferers), mothers-to-be, tough crofters, seamen home on leave, even children, had their own tales to tell and, as their nurse, I was told far more than many an incomer would be privileged to hear.

All district nursing, no matter where, has a certain predictability about it and at times it can be repetitive and monotonous. But our unusual, often harsh location meant that such work was frequently punctuated by considerable excitement: near-drownings and other disasters at sea, fights between drunken crofters, cars in ditches, tramplings by cows (or bulls) and, now-and-then, a gunshot wound – usually a poaching expedition that had gone wrong.

But sometimes, just sometimes, when my relief nurse was on duty, George and the boys were away for some reason, the animals fed and the chores finished, it was good just to *be*. Maybe on the shore as now or, in winter, sitting in the little porch at the front of the house, where I could gaze across the snow-covered crofts to the slate-grey of the sea and the white mountains in the distance. Nearer, the village would seem to be slumbering under its duvet of snow, as work slowed and cattle were driven into the byres for warmth. Footprints of rabbits, birds and even deer would pattern the slopes near the house, only to be obliterated when the dogs were let out to rush about with delight, to eat lumps of snow and roll in ecstasy on the cold ground, barking with excitement.

Now, lazing on the shore, musing in this way, I had not been aware of the approaching figure until the crunch of boots on pebbles brought me down to earth. I squinted up into the sun to see Alice gazing at me with some amusement.

'You were far away. What were you dreaming about?' she asked as she eased herself down beside me.

'I was just thinking how lucky we are to live here; especially on a day like this.'

'I know,' she replied. 'I feel just like that, too.' She paused, looking at the waves and at the sky. 'But, I think we should make the best of the next hour or so. Alistair predicts a storm by lunch-time. That's why I'm out early, gathering these for the garden.'

In her hand were some seed heads of sea pinks – obviously destined to spring to life in her garden next year. Alice was a great gardener. *Real* gardening: growing flowers and unusual shrubs as well as taming the wild, scrubby cliff plants, was her passion and everything that she touched grew and flourished in spite of rain, hail, cold, thin soil and the nibbling of rabbits and deer. Most folk had trouble so much as nurturing a cabbage!

After a brief rest, she sighed. 'I'd better get back. Alistair and Ben are out checking the anchor's on *The Spajag*. They are regretting commissioning her so early in the season, I think.'

We walked back along the shore together and even as we approached Dhubaig the skies were darkening; the wind had changed direction and was now stronger and blustery, while the sea, so inoffensive a few moments ago, seemed to be gathering its forces for an onslaught. The waves were now some eight or nine feet tall as they crashed over themselves on to the pebbles and out in the bay we could see the figures of Alistair and Ben being tossed about as they chugged back to shore in *The Spajag*'s small tender.

Ben was an old seaman, who lived in a cottage on the point near Alistair and Alice's house. He helped to maintain the boat and often accompanied Alistair on his trips around the various islands. He was indispensable, as Alistair had more enthusiasm than expertise and without Ben he would probably have been at the bottom of the sea long ago.

Belatedly very aware of the impending storm, we parted with a quick wave. There was now anger in every cloud and great bands of orange and blue streaked to earth in the blue-black sky. The mountains, so recently anodyne, were black with menace as they seemed to hunch their shoulders against the fury of the wind. We were used to this preamble, this gathering together of nature's forces so that, alongside our awe and admiration for the glories of sky and sea was the pragmatic rush to batten down everything that was movable.

Nick and Andy appeared and helped me to secure the chicken house, the shed doors, the house windows and park the vehicles where they would receive some shelter. Even cars and caravans were sometimes toppled by the force of the wind. We tucked ourselves indoors by a roaring (if rather smoky) fire and listened to the tumult outside with a smug feeling of security.

Not so Alistair and Alice!

At about the same time, Alistair stood at his sitting-room window with his binoculars, watching *The Spajag*, his pride and joy, being tossed from wave to trough and back like a matchbox. Scarcely visible through the lashing rain and the spindrift from the mountainous seas, she appeared and disappeared, first bow up then stern up, completely at the mercy of the elements. Ben, too, was at his cottage window, but he, like Alistair, knew that there was nothing that they could do but watch.

Suddenly, the boat was tossed higher than ever and immediately spun round. The forward anchor had broken and *The Spajag* was wallowing about on the stern anchor only! Both men knew that it would be only a matter of moments before that dragged or the chain broke. Sure enough, the boat began to move down the loch towards the open sea. Slowly at first and then gathering speed, she disappeared round the headland.

'Alice! She's gone!' Alistair knew that no rescue was possible. He loved his boat and was sure that he would never see her again. Alice joined him at the window and was about to put a sympathetic hand on his shoulder when she stopped.

'Al, look!' She grabbed the binoculars. 'She's floating *up* the loch. Look!'

There was *The Spajag*, floundering *up* the loch this time. After his initial relief, Alistair realised that this was not a much better scenario than before, as she would probably collide with one of the rocky islets with which Loch Na Caillach is littered. But at least it might be possible to salvage what was left, he supposed.

'She's well built,' he muttered to himself. 'Clinker built. Good and strong.' He pulled out his pipe and began the pointless task of packing and lighting it: pointless, because he was rarely successful and usually ended up with an unlit pipe full of dead matches.

Alice spoke again. 'Al, she's coming back *down* the loch now.'

And there she was – back again, heading for the open sea once more. Poor Alistair! For several hours, he was forced to watch his beloved craft drifting up and down the loch, tossed and buffeted, but amazingly, still afloat. On one occasion, when she reappeared, she had lost her mast.

Eventually, the storm abated and there was *The Spajag*, battered and bruised, minus most of her superstructure, wallowing in the little bay below the house, rather like a dog that has been off on a spree and has come slinking home.

The cruiser was restored to her former glory in the little boatyard at Dalhavaig, but Alistair sold her the following spring. He felt he was getting too old for all this maritime drama!

IO

A Damp Delivery

IN OUR HEBRIDEAN home, I was lucky in that even the washing-up was done looking at the view. As I clattered about, I could watch the gauzy mist of a November day drift in and out of the dark peaks of craggy mountains, or marvel at lightning snaking to earth through navy blue clouds. And on calm summer evenings I could revel in the golden serenity of the sunset mirrored in the glassy sea.

Occupied in this way one day, I saw a low-loader making its cautious way up the track on the opposite side of the glen. As I watched, it lurched onto a croft and came to rest in front of a ruined house. There it began to disgorge its burden – a long caravan, part yellow, part blue. Several figures, diminished by the distance, were waving their arms about and running to and fro. Eventually, the caravan was positioned and the figures sat on a nearby wall for a smoke.

I knew this to be the temporary home of Danny GG whilst he rebuilt the croft house that he had inherited from his grandparents. The 'G' was added because there were so many Dannys (often with the same surname, too) that identification became difficult. This problem applied throughout the Highlands and Islands as a result of the traditional habit of naming children 'for' fathers, mothers, grandparents. There are countless beautiful names from which to choose, so I found these self-imposed restrictions hard to understand – but that was the way it had always been done. It would probably take many more years and frequent appearances of romantically named film stars in the far-flung cinemas to change these ingrained habits. One family in Dhubaig had further compounded the confusion by naming *both* sons for the father: 'Shoras'. When the second child was born, it was necessary to differentiate, so the first-born became 'Shoras Mor' (Big Shoras) and the baby was 'Shoras Beag' (Little Shoras); but as they grew up, 'Shoras Beag' grew much taller than 'Shoras Mor' so with deadly Celtic logic, one became 'Shoras Mor Beag' and the other 'Shoras Beag Mor' – big, little Shoras and little, big Shoras!

* * *

The delivery of Danny's caravan reminded me of the arrival of our own for we, too, had occupied a residential caravan while our house was rebuilt. We had bought ours from a large city dealer on the east coast of Scotland so the delivery was bound to be long and complicated.

In this remote location, the delivery of anything from a roll of carpet to a septic tank depended on the availability of a lorry, the whim of its driver, the reliability of its engine, the tides, the weather, the steepness of the hills and the state of the narrow roads. In our case, all these variables were further complicated by the lack of any kind of track to our croft. We had to rely on the unlikely blessing of a dry spell to ensure that our goods did not get bogged down on the long-suffering Roddy's croft next door as we trundled back and forth across it.

Our caravan salespeople were apparently having difficulty finding a haulier willing to undertake the hazardous journey to Papavray. This included driving a forty-foot low-loader onto a roll-on roll-off ferry, a feat that required considerable skill in high seas or low tides. Added to this was the further sea crossing on a steamer and the negotiation of the notoriously awkward pier at Dalhavaig.

Many phone calls eventually led to its arrival in Dhubaig: but only to a point on the narrow lane, where it clung to the hill behind the two crofts. There it stayed beside the road for two weeks while the rain fell in a steady downpour and we lived in our tiny tourer. No-one could even contemplate trying to get it across the morass of Roddy's croft in that weather!

Then, quite suddenly, the rain stopped and the land dried out – a bit. I raced to the post office to phone the garage and tell them that we were ready for them to tow our monster into place. I should have known that it would not be so easy, but I was still very new to island limitations!

The driver-cum-garage-owner-cum-undertaker was very sorry, but the lorry had 'broke' and was being 'sorted'. In Scotland, one does not 'mend' anything or 'fix' it in any way. One 'sorts' it.

'When will it be ready?'

'Ach. I'm no sure at all. Maybe Friday.' And with that, I had to be content.

Friday dawned, bright and brittle, but before I could walk the short distance to the phone, a dispirited drizzle began to fall. The ground quickly resumed its spongy texture, as the drizzle turned to the now-familiar downpour. Saturday was no better and no-one worked on Sunday. Well, the positioning of a home was not a 'necessity' or an 'emergency' and I'm quite sure no-one felt like extending mercy in that weather, so the 'no-work on the Sabbath' rule was honoured and everyone went to church.

On Monday, however, the driver, the lorry and the elements combined to favour us and at about two in the afternoon, the rumble and clank of an ancient vehicle was heard in the glen. A dilapidated contraption came into view travelling at about six miles an hour. I heard, later, that it was a modified American army lorry left behind at the end of the Second World War. I'm not really surprised that they *did* leave it behind. The tow-hitch arrangements were no less antiquated and it took four men (some of the crofters had joined us) half an hour to secure the caravan, to their voluble satisfaction.

'Do you no' think we're needin' an extra bit rope on here?'

'Ach, no. You're worrying, man. These wee bolts will hold.'

'They're no' very big!'

The driver, very much in charge, was losing his cigarette from his bottom lip where he managed to balance it at all times. The argument had to be brought to a close.

'I'm tellin' you, it's as safe as yon hill!'

Totally unable to follow this logic, everyone gaped at the hill, thus singled out as the safest among so many; but the driver obviously felt that he had won the day and smugly clambered into the cab.

So the long, slow descent to Roddy's croft started. A narrow, curving track lay at a steep angle and culminated in a gateway that allowed less than a two-inch clearance on each side (we had measured it). And beyond that, the still soggy field had to be negotiated. The driver began to inch forward in his old wreck with our bright, new and expensive home slewing and rocking wildly from side to side, slithering and bumping down the steep slope.

Almost all the men from the village had now arrived to watch and varying instructions, interspersed with depressing prophecies, were yelled by one and all. The driver, however, gave no sign of having heard. Poker-faced, he disregarded every observation or piece of advice so generously given and at no time during the four-hour struggle did his hearing appear to improve. Sucking the muddy cigarette, with his eyes screwed up in an attempt to see through the filthy windscreen, he rattled and ground his gears, pumped the inadequate brakes and cursed absent-mindedly. No-one took the slightest notice of the tense female figure wringing her hands in an agony of frustration whilst watching many hundreds of pounds worth of bright, shiny metal lurching to what looked like undoubted disaster.

Suddenly, he arrived at the gateway. The truck squeezed through, but due to the haphazard arrangement of Roddy's outbuildings, the monstrous caravan could not follow at the same angle. So the whole weary business of unhitching, manoeuvring and re-hitching began again and a precious half hour was wasted. It was beginning to cloud over and the rain, never far away, had begun to fall in a light drizzle. My impatience increased; if they did not hurry, the field would soon be so wet that the entire assemblage might bog down and then it could take weeks to persuade anyone to attempt a rescue.

At last we were ready and, after stolidly lighting another cigarette, the driver climbed laboriously into his cab. He let in the clutch with such ferocity that the old rig, taken by surprise, leapt forward as though suddenly remembering the vitality of its far-off youth. The caravan careered through the gateway. There was a sickening crash and a splintering of glass. The large picture window at the front of the caravan was no more!

Several hours later our new home was in place. With much manhandling, strange oaths, sore hands and soaked clothing, we pushed and shoved in response to the bellicose orders growled wheezily between puffs of the inevitable cigarette. There were many opposing opinions as to how the 'van should be parked.

'You could have it face the croft.'

'If you put it over there, you'll no' get the sun.'

'Murdoch, you come to this end and push.'

'This is the end I'm standin', so this is the end I shall push.'

'Archie, pull yon side round a bit.'

'What for would I do that?'

And so the arguments continued, demonstrating once more the fierce individuality of the Gaels. But it was done, as things always are, with good-natured disputes ending in laughter.

The picture window with its shattered pane was receiving the full force of the driving rain for it faced the sea, each raindrop being caught by the wind and hurled in through the gaping hole.

'Archie, Roddy – do you have a tarpaulin that I might borrow?' I begged.

The driver overheard. 'Ach, a wee drop rain'll do you no harm.' A derisive smile hovered around his mouth, threatening to dislodge the latest cigarette. Obviously pleased with this sally, he reversed his lorry, now free of its burden, and, with the raising of one finger in salute, trundled off into the darkening evening.

It was four weeks before I could convince the island's only glazier to come to Dhubaig and then he calmly told me that he had only come to measure the 'wee windy'. Another three weeks elapsed before the glass was finally in place. We only just dried out for Christmas!

I I

Guilty or Not Guilty

DOCTOR MAC HAD been visiting an old patient in Dhubaig and had dropped in for a cup of tea. He drank more tea than anyone I have ever known and often turned up at our house looking hopeful.

We were chatting quietly when there was a rap on the door followed by a shout.

'Are ye there then, Nurse?'

Although it was about 6pm, I knew it would be Postie. This was our usual time for the mails to be delivered. One of the contradictions on the island was that the postman was termed the 'postie' but the actual post was called the 'mails'. So we had the 'postie' delivering the 'mails', but no-one, other than myself, thought this at all odd! On Fridays, he delivered the local newspaper as well.

I called, 'Come in.' And into the kitchen marched Postie.

'You'll be wantin' to see this, Nurse – Doctor too, I wouldn't wonder.'

He slapped the paper down on the table and stood back with the air of a magician who has successfully pulled off a difficult trick.

The headline read, 'Island Nurse Charged with Murder.' Doctor and I read on with mounting horror and disbelief.

'Angela Robertson, who has served as a district nurse on several of the Western Isles was today (that was two days ago, of course) charged with the murder of her estranged husband who was found in his car outside her house with a fatal stab wound to his chest. The nurse…' and so the article went on.

Briefly, it seemed that the husband had returned to what had been the family home that Angela now owned and lived in. It appeared that he had not attacked *her* in any way, but his blood was discovered on her coat and a blood-stained knife was found in the kitchen. She denied the charges.

Doctor Mac and I had been involved with Angela when she did duty as my relief nurse on Papavray the year before. Her husband had discovered her whereabouts, came demanding money and abused her badly. It then transpired that she also had epilepsy and Doctor Mac had recommended that she be allocated a nursing post where her health could be monitored regularly. We had heard nothing further. Life and duties had taken over and we had all but forgotten the incident. Now this!

'I don't understand this at all,' muttered the doctor. 'She was more like a frightened mouse than a vengeful wife when we knew her. And now they are saying that it was an unprovoked attack! Surely, we know better. I remember him as having a dangerous temper. But, if they are estranged, what was he doing at her house, anyway? I am not inclined to believe a word of this.'

Postie spoke up. 'She looked after the caillach when she had pumony and she was a gey shy, quiet sort of person then. No like you, Nurse.'

I was not sure how to take this.

'Aye, well. We'll doubtless hear some more rubbish soon. I'm no' sure they know what they are talkin' about, at all.' And with this didactic pronouncement, Postie departed in some triumph.

I was worried. Angela had seemed very vulnerable. 'I wish there were something that we could do.'

'No,' said Doctor Mac. 'We will have to wait and see what happens, I suppose.' He finished his tea and left for his home at Dalhavaig.

I sat thinking about Angela and how unsuited she was to the life of a district nurse in the harsh and often difficult environs of the Western Isles. Epileptic, shy, nervous? No. We needed to be tough and resilient in bad weather, on bad roads and sometimes with little or no back-up in emergencies. But I knew that it was not easy to find nurses willing to come to these islands and the Nursing Services were none too fussy about their recruitment methods. I remembered with amusement my own appointment.

* * *

It was only three weeks after we had arrived on the island and we were still living in a large, residential caravan while we waited for a builder to renovate the croft house.

One day, I was in the old house clearing out some of the filthy, mouldy rubbish that had been left there, when I heard a voice.

'Hallo-ow! Anyone there?'

I was wearing the oldest trousers that I possessed and had donned several old pullovers as the house was cold and damp. Cobwebs adhered to my hair and my hands were black. I did not relish visitors!

However, 'I'm here,' I shouted to the invisible owner of the voice.

Some puffing and wheezing came nearer and through the door came a very round, very breathless and *very* smart lady. The badge on her ample bosom identified her as some sort of health official. I wondered why she was here. Something to do with the insanitary state of the old croft, maybe? Did they think we were going to live in it in this state, perhaps?

'Ahh,' she said uncertainly as she extended her hand. I looked pointedly at my filthy one. She changed her mind and put her hand in her pocket. She looked me up and down and hesitated.

'Might we have a chat?' She peered about the dirty, empty room.

'We'll go down to the caravan,' I said.

I led the way, pausing to swill my hands in the stream and remove the topmost and dirtiest pullover. The caravan was bright, warm and clean and while I scrubbed the filth from my hands I could see relief on her face as she realised that I was possibly civilised after all. Over a cup of coffee, Miss MacFarlane, as she was called, relaxed a little. It transpired that she was from the south and had never been to any of the islands before, so she was well out of her comfort zone.

'You'll be knowing that Nurse Andrews is retiring,' she began.

'No. Neither do I know Nurse Andrews,' I replied.

Surprised, she said, 'But Nurse Andrews has been here for twenty-five years.'

Maybe, but I had been here for about twenty-five *days*. But light was dawning as she rambled on about the great job that the redoubtable Nurse Andrews had done during these twenty-five years.

Finally, she said, 'I hear you are a qualified nurse.' I nodded.

'Health visitor?'

More nods.

'Would you consider taking the post? We can't find anyone willing to come to the islands.'

Not very flattering, I thought. A last resort! 'Would I fit in? Would the islanders accept an English woman after having a native of Papavray for so many years?'

'Well, it might take a while, I suppose…' She trailed off. 'But you see, we are rather desperate.'

'Would I be working with the GP?' I had already met Doctor Mac.

'Oh yes! And once a week, a relief nurse would cover your day off.'

'And she lives here, I suppose?'

'Oh no! She would come over from the mainland.'

'Hmm.' I was doubtful about this. Even in the short time that I had been here, I had begun to realise that 'coming over from the mainland' on a regular basis was not a certainty. Storms, fog, sailing schedules and frequent engine failures were the reality.

'Well, we are rather desperate, you see.'

A thought occurred to me. 'How did you know, away down in Head Office, that I was a qualified nurse? Or that I was here at all?'

'Ah, well, you see, I have an aunt who lives in Kirkanbearah, just over on the mainland, and her nephew's friend's daughter lives in Coiravaig and she knows…'

'Archie and Mary,' I finished for her. It had to be! I already knew that Archie and Mary had their fingers very much on the pulse of everything that happened on the island.

'Yes.'

'And what now?'

'What do you mean?'

'Well, if you are offering me the job here and now – and I gather you are, because you are desperate – don't you want some proof that I *am* a qualified nurse? You see, all my papers are in storage until we get the house restored.'

'Oh, well, maybe. But you would be able to supply all those details for your first month's salary, I expect.'

'But I would already have been let loose on the patients by then!'

'Ah, yes. But… umm.' Yes, I knew – she was desperate!

I began to doubt the woman's sanity. Here was I, cobwebbed and filthy, only just arrived on Papavray and English to boot. She had heard third- or fourth-hand that I was a trained nurse and she wanted me to replace one who was a native of the island and had nursed here for twenty-five years! She was desperate indeed!

I told Miss Macfarlane that I would think about it and let her know. She looked quite affronted. Perhaps she felt that I should show more gratitude, and indeed, I was not ungrateful but everything was moving so fast. This was supposed to be a 'get away from it all' venture but, suddenly, it all seemed to be coming with me. I had been a health visitor in England before the move.

A rather put-out lady departed, teetered across Roddy's croft in smart shoes and drove off in an equally smart car.

Later the same day, Andy and I took Duchess for a walk on the shore. On the way back, Morag Macdonald hailed me from her doorway.

'I'm hearin' that you are to be our new nurse, then, Mrs Macleod.'

I suppose I should have realised that the arrival of a smart stranger in a smart car would not have gone unnoticed and the aunt's nephew's sister or whoever it was, had supplied the details which would have been faithfully broadcast by Mary. I didn't have the heart to tell Morag that I was only thinking about it.

But within a week I was kitted out in a uniform, allocated a 'Crown' car and was, once more, a working woman.

*   *   *

In the case of Angela Robertson, we had to be content with snippets of news in the local paper for, although grisly, the murder was not high profile enough to warrant dynamic reporting. On one occasion, however, we read that she had changed her plea to Guilty.

'Ridiculous!' Doctor Mac was incensed. 'She can't be guilty. She is just not the type to take a knife to anyone. She must be protecting someone.'

Archie was present. 'Aye. I'm no sure the polis down in England know what they are about. As if she would use a knife from her ain kitchen to make away wi' him!'

'And she didna even wash it after,' chimed Mary, who seemed more concerned with the apparent lack of hygiene than the incriminating evidence.

Doctor Mac sighed. 'We will have to wait and see what happens. I just hope she has a good lawyer.'

'Huh. Lawyers! They are no better than the polis!' Archie delivered this opinion in heavy tones and departed to milk the cow.

Months went by and the papers forgot the case – for the time being, anyway…

12

Riding Sunshine

JOHN HAD JOINED us on this spring day to help George with a few odd jobs, but the weather had seduced us all into sitting at the front of the house on my newly finished terraced garden. The ground dropped fairly steeply here and I had levelled and planted so that we could put chairs and rugs out to take advantage of our few warm, sunny days.

So we lazed, John, George, Nick and I, while Andy chased about with the dogs some distance away.

The cerulean sky was alive with nature's sounds. Gleaming white gulls leaned on the warm updraughts, brilliant against the clear heavens as they called to their mates nesting near the shore. A huge bumble-bee fanned the air with his wings as he searched for the sweet nectar among the burnished blossoms of early flowers.

The sea moved sluggishly, restlessly eddying into caves, shushing among the pebbles, the waves continuously folding and unfolding in their timeless dance.

A voice in the distance seemed out of place; an intrusion, an unnecessary sound, striking a discordant note, but it floated away – fragmented and fragile – to be blown to oblivion on a breeze so gentle that it felt like warm liquid on one's face. We dozed on.

Our peace was shattered, momentarily, by the singing wings of a pair of swans flying in perfect harmony, their long necks ululating as they wheeled towards the small lochan where they had been repairing last year's nest. Soon they would lay their clutch of perhaps two fat eggs and would noisily guard them against rats, otters, dogs and even golden eagles.

Andy approached, tired of his game, and the dogs departed to the burn for a long, cool drink.

John looked up. 'What about a ride on Sunshine?' he suggested, as Andy seemed at a loss to know what to do next. Nick and John were not keen on riding but knew that I was trying to teach Andy how to manage our rather naughty Highland pony. 'It's a perfect day, the ground is dry and as it's warm she shouldn't be too frisky.'

So off we went to Sunshine's twenty-acre field. I caught her with no problem as she was greedy and readily came to me for the 'nuts' that I held. Saddled up, she stood quietly while we helped Andy onto her back. We all loved this chunky, good-tempered pony but she sometimes had a mind of her own and insisted that the rider went where *she* wanted to go. As she favoured uneven, rocky terrain taken at considerable speed, this habit spelt trouble for both horse and rider, so we were trying to teach her better manners.

Andy had been badly frightened some time ago by the small white pony that we had bought for him. When we had gone to see the animal on an adjacent island, he had seemed quiet, biddable and soft-eyed. Perhaps we should have been suspicious when we learnt his name – Pepper. We swiftly renamed him Snowy, but it made little difference.

Almost immediately, he became fidgety and unpredictable, and within two weeks he was virtually uncontrollable. I rode him a lot myself to try to discipline and calm him but I was no expert and had little success, earning for myself a very painful shoulder caused by sudden and firm contact with the ground.

I did manage to calm him enough to get Andy into the saddle one day but Snowy shied on a steep hill, almost unseating him. I hung on to the lead reins and Andy clutched the pommel but, although he came to no harm, he was badly scared and we decided that he should not try to ride that young pony again. When Snowy added biting to his bad manners, I called the vet.

Iain-Angus listened to our tale and examined him (with difficulty) and soon formed the opinion that he had always been bad-tempered and that the folk who sold him to us had probably drugged him on a regular basis, possibly keeping him slightly sedated all the time in order to sell him. Obviously the drugs wore off once we had him and he had reverted to his crotchety self.

With the vet's backing, I contacted the sellers and asked them to fetch

Snowy and return the purchase price. It was far too easy so Iain-Angus was of the opinion that we were probably the last in a long line of folk who had found the pony to be unsatisfactory and that the owners would now decide to put him down. I was very sorry about this but it was a better scenario than an injured child.

While they were together, however, the two horses had bonded well – *too* well. When I rode Sunshine, Snowy rushed about the paddock, whinnying loudly and as soon as I turned Sunshine for home, she broke into a wild gallop to rejoin him. I only just stopped her from jumping the five-barred gate.

Andy was gradually regaining his confidence on her back and I hoped that he would one day enjoy riding as much as I did. It was not to be.

We walked beside Andy as he rode to the shore. I thought a nice gentle trot across the soft sand would be fine as we – or perhaps John – could keep up with them on the level surface.

What I had not bargained for was the change that last night's storm had wrought on the distribution of the sand and rocks on the beach. Where there had been stretches of clean, level sand yesterday, now there were deep holes and swathes of pebbles scattered across about half the area, while rocks had been exposed by the shifting sand and now stood proud of their surroundings, posing a considerable hazard to a horse. We all paused to rethink our possible destination.

Sunshine, however, had ideas of her own. She suddenly threw up her head, whipping the lead rein from my hand, and took off towards the sea at a fast trot. This was not too bad and I shouted to Andy to hang on tightly. John ran off and caught them up as the horse entered the gentle surf and trotted along at the tide's edge. All was well and Andy enjoyed the sensation of prancing in the water, but then Sunshine decided to set off back to the field (perhaps forgetting that Snowy was no longer there). With Andy clutching the pommel for dear life and John racing alongside, trying to grasp the dangling lead rein, that stupid horse wound her erratic way through every exposed rock on the shore, it seemed, and over the slippery, dangerous pebbles, gaining speed all the time. The rest of us came in from the side, trying to cut her off. She evaded our questing hands, but as we ran in front of her, she had the sense to slow down; my shouts of 'whoa' gradually seemed to enter her consciousness and she drew to a trembling halt.

I rushed to take Andy from her back while John held her firmly and began to walk her away from the pebbles. Andy was chalk-white and close to tears, but unharmed, and had done well to hang on.

It was not a good day, though, because it destroyed his new-found confidence and, although in the following years, even into his forties, he has tried and enjoyed most extreme sports, horse-riding has never figured among them.

A very subdued family returned to dozing in the sun, with birdsong and gentle breezes. It seemed a better option after all.

But a few days later, Sunshine redeemed herself as a sensible Highland pony rather than the wild, stupid animal, who was beginning to worry us. I had made arrangements with Dougall, the estate farm manager, for Sunshine to go over to the farm when the farrier was due to visit the island. There were very few working horses left so Elaine's horse, Rhueben, and Sunshine always joined them at the old Smithy to have their feet pared and new shoes fitted.

The Smithy was a sad place in the seventies, only used twice yearly, whereas the old folk spoke of the roaring fire, the constant stream of horses going in for shoes, and the resident blacksmith who made and mended all manner of crofting equipment up to the fifties. They told us that it was a warm meeting place in the cold winter days where stories were swapped and information passed on. Now, there was no welcoming warmth and cheer, no black-faced, burly smithy. Most crofters had tractors now and had to mend their own tools or buy new from the crofters' store, the old smithy was long dead and the place only came to life when the farrier came over from the mainland twice yearly.

Many of the islands have revived the old blacksmith shops to cope with the growing number of recreational horses and ponies that are now kept by incomers. They are also tourist attractions, making and selling fancy wrought iron work and garden ornaments – something the crofters would have scoffed at in our day.

It was a long walk, even taking a short cut across the open moors and hills, so I usually took Sunshine in the horsebox, but today George suddenly announced that he would ride her the seven or eight miles to the 'other side'. I was surprised and rather worried as George, having been brought up in a city, had only ridden a few times in his life and this was quite an undertaking. But he was determined.

'I'll meet you there with the horsebox in about three hours to bring her back.' I promised.

'Will it take me that long?' At last George seemed to realise how far he was intending to ride.

'Yes, it is very uneven terrain with bogs to avoid – so I would think you had better start now or you will miss the farrier altogether.'

Off they went at a very gentle pace. They would have to follow the road to the top of Loch Annan hill and then there were tracks cross-country towards Cill Donnan and the farm.

I busied myself at home in the house and the so-called garden in which

I was persuading a few flowers to bloom. Mimulas were about the only plants that enjoyed the boggy conditions but they were pretty and the bees loved them, so not *all* my efforts were in vain.

After the required three hours, I rumbled over to the farm with the horse-box. I entered the warm smithy to see Sunshine patiently standing for her hooves to be pared. She was very muddy and looked tired. I looked at George. If Sunshine looked tired, what on earth could I think George looked like? Covered almost to his waist in wet, smelly mud, he was slumped in an old basket chair, his head sagging, his arms hanging and his eyes closed in an attitude of complete exhaustion. I hid a smile but could not resist greeting him brightly.

'Hi! I see you have had a jolly good ride. Nice day for it! Good views from the top, I should think.'

A distinctly unappreciative grunt was all that emerged from among George's beard.

I relented and asked if he was alright. Angus, the farrier spoke up.

'He's about as dead as a living man can be, I'm thinking.'

He grinned at me in such a way that I could not contain myself any longer and burst into uncontrolled laughter. George looked such a sight! My merriment was not entirely appreciated but he did say that Sunshine had been very good and he'd tell me all later. He staggered off to the car and slopped his way into what had been a clean passenger seat.

I concluded the business with the farrier, boxed Sunshine who was remarkably biddable, and drove to her field. Leaving George asleep in the car, I rubbed the filthy pony down, fed her and then drove home. As I suspected, when George tried to get out of the car, he found stiff muscles that he didn't even know he had.

But after groaning his way into a hot bath and a rest in front of the fire, he was prepared to regale Andy and me with the tale of the long, harrowing ride.

All had gone well on the road to the top of Loch Annan hill, where he had stopped for a while but had not dismounted. It had not occurred to either of us that George had never mounted Sunshine from ground level. He had always had an old box that we kept in her shelter. Suddenly, out there on the open hill, he realised that once off the horse, he would probably have to walk the remaining four miles or so, because he would be unable to get on again. She was not very good at standing still whilst one mounted, and with no-one to hold her head *and* no box, he would be in trouble.

I had the greatest trouble containing my mirth through all this, but then he was telling us that he set off cross-country and, although he could see the outline of the farm buildings in the far distance, Sunshine seemed determined to veer off to the higher ground to the right. He tried to steer her back but she would not respond and plodded determinedly on in her chosen direction. He was getting very worried but then she started to swing round to the left again, bringing them back on course.

'I couldn't understand it for a bit,' said George. 'Then I looked back at the vast open space over which I had wanted her to walk and suddenly realised what the pretty white, fluffy plants were. Bog cotton!'

I had guessed, being country born and bred, that this was the case. Horses generally, and Highland ponies in particular, are able to recognise the signs of spongy, boggy ground that they know will not support their weight. So Sunshine had done a great job by calmly ignoring George's demands and plodding confidently along on solid ground and getting them safely to the smithy.

George recovered the use of his legs and ceased to walk as though he still had the horse between them but he did not offer to ride to the smithy again!

13

Father Peter's Quest

JOHN, OUR TRUSTY policeman, was on the phone.

'Nurse, get you up to Loch Annan. I'll ring Doctor. A visitor has just come and told me that Father somebody or other – a priest anyway – is in the ditch up yon. You are nearer – I'll get Doc and I'll come, too.'

'Is he badly hurt, do you know?'

'They didn't say how badly – but he's in pain.'

'I'm on my way. John, get Archie – his tractor might be needed if the Father is trapped.'

Long experience told me that frequently we had to drag a car out of the way before we could treat a crash victim who might be under it.

'What about Ramsey?' (The ambulance.)

'On the mainland, taking wee Alice to the maternity hospital.'

'Ahh.'

I gathered my first aid stuff and all the usual paraphernalia – blankets, small oxygen cylinder, a piece of carpet (often needed to crawl on in wet ditches) and other unlikely things which I had found useful on past occasions.

Speeding up the steep hill, I could see a group of people gathered around a large, black car, nose down in a fairly deep ditch beside a 'passing place'. On the opposite side of the track, squashed up against a rocky outcrop, was a battered truck belonging to Jacko from Dhubaig. He was standing beside it, looking sheepish. It was fairly obvious that the two vehicles had collided.

I called from the car window, 'Are you hurt?'

'No, no not at all, Nurse. 'Tis the Rev. who's poorly.'

As I got out (still in uniform from the day's duties) I was hailed with relief and a babble of voices.

'We didn't move him, Nurse. But we think he's in a lot of pain.'

'Thank you. Please stay around. Our policeman will be here soon and you can tell him how it happened.' I was used to people fading away before the cause of an accident could be established. I added, 'I might be glad of help, too.'

I stepped down into the ditch and peered into the car.

'Why! Father Peter! We meet again.' We had met last summer, when he had been on Papavray, walking for charity.

'I thought it might be you,' said the priest. 'How are you?'

I smiled, 'I am supposed to be the one asking *you* that.'

There was a red lump gradually appearing on his forehead and his right arm seemed to be stuck behind him somehow. His long legs were bent beneath the driver's seat, which had slid forward.

'Where is the pain?'

'Seems to be in my arm… or perhaps my shoulder. It's stuck somehow.'

And stuck it was! Jammed between the back of his seat and the door, the arm was bent in an unnatural position. Collar bone? Humerus?

'Doctor will be here very soon and will be able to give you something for the pain. You have a bump on your head. Were you knocked out?'

'Nn-oo. I don't think so.'

A tourist spoke up. 'He was conscious all the time, Nurse. We saw it happen, and he was asking how that young fellow was – not worrying about himself at all.'

'Can two of you gentlemen come with me round to the other side and we will see if we can open the door. That might release this arm.'

Two men began to shuffle their way into the blessedly dry ditch and round to the driver's side of the crumpled car. Father Peter tried to smile his thanks as they wrestled with the twisted door. But it was wedged firmly.

'Can we, perhaps, move the seat and release the arm that way?' asked a small, slim bespectacled man. 'I could just about get into the back, I think.'

But try as we might, we could not budge anything: everywhere was so bent!

'Doctor will be here in a minute – he'll give the Father something for the pain and then we might be able to prise the arm out, but it would be too painful to try just now. Father Peter, Archie will be here with his tractor very soon and he might be able to lift the weight of the car,' I went on, trying to sound practical and positive, all the time wondering why the good doctor had not arrived.

Then, both he and Archie appeared at the same time from opposite directions, one gliding quietly towards us, the other rattling and groaning up the steep hill in a cloud of black smoke.

Although disguising it well, the doctor was angry. He had been held up by a selfish and very foolish tourist, who would not pull in to a passing place to allow him to overtake. We often had this problem. Some tourists seemed to think that such passing places were only for oncoming traffic, forgetting the need sometimes for overtaking, particularly if there was an emergency of some sort – as now.

'Right! What have we here?'

I explained and gave a brief report of what we had already tried.

'Father, you are in a lot of pain, I can see. This will help, and then we will see what we can do.'

An injection was quickly given, by which time Archie was plodding to and fro assessing the possibilities for lifting the car out of the ditch.

'Can we be doin' anything yet, Doc?'

'A moment, Archie, to let the pain killer act. Then I think you could pull the car up a bit to release that door.'

'Aye. I'll be gettin' the ropes ready, then.'

There were many willing hands to help heave a heavy rope off the tractor and wind it round parts of the car.

'I think we could go ahead now,' said Doctor Mac. 'Father, this will be bumpy, I fear.'

I had managed to get into the passenger seat to hold the Father so that the motion of the lifting car would not be too sudden. We still did not know if there were any broken bones, of course.

The old tractor chugged its slow way up the track until the ropes took the strain then, little by little, the car began to grind its jerky, protesting way up and over the edge of the ditch and onto the passing place. Father Peter was amazingly brave, but every jerk obviously caused great pain.

Two of the tourists pulled the mangled door open so that Doctor could see if the trapped arm could be released.

'Ah,' he said. 'At least it's free and now we can get to it, but I fear that the clavicle is broken and the whole arm in a pretty bad state.' I could see huge gashes and strips of skin just hanging off.

Between us, Doctor Mac and I cleaned the wounds, cutting away his clothing (just a dog collar on a black shirt). Even with the pain-killing drug, all this must have been agony.

'That's enough, Nurse. If you can support his arm and shoulder, we can get him into my car.' Turning to the Father, he added, 'X-ray and theatre for you, I fear; and a spell in the hospital.'

'Not quite what I had planned, but thank you all.' Father Peter's smile encompassed all the helpers.

'Don't worry about the car, Father,' said Archie, as he wound the rope back on the tractor. 'I'll go back for Murdoch and we'll tow it to the garage.'

John had now arrived to talk to the witnesses.

Suddenly, Archie shouted, 'Doc! Doc! Nurse! Look at Jacko! He's no right!'

Jacko had said he was unhurt and so we had ignored him. Now he was slumped against the rock, unconscious and deathly white!

Doctor felt his pulse – very weak – and listened to his breathing – shallow and fast. He did not respond when shaken slightly.

'Internal injuries, I suspect,' was the doctor's opinion. 'Jacko is now our main priority.' He thought for a moment. 'Jacko into my car – John, come too, to give CPR. Nurse, we'll have to get the Father into your little car and you follow us.'

'No!' shouted John. 'My car for Jacko. I have a siren.'

With many willing hands and the utmost speed, Jacko was installed in the police car, doctor jumped in and John took off, siren blaring. Meantime, willing hands had lifted the Father gently into the *doctor's* car instead of mine (everyone was confused at the changing plans) but it *was* a much bigger car and better for a long-legged, injured man. The only trouble was that I had never driven the doctor's huge, ancient – but still splendid – Humber.

Archie saw my concern. 'Ach, 'tis a big brute, foreby, but you'll do it, Nurse, no bother. I'll see to all here – Father's car and his stuff, your...' But I was already starting the powerful engine, thumping the clutch and spinning the wheels as I inexpertly drove off at considerable speed. I wanted to follow John in convoy, or as near as possible, to take advantage of the blaring siren. I didn't want to be held up by another selfish tourist.

In this highly dramatic way we all reached our little island hospital in record time. Having had no way of warning the staff, there was a degree of surprised bustle as we drove up to the only door. But soon Jacko was on his way to the emergency unit with Doctor Mac in attendance. More staff emerged and stretchered Father Peter into a cubicle. I waited with him, telling him that Archie would see to his car and its contents, my abandoned car and Jacko's old truck, too. What a blessing Archie and his cohorts were at such times!

Doctor Mac was right. Jacko had internal injuries and was brought back from the brink. This young tearaway had been so concerned for Father Peter that he had ignored his own 'belly ache' – as he later called the pain. John eventually established that the accident had been entirely Jacko's fault, as he was lighting a cigarette and not watching the road. But Father Peter refused to press charges and even persuaded John to 'forget' Jacko's lack of licence and insurance, as he realised that the lad had almost lost his life in his concern for 'the Rev.'. Jacko had to be transferred to the mainland hospital and spent four weeks – boring weeks, he said – before returning home. Some sages said, 'That will teach him,' but, of course, it didn't. When he saw his truck, he scarcely recognised it as Father Peter had had it mended, old dents (and there were many) knocked out, cleaned, fitted with new tyres, taxed and insured.

Father Peter himself was never in any real danger, but badly shocked and in a lot of pain. The lacerations took a long time to heal as did the fractured collar bone, but after a while in the island hospital, I collected him and installed him in our spare room for a night or two, until his car had been mended and another young priest arrived to drive him home.

George was rather anti-Roman Catholic at the time and the two had some lively arguments, but more interesting to me was Father Peter's reason for his visit to Papavray.

One day, he said, 'You knew Angela Robertson, I'm told.'

Surprised, I asked how *he* knew her.

It seemed that Father Peter had been moved from the Dublin parish, where he had been working when we had met him last year, to a parish on the west coast of Scotland. Angela was working in the hospital there and became one of his parishioners. She had sought his guidance on several occasions when her estranged husband had made his occasional drunken appearances.

'But this charge of murder is ridiculous,' said Father Peter, confirming our own belief. 'And, as for the change of plea to Guilty... well! But I wondered if you had any opinions about her in general which might help me to understand and to portray her quiet nature to the authorities. You see, I think she might be protecting her daughter. *She* is married to a rather shady character and there is a rumour in the church that he was involved in some way with Angela's husband.'

'Doctor Mac and I can confirm that she is a gentle, rather frightened person and that her husband's temper is highly volatile.' I told him about Mr Robertson's attack on Angela here on Papavray and his subsequent arrest.

'All that might be helpful and I shall try to get to the bottom of the plea change. I visit her in jail quite often to give her communion.'

George asked, 'She hasn't confessed anything?'

'No. If she had, I could not divulge the content but I *am* at liberty to tell you that there has been no confession.'

So the matter was left there. Father Peter returned to his parish and inevitably Angela's problems were put to one side as duties, family and everyday chores filled our days.

Then, one Friday, the headline was there. 'Nurse Found Not Guilty'.

'Good,' we all said. 'Justice at last!'

'Well,' said Doctor Mac, 'anyone of us could have told them that and saved the country a lot of money.'

The article went on to say that the son-in-law had been arrested for the murder. Angela's husband had been blackmailing him. He had tried (with some success) to frame Angela and had bullied her into that confession by threatening her daughter. We were reading that Angela was ill and suffering from the frightful and lengthy ordeal.

Again, the weeks went by and the whole matter faded from our minds. Then, I received a letter from Father Peter.

Angela and her daughter had decided to emigrate to New Zealand to forget all the horrors with which they had lived for so long.

'Best thing they could do,' declared Doctor Mac with satisfaction.

14

Bowler Hats

IN SPITE OF THE cold, windy weather outside, the room was warm and cosy: the fire crackled in the grate while the iconic smell of peat smoke wafted across to where I sat at the table, attempting to write up my patient notes. With a Rayburn at the opposite end of the open plan ground floor, and comfortable furniture, the renovated croft house was the epitome of a snug home.

Such a modernised croft house might be almost anywhere until you looked out of the window. Enlarged to take advantage of the view, the window looked out over the crofts and houses of the village dipping away to the front, encompassed by jagged outcrops and high hills on two sides with the pounding sea on the third. Another hill rose steeply behind the house – so steep, in fact, that the sun failed to surmount its summit for some four to six weeks during our northern winter, leaving us in shadow and envying the houses on the opposite side of the glen, which were bathed in weak but welcome sunlight. We relied on artificial light for much of this time, but had purposely installed lights resembling oil lamps so that they added to the general feeling of cosiness.

Living in such a remote and windblown location surrounded by the capricious sea had its disadvantages, of course, but oh, the compensations! The beauty of the majestic mountains with their hurrying, bubbling cascades, the glittering lochs, deep glens and the sight and sound of the surging sea gave my life a simple reality. The things that mattered were the changing seasons, the ancient culture, the timelessness of a way of life now almost unknown in the more sophisticated parts of the country, the challenge of the weather and the earthy, uncomplicated characters around us. All these things combined to give me a feeling of permanence and of being part of the earth on which I stood.

So here I was, writing patient notes. Andy was building something complicated with Lego while Pip lay dozing beside him. Nick was lounging on the settee, teaching Squeak his latest trick.

Nick had become quite the entertainer and had bought a bowler hat for some sketch or joke. The hat was now perched on his head as he bent forwards towards the waiting dog.

He asked, 'What do gentlemen do when they meet a lady?'

Squeak immediately took the brim of the hat in his mouth, whipped it off Nick's head and placed it on his crossed knee. The dog then sat back, head cocked, looking pleased with himself. He was praised for his efforts and they proceeded to the next trick.

Watching this little scene involving the bowler hat took me back many years to a time during my nursing training when I had a most eccentric colleague.

*　*　*

It was during my second year of training in a huge West Country hospital that I found myself on three months of night duty with Bernie. A tall, thick-set, third-year student nurse about to take her finals, she was easy to work with, if a little vague. Together, with the help of an orderly (an untrained assistant) we coped nightly with a forty-bedded female surgical ward.

This was 1951. Wards were vast, bleak, bare, but very clean. The elderly iron beds were arranged down the sides of the ward, about fifteen or sixteen on each side and the 'overflow' ten or so were placed in the middle. These poor patients had very little privacy as they had no wall behind them and were packed so closely together that getting the old-fashioned screens around them for treatments was nearly impossible.

But the hospital was still in the post-war mode of trying to catch up on all the surgery that had been kept on hold during the days of bomb casualties, maritime disasters and other war-related emergencies; all at a time when they had had to cope with a much reduced surgical staff. Many surgeons were only now beginning to return from work in the occupied countries, in military hospitals and in the Far East. On the whole, the patients were amazingly understanding and grateful that they were being attended to at last. We managed as well as we could in the difficult conditions, with far too few staff, rigid discipline and a working week of seventy-two hours, sometimes more.

At night, the nurses had a desk with a hooded light in the middle of the ward but fairly near the door. The recent surgical cases or very ill patients were arranged at this end so that we could attend to them or monitor their progress and, sadly, so that if one of these people should die, it was less distressing for the rest of the ward if we could remove them quickly and quietly, rather than trundling the deceased from one end of the ward to the other. Similarly, those who had been admitted and were awaiting operation or those who were near to discharge and were therefore not in need of constant surveillance, were arranged at the far end, away from the inevitable hubbub near the door.

This particular night had already been hectic. Several operations had taken place that day so we had five or six patients needing hourly checks, oxygen, aspirations, dressings and so on. There had been a road accident in the city and two of the casualties had arrived on our ward. About seven or eight other patients were still critical after surgery some days ago.

So we were very busy, but during a slight lull, Bernie sent me off to have my 'lunch' at about midnight. I trotted off to drink hot tea and eat a hearty meal, leaving Bernie at the desk writing up the report on the new admissions and monitoring the surgical cases. She would have her meal when I returned and, in view of my inexperience, I hoped that she would make it a quick one.

These arrangements seem haphazard and perhaps unsafe, compared to today's world of sophisticated monitoring machines, better staffing levels and smaller wards, but this was the post-war reality of a country trying to deliver a good service with out-of-date equipment, new drugs, hurried social reforms, a sudden influx of young, untried doctors and nurses, and a dozen other problems of which, from our humble positions, we knew nothing.

I returned to the ward before my allotted half hour because we were so busy. The orderly was clattering about in the ward kitchen and the sluices. I approached the desk and there, with her head pillowed on her arms, was Bernie – sound asleep! I could see at least two drips about to run out and a patient was calling for assistance. I shook Bernie, who jerked her head up, blinked and said, 'Whoops!'

I was her junior so I could say nothing, but I *thought* quite a lot as we rushed about, renewing drips, dealing with overdue treatments and taking temperatures. Eventually, Bernie began her overdue ward round while I dealt with some more basic patient needs.

She had reached the far end of the ward and was flashing her torch briefly over the not-so-ill patients, when she paused beside the bed of a very old lady who was awaiting discharge. A moment passed then Bernie came racing up the ward.

'Quick! Get all the hot water bottles that you can find.'

I stared at her, but I was used to doing as I was told without knowing why, so I hurried to the linen cupboard, found six bottles which I took to the kitchen where Bernie was filling both the huge kettles and placing them on the gas cooker.

She looked at me. 'Not a word to Night Sister if she comes round. Leave her to me.'

'What's happened?' I ventured.

'Old Mrs Light has died. *That's* what happened. I was asleep – didn't do the midnight round, did I? She's cold. I can't report it now. She's been gone at least two hours.'

I was appalled and frightened. Frightened for Bernie, but I wondered if I would get blamed too.

Bernie continued talking while watching the roaring gas as though trying to hurry it up.

'I don't think there was anything to be done for her – she must have gone in her sleep. What was she in for – I forget.'

Luckily, I had an odd ability which now came in useful. 'Florence Light, aged ninety-two, osteoarthritis. Fell at home two days ago. No injuries – only shock. Ambulant. For discharge to convalescent home tomorrow – today now. First hospital admission ever.'

Bernie looked at me. 'Gosh. Wish I could remember half that much.'

Already guessing, I asked, 'What are you going to do?'

'*We*,' she emphasised. (So I *was* going to be implicated.) 'We are going to warm her up for a while and *then* I shall report the death at whatever time that will be.'

She looked at her watch. 'We'll just about make it before the day staff comes on. That's good because *you* can do Last Offices – better than handing over to them.'

I was getting more and more frightened, but soon we were creeping quickly down the ward and surreptitiously pushing hot water bottles in among the blankets and some below the mattress. The old lady probably *had* died in her sleep as she looked very peaceful. I was relieved to see that.

'I'll pop back to move them now and then,' said Bernie. 'Go and see if you can find any more.'

I have to admit that my worry was for Bernie and myself. I did not think that we had contributed to Mrs Light's death. She was old – there were not many nonagenarians in the fifties. She was frail and had had a shock – two shocks – the fall and being admitted to hospital for the only time in her life. We did not have sophisticated means of resuscitation, but even if we had been able to try, a ninety-two-year-old was unlikely to respond, especially as we had no way of knowing exactly when she had died. It was not necessarily during the time that Bernie was asleep. In fact, it was probably before that, maybe just after her previous round, because the old lady was already cold when Bernie found her. So that side of the event was not heavily on our consciences, but I was revolted by what we were doing. But then again, I thought, as I dug out another hot water bottle, it was not going to make any difference to Mrs Light. Bernie, however, could be thrown out, as sleeping on duty was, understandably, an offence punishable by dismissal. She would not have been allowed to take her finals, due in a week, and would end up with no qualifications and no job.

I, on the other hand, would not be blamed for not noticing the death, but I would be in trouble for helping to cover it up. But what was the alternative? Run to Night Sister? Tell the Ward Sister when she came on duty? Bernie was a good nurse. Others before her had fallen asleep on duty, as much due to exhaustion as lack of self-discipline. She had been unfortunate.

I rushed about finishing all the night tasks and then waking the 'fit' patients with a cup of tea. The days began before six in the morning for patients in those days, because so much had to be done by so few staff. From time to time, I saw Bernie wander to Mrs Light's bed and eventually she walked up the ward with a bundle of bed linen. The bottles were being removed. Then back she went, trundling two screens which she quietly placed round the old lady's bed. Various patients appeared to ask her questions and she gently shook her head. She went to the phone in Sister's office.

On her return, she came up to me.

'Okay. I have reported the death as taking place at five o' clock. I told Night Sister that she must have popped off in her sleep, so I did not know the exact time. I told her that I was doing the six o' clock round when I found her. Doctor-on-Duty is on his way to confirm death.' She looked at me. 'Keep your head… in fact, just keep out of the way.'

I was only too happy to do just that, but my heart was hammering as the doctor appeared. Suppose he guessed, somehow, that she had been dead for several hours instead of only one?

Bernie, cool as a cucumber, accompanied him and they disappeared behind the screens. After only a moment, they came out, chatting quietly, the doctor signed various forms at the desk and departed.

'Right,' said Bernie, 'you can do Last Offices right away. The day staff are on their way – so get on with it.' She did not say this in an aggressive manner, but seemed at last to be feeling the strain.

I had to leave various lesser jobs and I knew that the day staff would grumble later when they found that things like some catheter bags had not been emptied and measured. I quickly gathered all the necessary bathing materials and linens, while Bernie went into the office to give Day Sister the night report. I did not even want to think about that.

As I pushed the trolley with all the paraphernalia behind the screens, I happened to glance under the bed. On the floor, for all to see, lay one of the hot water bottles! Bernie had missed it. It must have slipped from below the mattress. What should I do?

Ward Sister would be round in a moment.

I emptied its contents into the water jug on the locker and pushed the flattened bottle back under the mattress. I would wrap it in the soiled bed linen that I would remove when I had finished my task. All the time I worked, I was aware of that bottle lying beneath the mattress: the mattress that would be removed later for disinfecting – a procedure always followed after a death. At all costs, I must not forget to take it away before the porters came for the deceased.

At last all was done. I bundled the bottle in among the linen and hurried off to the sluice.

'All done then, Nurse?'

I jumped as Sister's voice came from the doorway.

'Yes, Sister. I'm just clearing up. Mrs Light is ready for removal.'

'Good. You have both been very busy, I believe. Nurse Birkett tells me that you have been invaluable – working very hard.'

The skin on my back prickled. This was Bernie making sure that I kept quiet by putting in a good word for me, ensuring my gratitude. I thought to myself that she would make either a clever criminal or a good detective. It certainly seemed as though we had got away with it. We went off duty, I to have a much needed sleep and Bernie to start her study leave for her finals.

It would be nice to say that we met up in mutual relief, but she was two years ahead of me and had her own circle of friends and colleagues, so we did not see each other again. In fact, she seemed to disappear and I sometimes wondered why I did not catch so much as a glimpse of her. But life was full, work was hard, off duty times were fun and she faded from my world.

So why did a bowler hat remind me of Bernie?

It was several years after the Mrs Light affair and I was qualified and a staff nurse by then. I was walking in the town one day when I saw Bernie. *Was* it Bernie? She had always been 'different', but this figure was amazing.

Striding along in an almost military fashion, pushing a rather old pram containing a fat, sleeping baby, was this outlandish figure in a man's overcoat which flapped open to reveal baggy dungarees. A pair of workman's boots with red socks clumped noisily as she walked and adorning her shaggy head was a bowler hat! She did not see me but I was able to watch her meet up with the man whom I later heard was her husband. He was equally startling. Wearing a cloth cap, a red and white striped scarf over an Air Force blue coat which was so long that it dragged on the ground, he sported a moustache and a huge, bushy beard. This unusual couple greeted each other with a passionate hug. The man picked the baby from the pram, cuddled it for a moment before restoring it to its nest of slightly grubby-looking blankets. He then took over the pram pushing and as they turned, I could see that Bernie was hugely pregnant. They strode off with flat cap and bowler hat close together as they chatted.

In 1951, girls wore feminine dresses or skirts. Generally, trousers were kept for sport, gardening, country rambling. We were a generation reacting to the austere times of war time clothes rationing. We had small waists, flouncy skirts, shaped coats and high heels, while nylon stockings were still prized possessions, expensive and difficult to get. We wore pretty hats for shopping and for visiting; we made sure that the seams of our stockings were straight. We prided ourselves on our femininity and prettiness. So Bernie's outfit was all the more startling when compared with the fashion of the time.

It seemed that she had left soon after her finals, married her man and had fallen pregnant almost immediately. He had inherited a lot of money so neither of them worked. They lived in an apartment in his parent's ancestral home.

Bernie continued to be seen in the town, usually pregnant and always wearing a bowler hat.

15

The Tangled Web

'INDEED, NURSE, I think they are very quiet.'

'Who is very quiet, Sarah?'

'Those two folk in yon caravan thing – in the woods.'

I was sitting chatting with old Sarah as she pottered about polishing the furniture, the rugs, the cups and saucers, in fact, everything in sight. Whenever I was in her house, I felt that I should keep on the move or I might get polished, too. In her late eighties, Sarah was getting very confused and I kept a close eye on her as she was becoming a danger to herself. Luckily, I had been present a few months ago when she set light to her clothes by standing too near to the fire. No real harm was done except that her only skirt was burnt to nothing. I smiled now as I noticed that she was still wearing the one that I had given her as a replacement at the time. I was about a foot taller than Sarah so it was long and cosy on her and every time I called, she thanked me all over again for 'the bonny wee skirt'.

'How do you know this, Sarah?' She never went far beyond her croft house now as she only had chickens to see to. She had decided that milking her cow was too much for her and had given it to Archie to look after so long as he took her some milk every day. Archie was delighted, promptly put the cow to the bull and now had a strong female calf.

'Old Roderick brought me ma goods and he said the car had no' moved in days.'

'Perhaps they are great walkers, Sarah, and just leave the car and go off on a ramble?'

But Sarah had lost interest and was telling me that young Donny the Sheiling had been to see her. Donny had been a recluse, living in the sheiling in the hills behind her croft and rumour had it that they had been sweethearts at one time. But Donny had been dead for ten years and Sarah's mind was back in the past.

'He's comin' again on the morrow, so I'll be gettin' the place cleaned up.'

'The place' was like a new pin, but cleaning gave Sarah something to do.

'That will be nice, Sarah, but remember that old cow of his often gets out and he has to fetch her back from the moor so don't be too disappointed if he doesn't come, will you?'

'Aye. 'Tis true. An awkward beast is that one.'

With the usual thanks for the bonny wee skirt, she waved me off. She had probably forgotten about Donny again by now. A conversation with Sarah always left me wondering if I was getting as mad as she was – talking about a cow that must have been someone's dinner over twenty years ago!

What had she been saying? People in the woods? Had Old Roderick really said something about it? Or was this Sarah's mind wandering again?

I had other patients to see, but I drove quickly down the little track behind Sarah's house to see if anything made sense. The caravan was small and rather battered while the car – a Mercedes – was new and shiny. But just looking at the scene told me nothing. Should I knock, on some pretext? What reason could I give for such an intrusion? Maybe I should see Old Roderick when I got back from duty.

'Aye, Nurse. 'Tis a wee bit worryin, foreby. I think they have been there some three full days, not countin' today, y'understand. Naebody seems to have seen them and they havena been to ma wee shop, but I'm not knowing if they might have been to Dalhavaig for the shopping.' Roderick rubbed his head. 'Do you think we should be doin' something, then, Nurse?'

'I just don't know, Roderick. I'll have a word with Doctor.'

'Aye. Good idea.' All the locals had tremendous respect for Doctor Mac: a respect which extended far beyond his medical knowledge. To them, he was the Oracle and the Muses all rolled into one beloved man.

But before I could speak to Doctor Mac, Postie, calling with the mails, also mentioned the caravan. He reported one of old Martin's dogs prowling around the van and scrabbling at the door. Martin had called the animal off but had not investigated.

I was getting really worried now so I decided to ring our policeman, John.

'Hmm. All a bit odd,' was the reply. 'I think I might go down there and have a wee look. I would like a witness though, in case I need to get in to the caravan for any reason.'

'What about Doctor?' I asked hopefully. I didn't like this at all and would have preferred to be left out of it.

'Surgery?'

'Of course!'

I could hear amusement in his voice as John said, 'You don't want to come, do you?'

'Frankly – no. But I'll meet you outside Sarah's house in half an hour.'

We met as planned. Sarah had seen us and ran to meet us, declaring that she would be coming with us. It took all my persuasion and John's heavier tones to impress upon her that it was no job for a lady like her. The term 'lady' did the trick and she returned with dignity to stand at her doorway.

The caravan curtains were drawn. We could see that the summer grass was already climbing the wheels of both car and caravan and that there were scratch marks on the door, presumably made by Martin's dog.

John approached and rapped briskly on the door. No reply and no sound from within. He tried again. 'Police here,' he shouted. Still no reply. He glanced at the window; there was a slight gap where the curtains met. Fishing a torch from his pocket, he peered inside.

'I think there is someone there but I can't see much. I'll have to break in.'

He went back to his car, returning with a hefty screwdriver, which he inserted behind the door handle. The flimsy metal of the door bent and with a grating sound it flew open.

We both took a step backwards as there was an ominous buzzing and a dozen or so flies zoomed past us.

'Ugh! I'll go in first,' said John. 'I think we both know what we are going to find.'

He re-emerged, his face a greenish hue and I was not surprised when he turned away and was very sick.

'Sorry.' He looked at me, wiping his mouth. 'I'm sorry but I need you to have a look, too.'

I held a handkerchief to my nose and gingerly entered the fetid area.

Two people, a middle-aged man and woman lay together, partially dressed, on the bed. They must have been dead for most of the three days that the 'van had been there, judging by the general pallor and blue extremities, but I knew I would be asked if I had ascertained life to be extinct (although it was very evident that it was), so I reluctantly felt the necks of the two. Of course, there was no pulse. John was watching from the door.

'What about Doctor?' I asked. 'I am not qualified to pronounce them dead.'

'I'll need help from the mainland for this and they will send the police surgeon. We had better not touch anything else.'

I was overcoming some of my revulsion and looking round. An unmarked bottle, still containing a few white tablets, stood on the table among the remains of what had been a steak dinner. An empty wine bottle was beside the only glass, which was half full. With reluctance, I looked again at the couple on the bed. Something had struck me as being very odd – not fitting. The man, even in death, appeared to be well dressed and had a groomed appearance, and there was a pair of polished leather shoes on the floor. The woman, by contrast, was in cheap underwear and a floral cotton skirt which was frayed at the hem. Her high-heeled shoes, on the floor beside his, were scuffed and dirty.

On the shelf above the bed was a folded piece of paper.

'John, a suicide note, I think. Should I pick it up? Fingerprints...?'

'Plenty of other stuff for fingerprints. Yes, please. Bring it out here.'

I noticed that John did not enter to fetch it, but waited by the door as I gingerly picked up the note and, glancing once more at the pathetic scene, went out into the blessedly fresh atmosphere. As the cold air hit me, my legs felt distinctly wobbly and I closed my eyes for a moment to try to rid myself of a belated feeling of nausea. What a terrible scene!

What had persuaded two middle-aged people to kill themselves? Out here, the birds were singing and I could smell the resin in the pine trees. The sky was blue, with lazy clouds floating nonchalantly past the heather-clad hill behind the forest. A white butterfly fluttered gently back and forth. It was all so beautiful, so fresh and normal, and yet in that caravan, two people lay dead, putrefying among decaying food, dirty dishes and flies.

Outside, we sat a little way off on a fallen tree and looked at the note.

'No envelope,' said John. He unfolded the single sheet. There were two letters, each in very different writing.

'My Dear Gerald, I am sorry for the hurt that I have caused you. I can't continue our lives together. Tell Ellen that I love her. Margery.' This was in a neat, rather childish hand.

The second was in bold, rather sprawling writing. 'Dear Jennifer, I find it impossible to carry on. Life has been a nightmare for a long time. Bernard.'

I thought about the letters for a moment.

'John, these are not exactly suicide notes are they? One says that she 'can't continue our lives together' and the man just says he 'finds it impossible to carry on'. But neither actually says that they are going to kill themselves, do they?'

John nodded. 'This might make things very complicated. But that is for the team from the mainland to sort out, I'm glad to say. I haven't had anything quite like this to deal with before.'

'Neither have I, John. What happens now?'

'I need to stay here because I can't secure the door. So can you ring this number and give them the gist of things?' He handed me a card.

I nodded. 'I'll ring from home. If there is a return message, I'll bring it along to you.'

Leaving the forlorn-looking figure, I hurried off.

Once home, I shooed Andy off while I made the call, explaining to the mainland police that our local constable would remain at the scene until they arrived. They hoped to be there in an hour or so. Had I ascertained that life was extinct? (I knew it!) Yes, both were dead. Was the scene secure? While John stayed there – yes. Was there a suicide note? This was more difficult.

'Well, there is a note – of sorts. It will be up to you to say if it is a suicide note or not. John has it.'

'Hmm. Sounds intriguing. Do you not think it *is* a case of suicide, then, Nurse?'

I was not going to be drawn into this! 'I do not have an opinion,' I replied. 'I will tell our constable that you are on your way, shall I?'

He gave me his name and assured me that they would be there as soon as possible.

Andy and I set off to give John the message and to continue to the steamer to collect Nick and the rest of the Dhubaig pupils as it was Friday.

At Sarah's cottage, I turned up the track and gave a bored-looking John the news that the police would be here in about an hour.

'Can you give my wife a ring? She will be wondering what is happening.'

'Of course. Can Moira bring you a drink or anything?'

'No – because of the wee one. No matter.'

'If you are still here when I get back, I'll bring you something,' I paused and added with a smile, 'You could always ask Sarah, if you don't mind furniture polish all over your mug.'

'Thank *you* – I think not!'

The boys were agog when I told them what had happened and when we passed Sarah's cottage on our way back, we could see two police cars, flood lights, yards of red and white tape, several police and a sombre black van which we assumed would bear the bodies away – probably to the mainland. I was just accelerating away when a wild figure in long flowing clothes leaped into the road.

'Sarah!' I only just avoided her. 'You'll get yourself killed!'

'Nurse! I'm no liking all these policemen here. It's no' right to disturb those two folk like this. Like I said, they are quiet folk.' She was very distressed.

Neither John nor I had told Sarah anything about the deaths and obviously the police had not either. How do you tell someone as deranged as Sarah that two people are lying dead in a caravan a few yards from her house?

I asked the boys to talk to her while I walked over to the police.

'And say what, Mum?'

'Use your imagination.' I realised I was being rather unfair.

A large uniformed policeman approached me and, well within Sarah's hearing said, 'Just get that batty old woman out of here, will you?'

I resented being ordered around, but more important was the way in which he referred to Sarah.

'I shall talk to *Miss Sarah Burn* on your behalf, but you will treat her with respect, if you please.' I was glad I was in uniform. That uniform was a blessing in many ways – giving me dignity and credibility in situations like this.

He had the decency to look abashed. 'I'm sorry. But we can't have her interfering here, possibly destroying evidence etc. We shall be out of here in about an hour, but the area will remain cordoned off until tomorrow.'

'I think I will tell her that they are ill and that you are all helping them and will be taking them to hospital, and that she had better keep away because... because...' I thought rapidly. 'Because they are infectious! That might do it – but I can't be sure. She is very confused.'

'Worth a try.' The policeman nodded. 'If that does not work, I shall have to escort her to her cottage and put a constable, perhaps your own John, on the door to ensure she stays inside.'

I returned to where the boys were actually making Sarah laugh. I walked her back to her house, telling her the myth that I hoped would persuade her to keep out of the way.

Judging by the look of concern on her old face, I thought I had won, but then she said: 'But I could always give those nice policemen a cuppie.'

Oh Sarah! What are we to do with you?

'No, Sarah. No.' I had a sudden inspiration. 'Sarah, Doctor Mac said you must stay inside and not go anywhere near. He will be cross if you do not do what he says.'

It worked! At the mention of her beloved Doctor Mac, Sarah became compliant.

'Right, Nurse. I'll be doin' what the doctor says.'

With a sigh of relief, but still wondering if she would remember what the doctor was supposed to have said, I departed, promising to call the next day.

When I went into the surgery the next morning, a harassed John was talking to Doctor Mac. Apparently, all my so-called clever ideas had failed and just a few minutes after my departure, Sarah had emerged from her cottage and tottered into the middle of the investigation, bearing a mug of tea for Doctor Mac. Somehow she had arrived at the conclusion that the doctor was actually there. The senior officer had ordered John to take her inside and stay with her. Later he sent for a female officer (who had to come from Fort William) who stayed with Sarah for the remainder of the night and was still there this morning. John was at his wits end as the officer wanted to leave, the police needed to ensure that Sarah stayed out of the way and John had other duties to attend to.

'They will be finished by midday they say,' said John.

I could guess what was coming.

Doctor Mac turned. 'Nurse...'

'Yes, of course,' I answered his unspoken request and hurried off to do the essential insulins and then make my way to Sarah's cottage. A weary policewoman greeted me with her finger pressed to her lips. Sarah was asleep on the old couch. With scarcely a nod, the officer departed at speed.

There was still a lot of activity in the little clearing but the car had gone and the caravan was being winched onto a low-loader ready for departure. Several police were still examining the surrounding area. For what, I wondered? To me, it certainly *looked* like suicide but I suppose those letters were not conclusive, so they must be investigating every possibility.

I sat quietly with Sarah as she slept. I wondered how long we would be able to let her stay at home. She was getting rapidly more confused and forgetful and I could think that she might start to wander off, maybe get lost, stay out all night, get hypothermia... the possibilities were horrifying. But apart from the odd time, she was happy in the home she had lived in all her life, managed to wash and feed herself after a fashion, and pottered to and from her chickens. All the excitement had undoubtedly upset her, so she might be better when everyone had gone away. Doctor Mac and I would have to have a talk. I, too, had great faith in the wisdom of the good doctor.

In sharp contrast with the hectic two days, we heard nothing at all of the investigation for some time. Even John heard nothing. Then a tiny paragraph appeared in the local paper in the 'deaths' column to the effect that Margery would be 'sorely missed by her loving husband and her daughter, Ellen.' Why in the local paper, we wondered? The police had said that the couple were from London.

Then, a few weeks later, I had a visit from Detective Inspector Bligh, asking me to go over what I had already told them. Yes, I had felt the pulses – absent. Yes, I had seen the bottle with tablets in. How many? No idea. No, I had not touched it – in fact nothing except the note and the necks of the two deceased. So it went on. I felt it to be pointless repetition, but I suppose they had to check every possibility and he was probably comparing my story with John's.

But after a cup of tea (bribery), he gave me an account of the investigation. Should he have done that, I wondered, but I was too curious to question his decision.

The identification of both parties had been easy as there had been no attempt at concealment. The man was a fifty-six-year-old successful business man, living in West London. The inspector had visited the beautiful house and broken the news to an equally beautiful wife. Although shocked, she did not display grief and was unsurprised to hear the he was with a woman. She had been aware that he was depressed and on medication, but had not thought him to be suicidal. There were no financial problems, but she had thought for a while that he was trying to make up his mind to leave her.

Then the Inspector had visited a very different address. The woman, Margery, had lived with her husband, who was a taxi driver, in a little semi in a dingy street near Bernard's more opulent avenue. The little man was devastated when the news was broken and refused to believe that his wife had been with a man. He also fiercely resisted all suggestion of suicide. His wife was a staunch Methodist, believing that life was God-given. (At this point in the narrative, I remembered the single wine glass – as a Methodist, she would be unlikely to drink.) So what did he make of the fact that they were in bed together in a caravan, far from home? He maintained that she would not have been unfaithful to him unless... And here, apparently, another most interesting fact emerged. She had been the cleaning lady for Bernard and his wife (who was outraged when told her identity) and had mentioned to her husband that she was concerned about her employer's depressed state. He must have played on this in order to gain her sympathy, having none from his wife.

The Inspector went on to tell me that she was a very impressionable lady, not at all intelligent, gullible, perhaps, and naïve. She was also being treated for a very bad menopause. By piecing everything together, he concluded that she had been persuaded to go on holiday with Bernard 'for the sake of his health'. She thought that her husband would stop her (!) so it had all been arranged in secret. So far as she was concerned, it seemed that she was not expecting to sleep with him. Could a woman be this naïve?

When he forced himself on her (evidence showed this to have been the case), she was probably overcome by guilt and was persuaded to join him in a suicide pact. The notes implied something like that.

'Are you sure of all this? How can you know what went on in her mind and between them when they were alone?' I was very sceptical.

'As with many rather feeble-minded women of that age, she had inflated ideas of her own intelligence and allure and kept a somewhat fragmented diary full of all sorts of romantic notions. In spite of her capacity for self-delusion, it seems unbelievable that she had no idea that he wanted sex with her. She thought their relationship was "beautiful".' He shook his head. 'Incredible.'

'What did she think he wanted, if not sex?' I asked.

He shrugged. 'I can't imagine what went on in her head. I'm very sorry for that nice little man, her husband.'

And that was the end of it all.

I could not help thinking that Sarah's dementia was far more understandable than the selfish, manipulative, depressive behaviour of the man and the unimaginable rubbish that must have washed around in that poor woman's head.

But it was not *quite* the end of it all.

Some months later, Margery's husband made his way to Papavray to see where his wife had died. He called on me to thank me for what I had done (actually very little). I felt overwhelmed and very humble. Why, oh why did Margery turn her back on such a thoughtful man, who obviously loved her dearly?

Yes, indeed. What a tangled web…

16

Eggs, Eggs and More Eggs

THE WIND WAS howling ever louder by the minute. We could scarcely see out of the window, it was so thick with salt. The sea was throwing up huge spindrift which was flung inland on the cusp of the pugnacious gusts. The wind and the lashing rain assaulted the bruised hillsides, uprooting bushes and sweeping bits of hay and thatch, tree branches and other detritus past the house at a furious rate.

But we were snug: the chickens shut in their hut, two cats and two dogs asleep in front of the Rayburn while the family sat before the fire which belched peaty smoke into the room with every squall. Even Sunshine was safely tucked up in the hay shed. This weather had been forecast so I had had time to bring her home from her field, where her shelter was showing signs of rot and might well take flight in such weather as this.

Secure in our sturdy – if smoky – home, George and I dozed while Nick and Andy played Scrabble. I think some strange words were being added to the English language. All was peaceful.

Suddenly, all the lights went out. We were used to power failures in such weather but, looking from the window, I could see lights still on in the croft houses in the village, so this was obviously not general. There must be something wrong here. And there was! As we peered out, we watched in fascination as the electricity pole with the big, metal transformer at the top began slowly to bend, creak and, finally, break. The top half, with its burden, fell slowly to earth. It bounced twice and we could hear the sound of shattering metal. A few sparks added to the spectacle.

George sighed. 'Well. That's that. We can't expect Young Doug to come out in this!' 'Young Doug' was the linesman who had installed the pole and the transformer in the first place and who did all the local maintenance work for the electricity board. He was unnaturally enthusiastic about his work.

'I don't think we will ask him,' I replied. 'He would probably come out in an earthquake let alone a storm!'

I was recalling the occasion of the initial installation.

* * *

When we bought the old croft house in 1969, electricity was already conn-ected to the village but the mains supply was insufficient to take an extra property, so we had to have a pole and a transformer. All at vast cost, of course. The only place for a pole was in the area that we had already made into a sizeable chicken run, but this was no problem to Young Doug, appar-ently, although his job was to fix the transformer to the top of the pole.

Along he came and drove his van as close as he could to the pole, emerged and untied a tall ladder from the roof rack. There was a brisk wind blowing on that occasion, too, but I wondered – was his unsteady gait due to the elements, the weight of the ladder or had he been drinking? I was horrified to think that he was about to climb so high, shouldering the transformer, a sizeable and doubtless heavy object, and then cling on while using both hands to affix it. I could see that he was having trouble even placing the ladder against the pole. I ran outside hoping to delay and possi-bly sober him a little.

'Would you like a cup of coffee?' I shouted.

'Ach, no. I never drink the stuff.' (Later, I learnt that very few crofters drank coffee.)

'Tea?'

'Ach, no. I'll be gettin' on wi' this the now.'

Once at the top, he somehow balanced the transformer while he put a strap around himself and the pole. It promptly came undone and fell to the ground.

I ran to pick it up from the mud.

'Ach. Leave it be. I'm no' needin it.'

And there he dangled. It was a foolish and dangerous thing to do for a *sober,* man but Doug was very far from that. I watched for a while but I felt that he did not like my attention, so I went indoors. The job was done, eventually, and I persuaded him in to the warmth and finally to drink a cup of tea. He slouched on the settee, almost lying rather than sitting. I think the sudden warmth must have rekindled the effect of the whisky (and I had been here long enough already to know that it would be *whisky*) so that he seemed almost asleep.

Then he said, 'I saw the eggs.'

'Sorry?'

'Eggs. I saw them.'

'Oh! Are there any today? We have not been getting any recently.'

'Ach, no. You'll not get any wi' the mud.'

'How do you mean?'

'I saw them eating the eggs.'

I looked at the bleary face. What was he talking about?'

'Who was eating the eggs?'

'The chickens, foreby.'

The chickens? Eating their own eggs? I decided that he was more drunk than I had thought.

'Aye, well. I'll be on ma way, then.' He lumbered to his feet.

'But… would you like another cuppie?' I asked in desperation. He was still in no state to drive.

'Ach, I'm away.'

I took a deep breath. 'Doug, you are in no fit state to drive, you know.'

He drew himself up. 'Indeed I am. I'm able to drive no matter how many drams I have. And you have only given me tea.' He made it sound like an accusation.

I persisted. 'But what about other people on the road?'

'Ach. They are alright. They'll be no so drunk as me.' And with this incomprehensible sally, he drove off. Very slowly and most carefully.

What can you do with a man like that?

Hesitantly, I rang John, our policeman, whom I did not know well at all so early in our time on the island.

'Well, Nurse. It is difficult. I know he drives when drunk but the thing is, he always drives much more safely and slowly when he *is* drunk than when he's sober and that means I can't easily catch him.'

There were no breathalysers then and drunken driving on the island was shockingly commonplace. It was accepted with the same resignation as the weather. I would soon discover that there *were* accidents related to drunkenness but remarkably few. I can only think that they all had Doug's tendency to drive more carefully when under the influence.

But what did Doug mean about the chickens eating eggs? I consulted Archie. As the months and years went by, I turned to Archie for almost all information concerning crofting, fishing and anything local.

'Young Doug told me that he saw the chickens eating the eggs. But he was drunk and literally up the pole at the time.'

'Ach, that mannie! I don't know how he stays up the poles at all – he's that drunk all the time.' He paused. 'But he's right about the chickens. They sometimes eat the eggs for the shells. We have had a lot of rain – is your run wet and muddy?'

I nodded.

'Aye. That'll be it then. And have you not given them any grit?'

Grit! I suddenly remembered my father giving the chickens grit when I was a child. I had forgotten and while the ground was fairly dry and sandy, they had been fine, but chickens need access to some hard, gritty substance to help the corn break up in their crops. The recent heavy rain had washed the sandy soil away, leaving soft mud. The poor things must have been desperate. They were soon given grit and we had eggs for breakfast again.

My next well-meant innovation for the chickens was not crowned with success either. We had built the chicken house on stilts to foil any hungry foxes but so far I had needed to lift the chickens in at night as they had had their wings clipped to prevent escape and had trouble flapping their way up to the doorway. This was a chore, as catching them was considered by them to be a game. In the morning they were so keen to get out that they launched themselves from the doorway and landed with a plop on their beaks or stomachs, risking injury. Something had to be done! I built a ramp which I placed up to the door of the hut in the morning, taking it away at night. The chickens clucked fussily over it for a while but soon got used to a rather more comfortable exit in the morning. Eventually, I raised some lovely, fluffy, yellow chicks who, when they left the protection of their mother, joined the flock in the hut.

One evening, I went to shut them all up for the night only to find that the ramp had slipped away from the doorway and fallen flat onto the ground. Under it was one very dead, very squashed chick! I was most upset and made sure that the ramp was better secured after that.

But in spite of all my precautions, we began to lose chicks – about one a day. This was a mystery until I happened to see the culprit in action. A large gull used the electricity pole as a lookout and as soon as a chick wandered from the protection of the flock, he dived and made off with a nice fresh, fluffy, yellow dinner.

I was now down to three chicks, which were growing very quickly. It soon became obvious that we had just one hen and two cockerels and the pen was turning into a battleground as these two took to fighting at every opportunity. Egg-laying suffered as the noise and ferocity of the war upset the hens. Again, something had to be done and this meant that one cockerel had to go.

George and I were both squeamish when it came to neck-wringing, but a friend happened to be staying with us and was very used to such things so I asked him to do the grim deed and despatch 'Eric'.

The other cockerel, 'Russ', was a beautiful russet colour and was friendly to all. Eric, however, was the worst-tempered bird I have ever met. No-one was safe from his claws and beak, so the sacrificial choice was easy. Having explained all this to my friend, I departed in cowardly fashion, leaving him to do the dastardly deed. A while later, he entered in triumph with the dead cockerel swinging from his hand.

It was the wrong one! It was my beautiful, friendly Russ!

And so the disasters went on. I persevered for years, but eventually gave up the unequal struggle and gladly accepted eggs from grateful patients. They knew a lot about keeping chickens and were inclined to laugh at my pathetic efforts.

* * *

When the weather subsided, we contacted Young Doug to come and replace the broken pole. To our surprise, he brought a young man with him. The lad did all the climbing and heavy work while Doug stood by in lordly fashion. But I noticed that he was sober and encouraged the young man to use the safety harness. Did we have a reformed character here? Almost. What we did have was Doug's young son doing an apprenticeship and Doug himself displaying sense and caution. I was most relieved.

At about this time, we began another eggy venture which started one evening when we were having dinner with Alice and Alistair. The starter was an enormous hard-boiled egg, halved with the yolks mashed with something very tasty, topped with a sprig of mint. I was intrigued and enquired what exotic bird had laid these eggs.

Alice laughed. 'Hardly exotic. Seagulls.'

'But they are not at all fishy to the taste!' I said. (I don't understand even now how the eggs of fish eating gulls could *not* taste of fish.) 'And how do you get them?'

Alistair and Alice's house overlooked Loch Na Caillach, There were several tiny, rocky islets scattered here where seagulls nested. Alistair took his dingy out to two of them in the spring, located the nests and destroyed any eggs already laid. From then on, he would return daily and collect any newly laid eggs secure in the knowledge that he only had fresh ones. As their eggs were predated in this way, the obliging gulls laid more but as the spring wore on, Alistair would stop his visits to give the gulls their chance to raise a brood. Good for the gulls and good for Alice's delicious dishes next year!

Humbly choosing a different isle, we began the same piratical visits, turning them into picnics on the islets, exploring the rocks and pools. We enjoyed watching the faces of dining visitors when they were told where the tasty eggs came from. I felt a little guilty as the poor gulls kept laying to try to raise a family, but, like Alistair, we stopped our thieving in time to allow at least one hatching of these vociferous monarchs of the sky. How beautiful they can be with their white plumage stark against the blue-black of an approaching storm! At such times, I can almost forgive the one who took my chicks.

17

A Four-Legged Sailor

'HAS ANYONE SEEN ma wee dog?' Amy Macdougal poked her head into the surgery waiting room.

Amid the coughs and sneezes, there was a general shaking of heads. 'That animal is queer in the head. He's always away,' observed old Callum dourly.

'Aye, he's a funny wee fella, right enough,' agreed Amy. 'He's usually up the hill or happen at Danny the butcher's. Sometimes Postie brings him back with the mails.'

I was passing through the waiting room on my way to my first call.

'What is his name so that I can call him if I see a lonely looking collie?' I asked.

'Ben. But och, he's that deaf, he'll no be hearin' you, anyway.'

How was anyone to recognise a collie as being the escapee if he could not hear his name being called? They were all black and white!

'Aye, well. He'll no doubt turn up,' sighed Amy and opened the door to leave. She appeared to be about to chat on but a chorus of 'shut the door' caused her to scuttle away into the brisk wind that was whistling round everyone's ankles.

Two days later, the dog had still not been found. Amy extended her search to the harbour, asking all the boat owners if they had seen him.

'There was a collie here tryin' to steal ma fish,' said a lad who was fishing from the harbour wall.

'Aye, he'll be hungry indeed.' Amy was beginning to hope. 'And where is the rascal now?' She peered about.

'Och, he's no' here,' the captain of one of the larger vessels spoke up. 'He boarded the steamer to Mallaig.' He paused. 'Why? Was there no-one with him, then?'

Amy stared. 'Are you sure? On the steamer to Mallaig? He must have gone by himself then. There is *naebody* with him.'

The captain roared with laughter. 'He'll be getting himself a free ride, then.'

Amy drew a deep breath, 'I'll have to be getting to Mallaig mysel',' she said.

Again the captain's laughter rumbled out. '*You'll* no be getting a free ride, I'm thinkin'.'

'No, indeed,' said Amy, unable to see why her predicament should be the cause of so much hilarity – she was not a good sailor.

She boarded the departing steamer right away and when it came alongside at Mallaig that afternoon, a rather wan-looking lady disembarked. For once, there was not a collie in sight, so she started to walk up the hill in the steep little town. Ben would likely be hungry, she thought, so she made her way to the butcher's shop. But Lachlan the butcher had not seen him. The post office was unable to help and neither was the pub.

There was only one steamer per day, so Amy would not get home that night. But she had a cousin in Mallaig, and Bella was delighted to see her and happily offered her a meal and a bed for the night.

'There's a ceilidh at Geordie's the night,' she said. 'You'll likely see everyone, I'm thinkin'. And maybe someone there might have seen that mutt of yours.'

So they set off for an evening of chatter, singing and storytelling. Amy met up with many old friends and they asked everyone if they had seen Ben.

A stalwart young fisherman frowned, 'Aye,' he said, 'I saw a lost lookin' collie that I didna know yesterday.'

'Where? Where?' asked an excited Amy.

Seriously, the young man replied, 'He was boarding the steamer for the Isle of Muck.'

'The Isle of Muck?' stuttered Amy. 'Why, that's... Och, indeed...!' She was totally nonplussed.

Bella was very concerned, 'You'll no get there, Amy. There's only one steamer a week for Muck. I know 'tis not far, but there are only about a dozen people living there, so the boats no bother with it much.'

'Well, it went yesterday so it will no be going for six more days,' said the dour young fisherman, counting on his fingers.

'What am I to do?' Amy was very worried about her adventurous canine. 'Will they be good to him? I don't know anyone on Muck.'

Lachlan, the butcher spoke up. 'I'm away over to Muck for some beef tomorrow in ma own wee boat. I'll fetch him back.'

'Oh! but how will you know him? He's that deaf, he'll no hear you call his name.'

'On Muck, every dog and every cat is known to everyone and possibly every chicken too. Certainly all the beasts are known by name and some-times they don't like to slaughter them and I have trouble getting ma meat. So you see, if your wee dog is there, they will all know he doesna belong.'

It all seemed so simple that Amy was happy for the first time in days and true to his word, Lachlan fetched the dog back to Mallaig the next day and Amy brought him home to Papavray in triumph.

The next week the local newspaper carried the headline, 'Local Dog takes an Island-Hopping Holiday'. And there was a picture of Ben, tongue hanging out, one ear up and one down, sporting a soppy grin. But that was not the end of it. Not by a long way! The imagination of the *national* press was excited by the bizarre adventures of the sailor dog and ran the story, with many embellishments, in one of the well-known dailies. Amy found reporters on her doorstep and photographs of her and Ben graced the pages of more than one newspaper. Next came the animal magazines. Some were genuinely interested, but some carried ridiculous articles accusing her of negligence or glory seeking. Amy didn't know what to think and was relieved when, after a few days, they lost interest.

But a short while later, she was amazed to see postie staggering over the croft to her house with a bulging mailbag. Fan mail was arriving! The letters were mostly addressed to Ben and various gifts were sometimes included. A warm winter coat: Amy didn't even know what it was at first. Tins of expensive dog biscuits: a brilliant red studded collar (Ben had never had a collar on in his life) and a long, bright chain with a handle on the end.

Amy studied this for some time and then said, 'T'will be handy for bring-ing the cow down from the moor.'

18

The Lure of Papavray

IT WAS A GLORIOUS day in June: cool but dry and sunny. It was just the day to get on with the job of stacking the peats. George and I had cut the brown, wet rectangles out of the soggy bog early this year as we had enjoyed a blessedly dry spell in late March. They lay on the tussocky grass where we had placed them and were now crisp and brittle. I needed to stack them into the required pyramids to ensure that the wind blew through them to complete the drying process.

So here I was, 'in the peats', glad of the stiff breeze which kept the midges away. Digging or stacking peats was almost impossible if the midges were about. As soon as a breeze dropped, they appeared in their millions from goodness-knows-where to torment us. They got up your nostrils, in your eyes, among your hair, up sleeves, down shirt necks and generally lived up to their name of 'the scourge of the Highlands' or in this case 'Islands'.

After a while, a dilapidated Ford drew up on the narrow, undulating road and Fergie H emerged. He strode purposefully towards the next peat hag to ours.

'Ah. It's you, Nurse. 'Tis a good day for the peats, indeed.'

We worked in companionable silence for some time and then Fergie produced a bottle from his pocket.

'A dram, nurse?'

'Fergie. You know me better than that. But I have a thermos and you could have some of your whisky in a cup of tea.'

'That would be grand, just.'

We sat on a small tump and drank tea (heavily adulterated in his case) and munched clootie dumpling.

Fergie pointed a peaty finger, 'That worn-out hag was ours when I was a young boy.'

'It's a long way from Craig Mor where you were raised.' I observed.

'Aye, and we had to walk it wi' the peats in a basket on our backs from the age of about seven or eight, I recall.'

'It must have been tough back then.' I was purposely encouraging him to talk about his boyhood, as I loved to hear the crofters' tales of their young lives when, for most of them, times had been tough.

Although I loved the simplicity and traditional ways of the island people, I was sometimes amazed at the stoicism with which they accepted the difficulties, hardships and lack of much real comfort in the crofting way of life. But the older folk remembered the days when life was *really* bad, with cold and hunger and general poverty and deemed themselves lucky indeed to have the small comforts of today.

'Aye, it was different then, foreby.' Fergie had risen to the bait and was soon deep into the past as he recalled his childhood.

His father had been shepherd to Stephanie Smythe's grandfather and father when the Craig Mor estate had been busy and profitable. Fergie was the youngest of six children born to Alec and Flora. They lived in a tiny estate cottage which was dark and damp, the Smythe's factor refusing to carry out essential maintenance on any of the workers' homes. If they complained, they were evicted, losing their jobs as well as their homes. These were not crofts houses with the few acres on which to keep animals or grow potatoes, they were built as housing only for the workers on the estate, so all but the most foolish accepted the poor conditions in order to keep their jobs and feed their families. The men would try to maintain their own cottages with bits of wood from the shore, tin drums straightened out to patch leaking thatch and any other useful bounty from the sea.

'Aye. But we children knew nothing else and we had each other and the other estate children to play with and we were a happy bunch. I suppose we lived on porridge and potatoes mostly, but so long as our stomachs were full, we didn't care.' Fergie paused, gazing unseeingly at the distant mountains where fluffy white clouds were playing hide and seek between the peaks.

'But we children grew and there was no room in the wee house for all of us to sleep. Ma and Dad slept in the box bed in the kitchen and the rest of us were all in the only other room. Gordon and I were the only boys and as he was much older than me, it became awkward for the girls. We were lucky in that we had a cow and father had a horse for his job, shepherding in the hills. These animals were housed in the byre which was attached to one end of the house. Father decided to partition off a small area with some planks he had found on the shore. He made two little beds out of the same rough wood and that became a bedroom for Gordon and me. The warmth from the animals, coming through the thin panel of wood kept the place reasonably warm in winter but boy, the smell! It must have been bad for me to remember it, I mean, because we were used to smells back then. So long as we didna mind cold water, we washed in the burn but, with no proper sanitation, houses were often smelly and fly-ridden.' He paused. 'The worst thing about that so-called bedroom was the floor. It sloped towards that end of the byre, so when the animals wet or sh… or so on, it all trickled past our wee beds. We had to go in to the 'room' in our boots and prop them on the end of the bunks. Woe betide us if we kicked them off in our sleep!'

Fergie laughed heartily at this point, as I listened in mounting horror.

To him, it was his past – just the way it had been – nothing more. To me: well! I was talking to someone who had lived like this and thought little of it.

Eventually, Gordon went to the senior school which was far away, with no designated transport as the scholars had now. He came home only at holiday times so Fergie slept alone in the byre during term time. He did not care for this.

I had noticed how crofters like company. Not for them the solitary moments that I cherished: they were happiest among their family or at a ceilidh. Perhaps, coming from the south with its teeming crowds and cheek-by-jowl houses, I needed the quietness of my moments alone, but these folk were surrounded by space, houses set in several acres, villages sparsely populated, towns almost unknown, 'traffic' mostly just a few cars and tractors so their need was to gather together for company – for human contact.

Fergie's sisters gradually left to go into service or perhaps to 'better themselves' in some way and finally Fergie followed Gordon to the mainland school. He liked school and was a very bright pupil enjoying the sciences particularly. When he passed his final examinations, he decided that he wanted to study medicine to become a doctor. There were no grants or bursaries for people like crofters in those days but his oldest sister, Gwenny, had a surprisingly well paid job in the early days of radio and undertook to pay for Fergie to go to medical school. In this way, he completed the first two years, working in the holidays at whatever job he could find to help with the expenses.

Then disaster struck. Gwenny was diagnosed with tuberculosis and had to give up her job so there was no money for Fergie's training. The family, most of whom had some sort of job by then, pooled as much as they could of their meagre earnings to send Gwenny to Switzerland. The clear, dry mountain air of that country was accepted as the best possible treatment (although cripplingly expensive) for a disease that, in less than twenty years, would be cured by the early form of antibiotics.

So that was the end of Fergie's ambition to be a doctor. Not only had the money stopped but he joined the rest of the family in contributing to Gwen's treatment.

'That was really tough, Fergie. You must have been devastated.'

'Aye, indeed. It was a disappointment, foreby, but that was the way of it. I got a job in a pharmacy, having a bit of knowledge of drugs y'see, and got on well. Then the war came and I joined the navy. I got a commission and saw some action...'

'Mary told me that you were decorated for bravery, Fergie.' I did not have much hope that he would tell me about that, though. They never did, these brave men.

'Aye, well,' was all that Fergie was prepared to say.

After the war, he became a successful salesman of medical paraphernalia, drugs and special foods, but he always wanted to get back to Papavray. His parents had died during the war and some of his siblings had emigrated. Gwenny had recovered well from the tuberculosis only to be killed in an air raid on London, so Mary, his cousin, was his only remaining relative on the island. The old house had fallen into ruin, the estate was run-down and Stephanie was just about keeping it ticking over.

'Aye, there was nothing left of what we knew as children, but Miss Smythe is doing her best to keep the farm going. She is good to her staff. If only they knew...' He even grinned as he remembered the bright apartments in the main house in which the three present staff were housed and the contrast with his childhood home.

He sighed and smiled as a passing rabbit paused to inspect us. He looked up at the sky, at the mighty bulk of Ben Criel, at the mountains shimmering in the warm air and finally at me.

'Well. There you are. I think you will understand why, all my life, I wanted to come back to Papavray.'

Yes. In spite of the hardship of his childhood, the disappointment of his medical aspirations and later in his life, the loss of a daughter and of his wife, I thought that I understood the pull of the island for him. He was a part of the whole, someone whose roots were planted deep in the peaty soil of this harsh but beautiful, bare but bountiful isle. Yes, he belonged nowhere else.

As though he read my thoughts, he murmured. 'I'll never leave. I'll die here and be buried here so that I shall never leave.'

He straightened up, embarrassed by his show of emotion. 'Aye, well. We'd best be getting on with it, before the light goes.'

Just as we rose, Doctor Mac's gleaming Humber purred to a halt. He wound the window down and I walked over to the car. I would not have wished the immaculate doctor to tramp through the peat bogs.

'Nurse, I think you should see Sarah in the morning: perhaps bring her to the surgery if she will come.'

'Something wrong? I mean – more than normal?'

'Mairie, (Sarah's neighbour) popped in. Sarah did not feed her chickens this morning and when Mairie went to investigate, Sarah was just sitting staring into space. I don't know that it is anything particular but I'd like you to visit.'

'I'll be there first thing in the morning. Are you going to Dhubaig or Coiravaig?' I couldn't think of anyone who was ill in either village on our side of the Ben but the doctor was heading that way.

'No, I'm off to have a dram with Alastair. He has some new fishing tackle to show me.'

These two men were fanatical fishermen, always buying new and expensive equipment, but very rarely catching fish, whereas Nick and Andy had only the most basic of rods and lines and regularly caught quantities of mackerel!

As I approached Sarah's house the next morning, I could see that there was no smoke coming from the chimney. Not only would she be cold but, like so many of the older folk, Sarah cooked her sparse meals on the open fire. I could also tell by the noise that the chickens had not been fed.

I knocked and pushed the door open. There was Sarah, in a voluminous nightgown, sitting on the cold floor surrounded by letters, newspaper cuttings and tiny faded photographs which were spilling out of an old cardboard box on the floor beside her. The grate was cold, there were dirty dishes on the table and, most surprising for the house-proud Sarah, there was dust everywhere.

'Sarah. Are you alright? What are you doing?'

'I'm sortin' stuff, Nurse. 'Tis a long time since I looked at all yon.'

'But you'll be cold without a fire, Sarah.'

'No matter. It will no be needed at all soon.'

'What do you means?'

'I'll no be here much longer.'

'Oh?'

'Aye. I wrote to Donald-Archie a whiley back to tell him the funeral will be next week.'

'Sarah, I don't know what you are talking about.'

She seemed suddenly to realise that she was talking to me not just to herself.

'I'm going to be dyin' in the next few days, y'see, Nurse.'

I was shocked. 'You don't know that, Sarah.'

'Oh yes I do. I've aye known that I'd no live into my nineties, so I've written to that place in America – New York, it is. He'll have the letter by now!'

'Who will?' I wasn't very sure if Sarah was still capable of writing or indeed if she *could* write. Many of our old folk had left school at fourteen and had only had a very sketchy education until then, having had to take time off to help with lambing and harvest.

'Why, Donald-Archie of course. My son.'

Had the world suddenly spun the wrong way for a moment? Sarah? With a son? Or was her mind wandering again? Surely we would have had a record of the next of kin. So far as I knew, Sarah was the last of her family.

'May I see his address, Sarah?'

'Ha! You think I'm havering, mebbe.'

She handed me an old, tattered notebook and on the first page was 'D. A. Burnett' – and an address in New York City.

'And this D.A. Burnett is your son, Sarah? I didn't know you were married, let alone had a son.'

'Nae. That's his father's name, "Burnett". I wasna wed to him. Ach, 'twas a long time ago and now I have to get on.' She seemed to lose interest and returned to her version of sorting things out. I had a sudden thought.

'Sarah, you don't want to throw all these letters away, do you? They are all that you have of your son. Would you not be better keeping them and then when you do pass on – one day, not soon – he could have them back.' What I was really thinking was that the letters might give Doctor Mac and me some idea about Sarah's background. I was beginning to realise that we knew nothing about her early life. That all took place even before Doctor Mac came here.

'Ach no. 'Tis not necessary.' Sarah sounded irritated. 'I have more than just the letters. I have the money, y'see.'

I was even more puzzled, so decided to change the subject.

'Doctor Mac would like to see you, Sarah. He is a little worried that you are… well… not looking after yourself very well.'

'Yes, I am.' Sarah was indignant.

'Well you are very cold with no fire, to start with. The cold can make you ill. I'll take you to the doctor in my car.'

Sarah brightened. She thought cars were the height of luxury so she nodded and immediately got dressed. I noticed that she was still wearing the skirt that I had given her. What was all this about dying next week and a son and money?

Doctor Mac saw her, I took her home and went back to talk with the doctor.

'I have no record of a son or of any remaining relatives, nor has she ever mentioned a child in all the years that I have known her. She was healthy until the dementia began about eight or nine years ago so I actually saw little of her.' He was shuffling Sarah's old notes.

'What do you make of this "dying next week"?'

'I don't know but we will keep an eye on her. We must hope that this son will materialise – if he exists.'

And so the matter was left and I dropped in on Sarah for several days, often lighting her fire and checking that she had food in the house. She was quiet and uncommunicative and there was no sign of 'sorting out'. I wondered if it all been a figment of her imagination, although Postie remembered posting a letter for her some weeks ago. He said it was the first in years. (Postie often collected letters to post for the old people.)

Then one morning, the phone rang. It was Mairie, Sarah's nearest neighbour, ringing from Dalhavaig post office.

'Nurse! 'Tis Sarah. She'll no get up from her bed and she'll no even take a cup o' tea.'

'Has she told you what's wrong, Mairie?'

'Naught that makes sense. She says she is due – that's the word she used, "due" – to die today and she would prefer to be in bed. I canna make sense of it all and I have to get back for wee Hugo.'

'I'll go to see her right away, Mairie.'

I opened Sarah's door. She was curled up under the bed-clothes in the old box bed in the kitchen. I pulled the bedclothes back. She was very still and a shiver went down my spine. I felt for a pulse – nothing. I pulled my stethoscope from my bag and, ripping away the old nightie, I listened to her chest. Not a beat!

I sat suddenly on the side of the bed. She was warm, her colour was still good and her eyes were closed as though in sleep. But she was undoubtedly dead. It could not have been half an hour since Mairie had rung – the road had been good and I had made good time. And yet she was dead! I was shocked. I was used to death, some expected, some sudden, some tragic and, worst of all the death of a child, but this was weird beyond anything that I had experienced.

I jumped up and ran to Mairie's house. Mairie was sitting cosily before the fire, breast-feeding young Hugo. The scene was one of normality and contentment and served to steady my jangled nerves.

'Mairie, can you run to the post office and ring Doctor. I'm sorry, but I need to stay…' I nodded towards Sarah's house, 'but I need Doctor.'

Mairie was buttoning her dress. 'Is she gey bad, then?'

Do I tell her? 'Well, Mairie, she seems to be dead.'

Mairie stopped in the act of putting Hugo into his cot.

'But… but…'

'Yes, I know. That's why I need doctor.'

She picked him up again and, wrapping him in a shawl, tucked him into the crook of her arm and set off at a run. These days, I would have stayed with Sarah and rung the doctor on my mobile. Or even before mobiles, most homes in the south had landlines by the seventies. But this was Papavray.

I returned to Sarah's cottage and looked around to see if there were signs of tablets or anything that she could have taken. Without a real search, I could not be sure, but there seemed to be nothing. Doctor Mac appeared in less than fifteen minutes, his home being very near.

'I don't understand this at all,' I said and told him of Mairie's call and my arrival so soon afterwards.

He examined Sarah and straightened up, shaking his head.

'Well, she has only been dead… maybe half an hour?'

'It can't have been much more, even if she died the minute Mairie left to phone me.'

'In all my days, I have not seen this… unless,' and he began to look around, as I had done, for any sign of drugs. 'It is not strictly necessary but

I will ring John. Perhaps then we will search the place for letters or anything... I shall request a post-mortem.'

I remembered the letters and postcards I had seen and I reminded the doctor about the 'son'.

'Yes, but I'll get John. You had better stay, Nurse, as it does not look as if there is a lock on the door.'

'Do I do Last Offices'? Or should I wait?'

'I'll get John,' Doctor repeated. 'Then we'll see. I must start surgery but I will come straight afterwards.'

John, the policeman, popped his head in a few minutes later to say that, as Sarah had been under the doctor's care, I could go ahead and that he would come back with the doctor later and we'd go through any letters.

Later that day, we found Sarah's entire life in that old cardboard box.

She was the illegitimate child of Sarah Mackinnon – father unknown. As this was a terrible slight on the mother's character, it was surprising that Sarah (senior) got a post as lady's maid to a Lady Leticia Briggs in the Outer Isles. I recalled Sarah telling me about this when I had seen all the beautiful but rotting dresses that her mother had left in her care. I belatedly remembered my promise to put her into one of these when she died. It was not too late: I could drape the remains of the best of them over the clean night gown that I had dressed her in.

Sarah (our Sarah) was allowed to live with her mother at the house. (We were all of the opinion that some male member of the household was probably responsible for the child. We could see no way that she would have been tolerated otherwise.) She grew to be a lovely young woman – there was a faded photo of her – and stayed on as parlour maid. History repeated itself and the son of the house fathered a child with Sarah. She was not allowed to keep the child and for many, many years she had no knowledge of his whereabouts. But he had been lucky enough to be adopted by wealthy people (again we wondered if these 'people' were some friend or relative of the Briggs family).

It appeared that Donald-Archie 'found' Sarah when she was about fifty years old. Having inherited her uncle's croft, she was living on Papavray as a simple crofter. Donald-Archie was already wealthy and, although he did not seem to have come to see her, he arranged for money to be sent to the Laird – Duncan's father at first – then Duncan himself. It seemed that, far from collecting her rent for the croft, Duncan's once-monthly visits were designed to give her the cash. Unknown to Sarah, her son had predeceased her by some twenty years, but had arranged for his solicitors to continue the payments from his estate. We realised that Duncan must know all this but he was away at the moment so he was not aware of Sarah's demise.

It was obvious from her lifestyle that she did not use the money. So where was it? There was no will. Crofters usually had so little that making a will was considered the height of sophistication.

'I'm thinking that she would have it stashed here somewhere. I don't think she would have trusted banks. The trunks?' said John.

'No. I had trouble opening the one with all the dresses: it had not been opened for years.'

The three of us scrabbled about, looking in boxes, old leather cases, under her bed – nothing.

Then I thought of what Mairie had told me. Sarah had insisted on dying in bed. She often slept on her old sofa, saying that it was more comfortable than her knobbly old bed. But she wanted to die in bed.

'The bed!' I began to strip off pillows, blankets, the old feather mattress and finally, the horsehair under-mattress.

There, still wrapped, were wads of notes! There must have been thousands and thousands of pounds. Old, white five pound notes were in the earlier bundles, while modern fifties were in others.

'Well.' Doctor stood back, dusting his knees.

'I have never seen so much money.' John gazed, mesmerised, at the bundles spread over the entire length and width of the planks forming the bed.

'What are we to do with it all?' I wondered.

'I'll have to get Fort William in on this,' declared John, alluding to the central police station for the area. 'We will have to count it all and keep it somewhere more secure than this.'

'We will talk to Duncan when he returns and see what he might know about her wishes,' said Doctor Mac.

I looked at him. 'I don't think she will have given it a thought beyond putting it away "safely".'

I thought of her meagre meals, the chickens, the cow, the damp croft house, the lack of decent clothes, the peat-cutting and so on. And yet she could have had a comfortable life. But to have such a life on Papavray would have set her apart from her friends and Papavray was undoubtedly where she had always wanted to be. She was wiser than many of those who win vast quantities of money and think that they can change their lives and themselves and yet somehow remain the same.

* * *

Sarah's post-mortem showed that she had died of natural causes. None of us ever understood how she could have known when she was going to die. Was this an ability that comes to some who live in simple surroundings 'close to the soil'? Wild animals sometimes know when they are about to die and some, like the elephant, travel miles to a particular place to do so. So why not humans?

The money was spent in accordance with Donald-Archie's will 'To bene-fit the island of Papavray in whatever manner seemed fit to the Laird.'

Duncan had an old people's home built on Papavray because those needing care in their later life had always had to leave the island. The move away from their roots had killed not a few.

Now they would be able to end their days on the island they loved.

19

Island Animals

I AM CONTINUOUSLY amazed at the glory of the mountains and sea and the ever changing light of the Hebrides, the warmth and personality of the people and the huge variety of events that fill our lives here on the edge of the British Isles. But equally interesting are the animals without which the way of life on the islands would not survive.

Almost every aspect of life in the Hebrides is dictated by, or concerned with, animals: in fact, their needs rule the everyday lives of the crofters as no clock ever could. Husbands and wives take separate holidays so that there is always someone at home to milk the cow and feed the chickens. No-one gets married during the lambing season as everyone including the bride and groom would be far too busy. Wives hurry home from the bus after shopping in order to feed the hens rather than because they have any intention of producing their husband's meal on time.

Sheep shearing involves the entire family. The dogs gather and pen the sheep and the men shear the woolly beasts while the women struggle up to the sheep fanks on the hillsides with baskets of food and tea for everyone. Even the old folk are expected to help roll up the fleeces back in the byres.

Dogs – usually collies – are indispensable to the crofters who are often canny enough to be able to view a two-week-old pup and tell if it will make a good sheep or cattle herder. Cats, too, have an important role to play as without them the busily munching mice would sadly deplete the bins of grain and rats would eat the hens' eggs while they were still warm. Woe betide Rabbie Burns' 'wee timorous beastie' when the island cats were on the prowl!

We had been on Papavray for about a year when our old retriever came to the end of her long life. To minimise the sense of loss for the boys, we immediately chose our two collie puppies, 'Pip and Squeak'. They were completely untrained, but having been born of working parents, they had ingrained herding instincts. On one occasion, I very much wished that they hadn't. We were visiting friends in England when the dogs ran off, rounded up a herd of peaceful cows and brought them triumphantly into the suburban garden. Our host's lawn was never the same again.

There is a custom in all the Hebridean islands which is often a disturbing surprise to visitors and to incomers like us.

One afternoon during our first summer on Papavray, the boys and I were walking along a pebbly beach when I was startled by Nick's shout.

'Look, Mum! It's a bull.'

'Oh? Surely not.'

'It is Mum. I can see his... um.'

He was right. I, too, could now see his 'um', but I still found it hard to believe. We were still new to island ways and a bull on the loose was not something that we were used to seeing.

The beast, which turned out to be a Hereford, was massive: short of leg, large of head and with murderous-looking horns. He was strolling across the beach, attended by a slight figure in cap and wellies. Languidly flicking a thin twig – no, not a stout stick as one would have expected, but a fragile *twig* – the man shambled past us and, with a brief nod, followed the bull through a gate and out of sight.

On our way home, I sought Archie, to whom I already turned for information on all things local or crofting. Usually so pleased to air his knowledge, he was oddly reticent; even going so far as to say that he didn't want to discuss it. Puzzled, I reminded him that I was a nurse, wife and mother and had therefore been aware of the 'birds and the bees' for some time. Eventually, I was told that the bulls were owned by the Crofters' Commission and rented out to the various islands in the summer months, each township getting its own bull. The crofters paid so much per annum per head of cattle owned (usually just a house cow) and the bulls roamed freely with the cows. Although crofting life is lived 'close to the soil', strangely, the mating of these animals is termed 'getting married'! This is just one of the contradictions of life in the far north.

So the cow would have a calf every year and the problem of fresh milk and butter was solved. The calf would be sold or possibly slaughtered at about two years old and salted down, or more recently (since the 'electric'), frozen. So the mystery was solved. Our passive, old Hereford was not unusual in his affability on the beach that day, for as long as a bull has the freedom to roam and his cows to 'court', he takes little notice of humans and we became used to encountering these magnificent creatures in our everyday lives. All the same, when walking in the hills, we favoured a stout stick rather than the twig in which the crofters put their trust.

There was one morning when a stubborn bull almost caused the boys to miss the school bus to the ferry for the mainland. I was driving the three children of senior school age from Dhubaig over to the bus which left from Cill Donnan. We were high on the side of Ben Criel when, rounding a bend, I almost ran into a large black bull standing determinedly in the middle of the single track road, munching contentedly. This bull was known to be of uncertain temper if approached, so I blew the horn and we beat the sides of the car with our hands to try to move him. He took not the slightest notice, continuing to gaze into the distance and munch. But I noticed that his tail twitched and one front foot rose in the air. He was not happy! We continued to make as much noise as possible but nothing moved him.

'We are going to miss the bus, foreby,' said a worried Donald.

'Nurse!' Chris suddenly spoke. 'I have my bagpipes here for the school concert. Do you think if I played them out of the window, he might move?'

'Yes, Chris. Anything.'

Chris took the pipes from their case, warmed them up and started to play.

I have never seen a bull move so quickly! He was off the road and over the hill in a twinkling. They caught the bus.

These Commission bulls were removed from the islands in the autumn (hopefully having done their duty by the cows) and housed in the warmth of their winter quarters in Inverness. One year, I happened to travel on the mainland ferry transporting about twenty of these creatures from several islands. The sea was rough that day and the bellows and attempted stampedes showed just how little they enjoyed this trip. It all looked horribly dangerous, but I had lived on Papavray long enough by then to have complete confidence in the shouting, sweating men who were slipping and sliding about on the deck in the ample evidence of the bulls' distress.

There were still one or two working horses on the island but ancient tractors had replaced most as the crofters found it easier and cheaper to maintain these than buy winter feed, supply stabling and pay the farrier (usually just the blacksmith) and the vet.

Apart from the farm and working animals, many wild creatures were in daily evidence. Deer, foxes, rabbits, shrews, voles and many other small rodents were common while otters and all manner of sea birds enriched our lives. Deer, however, were often a problem, as they would descend to the villages in the winter to find food and many a row of winter cabbages has disappeared overnight, no matter how high one's fences.

Every spring sees the joy and wonder of lambing time when the hills are alive with the thin cries of the newborn and the worried bleats of harassed ewes. Lambs in the Hebrides are rarely seen to leap and gambol like their southern cousins born in lush meadows and warmer climes. The ewes here have a hard time finding sufficient food on the sparse winter pasture, so their milk is less nourishing and the lambs have little energy for frolicking. There was only one spring when I saw a 'school' of lambs playing together in the sunshine in a little dell while their mothers grazed contentedly nearby. It had been an unusually mild winter.

There are always the tragedies. Every year, some ewes, weakened by the winter privations and the burden of lambing will die, often leaving a motherless lamb. Many of the croft house kitchens are very busy at this time of the year and rows of baby's feeding bottles can be seen on the shelves although all the inhabitants may be over seventy years old. Cardboard boxes nestle by the stoves, each containing a white, fluffy and very vocal orphan.

We adopted a lamb ourselves during our first spring on Papavray. We called him 'Louis' and the little bundle of soft curls immediately enslaved the entire family, with everyone competing for the privilege of bottle feeding him. But little lambs have a habit of growing into big sheep and Louis was no exception. The soft fluffy curls became a stiff, wiry coat, the dainty hooves turned into sharp instruments of torture while the once pretty head began to grow knobbly horns. The only one to ignore this change was Louis himself. Having been raised indoors, he saw no reason to relinquish this privilege and jumped onto chairs, walked across the coffee table and tried to steal the family's food. When we could stand this no longer, we banished him to the outside world where he promptly launched a campaign of destruction on the back door. It bore the evidence for years.

At this time, we still had our old retriever, who had led a pampered life before coming to Papavray. Now here was this upstart challenging her superiority. Our 'small acre' (to quote Mary) became a battlefield, with head-on confrontations daily. The poor dog could not even get a drink from the burn without being butted into the water head-first. I suppose the sight of her elevated bottom bent over the stream was just irresistible to Louis.

Eventually he became such a menace that he had to go. The dog was a nervous wreck, the cats rarely came home and our friends had begun to desert us. Not many people care for an aggressive, fully-grown sheep, although they might have been delighted to cuddle the little bundle of fluff some months ago.

The menfolk of the family were vociferous in their demands that he should be made into lamb chops and teased me with much smacking of lips and talk of mint sauce. The female contingent spoke eloquently of rugs beside the bed and warm linings for jackets. But in spite of his naughty ways, I was quite fond of him so we gave him to the Laird's shepherd on the other side of the island. He had been neutered and was termed a 'wedder', and we knew that his only future was a butcher's slab, but for years, he evaded all attempts to load him into the float for market. He had no intention of becoming a lamb chop!

Inevitably, other events claimed our attention and we lost any contact with Louis until the Island Sheep Dog Trials about two years later.

The judges, the crowds, the shepherds with their dogs had assembled on the hillside near Dalhavaig and the competition had begun. The afternoon was going well for a while and then George touched my arm.

'Look! That's Louis!'

I looked towards the eight sheep which had just been released from the holding pen on the hill. One very large wedder was certainly familiar! There was defiance in his stance. The poor sheep dog puffed his way up the hill as directed and circled round the back of the little flock. Seven sheep began to move as expected but what was this? One large wedder stood his ground. The dog advanced threateningly but met with not only stubborn resistance but active aggression as Louis gave him a painful butt in the ribs. The dog stood quite still. This was beyond his understanding.

Louis took himself off while the men hastily released another sheep in his stead, but the dog was too confused to respond to his master's frantic signals and rushed forward, driving the new creature in totally the wrong direction. The last the crowd saw of these animals was two tiny dots on the far horizon, but on my way to a call about half an hour later, I saw the same dog still chasing the same sheep! They were both near exhaustion.

Sadly (or perhaps not), Louis was eventually caught and sent to market. We gave the money to the Sheep Dog Trials Fund. It seemed appropriate!

It was inevitable that I was often called out to ovine and occasionally even bovine births. Of course, the crofters had been helping their animals for hundreds of years, but their hands are usually large and work-roughened so the presence of a nurse with a small hand and a little knowledge of anatomy was too good an opportunity to miss. In most (but sadly not all) cases, I was able to help.

But one night my patience was stretched to the limit when I was once more expected to function in the dim light of a crofter's failing torch. The ewe was presenting one leg of a very large lamb and had been pushing for so long that she was exhausted. I couldn't see what I was doing and the poor beast's contractions were cutting off the blood supply to the hand that I had inside her. I know I sounded bad-tempered as I addressed the lethargic crofter.

'Can't you give me a better light, Johnny?'

'Ach, no. This is ma only torch.'

'Why don't you get the electric connected to the byre? Your house is only a couple of feet away.'

'Ach. It would cost me. We've always managed before.'

The 'electric' could have been run in for about three pounds and I was obviously giving my time for nothing so I felt that Johnny was being very penny-pinching.

I was unsuccessful and I suggested that he call the vet. He grumbled about the cost but ambled reluctantly to the nearby post office telephone. The vet, too, was unsuccessful and the lamb was born dead. I don't really know if it was Johnny's fault for leaving his ewe for so long, but I was so angry with his uncaring attitude that I said I would never come out to his ewes again.

But, of course, next spring I answered his call as usual. Still no 'electric', but I took my own torch!

20

Parents and Problems

MY PARENTS WERE coming to stay for two weeks. I had decided that it would be easier for them to take the large, once-weekly steamer to Papavray which came straight from Mallaig, without the need for ferry rides and buses or taxis. This weekly blessing was a summer concession only. The boat called at several other islands on the way, which was of great interest to visitors to the Hebrides but meant that it took so long that we rarely used it.

The great day arrived and we went to the pier to meet them. Rhuari emerged from his office (a small wooden shed).

'Ach, Nurse, they'll no be here the night, I'm thinking.'

'What do you mean, Rhuari?'

'There's trouble with the engine or the steerin': I'm no too sure which, but she'll no' sail the night.'

Thinking of Mum's panic at being stranded, I said, 'They'll get lodgings in one of the hotels in Mallaig, I suppose, and come in the morning if it's fixed?'

Rhuari shook his head, 'There's the festival. All the beds will be booked and gone for miles around, I wouldn't wonder.'

This was a problem, indeed! Mother didn't like wild, remote places anyway, and had taken some persuading to undertake the journey at all. I must have looked as worried as I felt.

'Wait you, Nurse.' Rhuari appeared to have had an idea. 'Wee Iona works on yon boat. I'll get in touch with the Harbour Master at Mallaig and see if –' Leaving the sentence unfinished, he wandered off to his office. We waited in the car – it had started to rain.

Back came Rhuari, all smiles, 'Wee Iona'll find them a double berth on board for tonight. They keep several of them free for company directors comin' to the islands sometimes, to have a wee look at us. They come from Edinburgh,' he added with disdain.

'You are a marvel, Rhuari!' My relief was intense.

'Ach, 'tis nothing, nothing at all.'

'I don't think I know Iona, do I?'

'Maybe not.' Rhuari pondered. 'She's from Lewis, y'see. Morag MacInnes's daughter. Ye mind Morag – that was.'

'Yes. I tended her for many weeks before she died.'

'Aye, I know. Iona is that grateful for what you did for her mother, that she's arranging all this at no charge.'

'No charge? How can she do that?'

Rhuari tapped his nose. 'She'll do it,' he said and pottered off.

I was still trying to think how to thank him, when he turned and said, 'I gie ye a call tomorrow when she's on the move.' (The boat – *not* Iona).

In response to a call from Rhuari, we arrived at the pier at about lunch time the next day. Down the gangplank came the parents, with one of the crew carrying their cases. They were smiling broadly.

It seemed that they had been treated to a slap-up supper of freshly caught cod and again this morning – a fried fish breakfast. They were mightily pleased to have been treated so well and astonished, when asking for the bill, to be told that everything was free. They had trouble believing this even when I explained about Iona and her mother. This kind of gratitude and generosity is not readily understood by those who do not know the culture of these islands.

Home we went and got them settled in and the long planned-for holiday began.

'It's such clear, clean water!' Father was enthusing about the crystal-clear water from the tiny spring on our land. Often in literature water is said to 'sparkle' – this really did! A jug of this ice-cold water from deep below the ground sparkled like diamonds when on a snowy table cloth, and it tasted as good as it looked. We were very proud of it.

'Hmm,' said Mum, unimpressed. 'It's a lot better than that brown stuff from the taps. Especially in the bath. It puts me off.'

'It's only the peat, Mum. The water passes through the peaty soil and picks up the colour and a few bits of vegetation sometimes. It's very soft water. Good for your skin.'

Mum prided herself on her soft skin, but was not convinced about the brown water.

'People drink it straight from the streams up in the hills, if they are walking or climbing,' said Andy, trying to allay her fears.

But there were secrets to this 'healthy' peaty water! We were used to bathing, cooking even teeth-cleaning in it, but for a decent drink, we always chose the water from the spring. The village water supply to the taps came from Loch Annan, situated in the hills on the side of Ben Criel. We passed the famous Loch on the infamous Loch Annan hill almost daily but rarely gave the water supply a thought. At the outgoing end of the loch, there was a small, concrete structure with a metal grid, which filtered out any large objects like branches of trees and stones, before the water descended to the homes many hundreds of feet below.

From time to time, someone from the 'water board' would toss an indeterminate amount of chlorine into this tank. What most visitors (and certainly my parents) did *not* know was that this was only done if a dead animal (usually a sheep) had been observed floating in the loch or caught in one of the small streams that fed into it. We were used to this doubtful system but it was a secret worth keeping from visitors – and parents!

One of the many things that Mum could not understand about our northerly location was the vast difference in the times on the clock and place on the compass of the sunrise and sunset in winter and summer. Being so far north meant that the school-taught concept of the sun rising in the east and setting in the west had to be stretched considerably. I tried to explain, when they arrived that, being high summer, the sun would not set that evening until about eleven pm, barely west of north and would rise just a few points *east* of north at around four am, tomorrow, and that there would be no real darkness in between: only twilight as the sun rolled along just below the horizon. I loved this strange, silver light, which bathed the far mountains with a ghostly mantle, while the lochs and little white houses were clearly visible in the fairytale glow. This was a truly magical time, and one that I had often experienced whilst helping with a difficult lambing out on the hill, or driving home after a night call. Then I would stop and watch to see the summer sun peep over the mountains to announce a new day.

At first, Mother would say, 'Oh, it's light in the evenings at home in the summer,' obviously thinking that I was making a lot of fuss about nothing. The only way to convince her of the huge differences between Papavray and 'home' (Somerset) was to show her. So we promised to stay up one fine night, for the parents to watch. Father, who had a much better understanding of the heavens, nevertheless wanted to see the phenomenon for himself.

So stay up all night, we did! Or at least until about four am. The only problem with this was that we had to be up in the morning for work and school whereas drinking tea in bed was about the most taxing thing that the parents had to do. But it worked! Father talked about it for weeks apparently: and even Mum had to admit that it had been an 'experience'.

I took Mum with me sometimes when I visited some of my elderly, female patients. She chatted away to the patients' families and when we were given the inevitable cuppa, she praised the cakes and dumpling. This kind of socialising was more to her liking and she was good at it, being undeterred by the heavy accents. Father was at ease with the crofters, being an outdoor man himself. During my childhood, we had had goats, pigs, chickens, geese, horses, dogs, cats, rabbits and white mice. But it was all only a hobby, however, so the crofters would probably have thought that it was not 'real'.

I took them both to the little townships, all the beauty spots that were accessible by car and even to the peat bogs, where I demonstrated peat cutting. When Mum saw the brown, wet rectangles being wrested from the squelchy ground, she was amazed that this was what turned into the dry, crisp stuff that she saw in the peat basket by the fire.

Mum had never been able to comprehend my love of the outdoors, for wild unusual places and for challenging lifestyles. I think I had been a mystery to her from the day she married my father, a year or so after the death of my mother, when I was five years old. She was either amazed *at* or disapproving *of* almost everything I did and always declared herself surprised if whatever it was turned out well.

But they enjoyed their holiday. Father was genuinely interested in the animals, the beauty of the surroundings and the unique culture, and Mum enjoyed the cosy house and the fires which we lit in the evenings. But I think she was glad to go back to 'civilisation'. I'm sure a lot of people would sympathise with her outlook, as we must have appeared to be most eccentric to southern, perhaps town-bred, people.

* * *

But among our friends on Papavray, there was one couple who appeared eccentric even to us. They seemed to live and think in another era altogether!

Quentin was an archaeologist of some repute, seeming only to be interested in ancient cultures and artefacts. He was often entirely oblivious to the modern world. Their home was in an outstanding position overlooking their own little bay with the garden running down to the shore.

One afternoon, soon after we met them, we were invited to take tea on the lawn, looking at the fantastic view of shore, sea and distant mountains. We watched oyster catchers skimming the shining water and enjoyed the sunshine with Quentin, while Barbara was indoors preparing tea. Quentin was about to embark on a very interesting dig in the Middle East and was enthusing to us about its prospects. We were genuinely interested and, not knowing him well, were too polite to mention the large black cloud which had just appeared. Then a gentle drizzle began but, Quentin, back in 3,000 BC, failed to notice. Neither did he stop talking when the drizzle rapidly turned to rain.

Just at that moment, Barbara appeared in the doorway carrying a tray. Seeing the rain, she stopped in horror.

'Quentin,' she called in a very stern tone. 'Does it not occur to you that it is rather strange to be entertaining one's guests in the garden in the rain?'

Quentin looked at her and then at the weeping sky. 'Oh! My word! It's raining,' he said, with surprise.

Quentin was also inclined to take everything literally, sometimes with hilarious results.

Mum (not with us on this occasion) had a fund of silly sayings which she would trot out whenever she felt that one might fit a story or situation. Among them, there was a very weird tale concerning a woman who 'waved her wooden leg smilingly to the crowd'. We never found out where this ridiculous piece of nonsense came from, but one day, in conversation, I was foolish enough to tell Quentin and Barbara about Mother's love of idiotic sayings, in particular – *that* one. As I finished, Quentin looked at me with great concern.

He said, 'I didn't know that your mother had a wooden leg.'

We stuck to archaeology after that!

* * *

At the end of their holiday, the parents were to catch the train at Mallaig and change at Fort William for Glasgow, the south and home. I drove them to the pier for the weekly big steamer and handed their luggage over to be stowed for the boat trip and then taken to the train station at Mallaig. All very straightforward, one would think.

I had just arrived home from my morning's duty, when the phone rang. It was Mother ringing from Mallaig.

She was frantic. 'They have lost our cases! They were not on the boat when we docked.'

Oh gosh, I thought (or something like that) this is all we need!

I thought quickly, 'You catch your train to Fort William as planned, Mum, while I try to sort something out here. They won't be lost – just put in the wrong place at the pier, I expect. There is a wait at Fort William of about an hour and a half, isn't there? Ring me again from there and I'll let you know what is happening.'

I put the phone down. I was pretty sure that 'Dougall the Pier' would have put the cases in the wrong trolley.

I rang Rhuari at the pier and explained.

'I'll go and have a wee look round, Nurse. They may be here yet. Ach, it's likely that Dougall!'

He rang back in moments. 'Aye. They are among some incoming luggage. Roddy is off to Mallaig in his wee boat with his catch just now so I'm giving them to him. He'll take them to the station as soon as he docks in Mallaig.'

'But the train will have left by then, Rhuari.'

'Oh, aye, indeed; that could be awkward, just.' There was a pause. 'I'm thinkin' that Alistair-the-bus, him at Mallaig bus depot, y'mind, will be away to Fort William soon. Aye, I'll ring him now before...' He left the sentence unfinished as he rang off, presumably to ring Alistair-the-bus.

A few minutes later, he was back on the phone. 'Alistair will take them. I've rung the stationmaster at Fort William and he'll keep the train to Glasgow as long as he can and Alistair will drive fast...' He paused for breath. 'It will all be fine, Nurse. You'll see.'

Thinking of the winding road from Mallaig to Fort William, I hoped that Alistair did not drive his bus *too* fast!

But Rhuari was right – it *was* all fine. Mother rang on arrival at Fort William. I calmed her and said that their cases were on the way and to go and have a cup of tea.

Some hour and a half later, she rang again. 'They are here! Must go. Train's waiting. Bye!'

I rang Rhuari to tell him and thank both him and Alistair (when he returned – with his bus). Rhuari seemed surprised that I should bother.

'Ach, not at all, not at all, Nurse. No, no. 'Tis no trouble at all.'

It was all routine to him and his team, but we were amazed at everyone's willingness to put themselves out to such a degree for a couple of suitcases.

I was remembering the last time that I had landed at Heathrow from Khartoum, when my two clearly labelled cases had gone to Karachi! It was five days before I was reunited with them, but here in the far north, ordinary, willing people do so much better. But *they* are the ones who are often deemed to be behind the times and not too bright!

21

Sunshine's Adventure

THERE IS A MYSTERY about Sunshine, our pony, which has never been solved.

One bright, calm spring morning, George took the hay to Sunshine in her vast field and returned somewhat perplexed.

'Mary J, she's lying down!' he reported.

'She never lies down,' I said, puzzled. 'Is she alright?'

Having been brought up in a city, George knew very little about horses. 'I don't know. Come and have a look at her.'

The clear morning air was invigorating and redolent of seaweed and salt. The neighbouring islands were so clear that we could see cars and tractors on the coast roads. The sea sparkled and two white sails of fishing boats could be seen idling and flapping as the slight breeze caught them. In the quiet, we could hear the voices of the men on board and the lowing of cows across the water as they rushed to croft gates to receive their hay. Although it was May, the grass was not long enough or rich enough yet to stop giving the animals their winter feed. Another week or two should see the end of the morning and evening chore, but after a brief summer, we would start all over again in September.

Sure enough, Sunshine was lying down in a hollow and had not touched her hay. I encouraged her to get up so that I could see if there was any obvious reason for her lethargy. I called and she rose slowly and came towards me to take the nuts that I offered. No limp, no sign of injury. After standing for a moment, she ambled over to the manger and began to chomp happily at her hay. We resolved to check on her again later in the day. What could have caused this uncharacteristic behaviour? Highland ponies rarely lie down unless they are ill, old, or very young. But a very *tired* horse might sometimes need to rest its legs. Sunshine was not normally afforded enough exercise to *get* tired. She had not been ridden at all for a week so why would she be tired?

On our way home, past the bay near the field, George pointed. 'Look! That's Richard's boat! Who on earth are those two?'

'Those two' were two youngish men in *suits*. No-one, but *no-one*, goes boating in a SUIT!

'Well, they can't row!' said George with contempt. 'But what are they doing with the factor's boat?'

We watched them make landfall and step fastidiously on to the sand. They pulled the boat up the beach, making much of this simple task. Ties adorned their smart shirts while highly polished shoes, now covered in sand, showed below the fabric of their dark suits. They walked towards a tiny, unmade-up lane leading to a derelict croft house, leaving dainty footprints in the damp sand. As we followed at a distance across the beach, intrigued to know what they were up to, I noticed something else.

'George, how many horses are there around here wearing shoes?'

'One,' said George, 'Apart from Sunshine, I mean. Rhueben, Elaine's horse.'

'He lives on the other side and, in any case, he is huge with shoes to match. Look at these!'

We both examined the hoof prints, clearly visible in the sand. They belonged to Sunshine: I recognised a small nick on the outside edge of the rear left shoe. The tide had ebbed and flowed many times since our last visit to the beach, so clearly she had been here early this morning!

George sauntered nonchalantly after the disappearing figures while I followed the tracks of the pony to see where they came from. We met up a few minutes later and reported our findings.

'They had a smart-looking car down that track. They got in and drove off in the direction of Loch Annan. For the ferry, I expect.' George sounded suspicious.

'The tracks come from the hills, over there. Once they leave the beach, I can't see them very well, but it looks as though they come from the direction of Kilcraigie.'

This was the ruined village a few miles from Dhubaig. Although the remains of the buildings were high on a headland, there was a sheltered bay at the foot of the cliffs where the fishing boats used to land their catches many years ago. It was possible to walk over the hills to this bay and on warm summer days, we often had picnics there and sometimes bathed – if we were brave enough.

'Let's go and have a look. We could take some lunch,' suggested George. 'We might find out what has been going on.'

We checked on Sunshine who was lying in the sun, went home, collected some food and set off.

It took us about an hour but finally we descended to Kilgraigie beach. There were the hoof prints again! Two sets. One in each direction!

'Curiouser and curiouser,' I quoted. The set leading onto this beach disappeared into the water at the edge of the tide, which had turned now and was just beginning to come in. The other set came from the edge of the sea and looked quite eerie; as though some creature had emerged from the ocean to invade the land. In addition, there were a lot of human footprints but I could not find any pattern to them: there were too many.

'So she came onto the beach, down to the water's edge and then back over the hills. There must have been several people with her, judging by all these prints,' muttered George.

I had been roaming about looking at the prints. 'You know, I'm no tracker but I think someone like John Wayne might have said that the prints entering the sea are deeper than those leaving it. Doesn't that mean that the horse was heavier when she walked towards the water? What do you think?'

George looked and was of the same opinion, 'So she had a load on her back. A person? Or something else?' He paused, 'These Highland ponies are bred to carry deer carcasses. I wonder...?'

I stood looking round. This bay was very remote and secluded and the hills above were teeming with deer, so poaching was certainly a possibility. But why had the factor's boat been used and how did those two men fit in? And why had Sunshine been in the sea? We looked around the beach but could see nothing unusual; so we had our picnic, trudged back over the hills and checked Sunshine. She was her usual amiable self but still rather subdued.

Although we discussed the mystery endlessly, we were no nearer a solution and Richard could not help as he had not missed his boat at that stage. John, our policeman, was equally baffled and felt that there was nothing that could be done, as it was all just conjecture.

The deer-poaching theory seemed to be confirmed some time later, when the estate shepherd found heads and entrails high in the hills. We never really knew what happened but, by employing some Sherlock Holmes logic and a good deal of guesswork, we all decided that a well-organised gang was probably at the bottom of the weird happenings.

Coming ashore at Kilcraigie, they would not be observed. They had killed at least eight deer in the hills and used Sunshine to transport the carcasses to a substantial boat of some sort. Then they had returned a very tired horse to her field. But where did the two well-dressed men come into the equation? Why row the factor's boat? Where from? Why were they landing on Dhubaig beach? Why in smart suits for such a trip? That those two men were involved, we never doubted, but no-one could shed any light on it.

Sometimes when Sunshine looked at me with those beautiful, dark eyes, I wished that she could talk. What a tale she would have told! But then again, I wonder if some of our innocent locals were rather glad that she *couldn't* talk. For there was one last question. How did an outside gang of poachers know that there would be a strong, healthy Highland pony in a field so well placed for their purposes?

22

The Echo in the Hills

'ACH, IT'S COARSE, coarse weather the day, Nurse, do you not think?' Morag dragged her coat farther round her plump figure as we approached Archie and Mary's house.

It was 'van time' and several of us were going to drink tea with Mary whilst waiting for the unpredictable vehicle to arrive – or not arrive at all, perhaps.

Ah, the vans! These malodorous vehicles travelled the villages and outlying hamlets once weekly, selling stale food at inflated prices. But the convenience of these mobile shops, which stopped as close to every croft house as the road would permit, was such that, apart from a mild grumble, the crofters seemed resigned. In fact 'van time' was always a good excuse for an impromptu ceilidh. Folk from distant crofts would descend on the lucky people who bordered the van's route and much tea and gossip would brighten the day. The van could be an hour early, two hours late or fail to appear altogether, but at least everyone had a good time whilst waiting.

'Aye, it's cold indeed for May,' agreed Behag. 'I'm thinking we'll no get the peats dry for a wee whiley yet.'

'I mind, one year, we didna get them in at all until November,' said Mary, handing round cups (no saucers) of tea.

Everyone began to reminisce about good and bad years for the peat. Although the islanders no longer relied exclusively on peat for their fuel, the unreliability of the ancient coal boat and the frequent storms around the islands made a steady supply of coal from the mainland a constant worry. So peat, with its blue smoke and acrid smell, was still cut and hoarded in huge peat stacks beside the croft houses; some as tall as the houses themselves.

At last, the van arrived and, one by one, we mounted the rickety steps and, amid ribaldry and laughter with 'Starky, the van man', who was a great clearing house for gossip, we purchased our goods and departed with the usual mild mutterings about the prices. As I turned for home, an old Land Rover rattled to a halt and Brian's cheery face grinned from the window.

'Mary J. Long time no see.'

'I'm used to that,' I said. 'You are always too busy, tucked away there up in the hills.'

Dij and Brian ('Bri' to all) ran Echo House as a climbers' hostel. Much extended and altered, it had been a primitive bothy and a byre but was now a warm and welcoming home-from-home, hidden away in a high fold of Ben Criel. Ben Criel was more than just one mountain; it was more like a group of craggy peaks running down the middle of Papavray, culminating in the highest point which was over two thousand feet. The lower slopes were used for sheep grazing and could be walked or scrambled up, but the higher slopes were sheer, rocky and remote: ideal for climbers of medium ability and much used for practice climbs before tackling the Alps.

Dij and Brian, now in their forties, had been climbers, and so knew well the requirements of the enthusiastic young people who came back year after year to the rough and ready but homely and welcoming atmosphere, with its big fires and lashings of good food; its comfortable beds and friendly faces. These two worked harder than anyone I have ever known: their task made that much more arduous because there was no electricity supply to Echo House. This meant that Dij had no freezer, so she was always drying or bottling food in order to preserve it and, with no washing machine, all the bedclothes, towels etc had to be washed by hand and dried at night in the vast kitchen, warmed by the old range. Brian spent much time on DIY to keep the crumbling old place going and made weekly sorties to the mainland for supplies returning with a groaning Land Rover. The house was almost surrounded by peat bogs and here, peat *was* essential as the coal lorry would not attempt Brian's steep, rough, three-mile-long track.

'No, we've been a mite busy,' rejoined Brian. 'But you'll know that we have got the electricity in at last.'

We had all been aware for several weeks of the muffled explosions in the hills, as rocks were blasted away to install the electricity poles. These had been sent from the mainland by ferry on low loaders but, of course, such vehicles could not negotiate the trek up into the hills, so they all had to be transferred to a tractor and trailer which kept getting bogged down in the soft ground. The whole enterprise had taken months and must have cost Brian and Dij a fortune.

'Yes. We have bought a freezer and a washing machine. They will make Dij's life a lot easier. Couldn't afford anything else. Anyway, we are having a party to celebrate. Lots of climbing friends, but local folk too. Can you come – all of you? By the way, the post office is going to use the electricity poles, so we are getting a telephone as well. All mod-cons at once!' And, with a cheery wave, he was off.

The party, later that week, was typical of Brian and Dij: no fussy finger-food or little things on sticks for these two! Large legs of chicken, venison steaks and beef joints together with mounds of home-grown potatoes and carrots, covered in tasty gravy were washed down with gallons of tea out of an enormous urn. They had taken the brave and unusual decision to run a 'dry' house – a move almost unheard-of in Scotland. This was not through any religious objection to alcohol – just that they felt that climbers needed a clear head, steady legs and a good eye and that the only way to ensure this was by a total ban rather than pallid half measures. This decision could have spelt disaster for their business, but their attention to the comfort of their guests was so caring and so in tune with the needs of climbers, and their personalities so bubbly that surprisingly, there was no problem at all. No-one minded!

Dij and Brian and two local girls who helped in the house sometimes bustled about during the evening, making sure that the thirty or so guests were fed (overfed?) and comfortable. Duncan and Felicity, Doctor Mac and Fiona, with her beautiful halo of white fluffy hair, my relief nurse, Sally, and several of the crofters mingled with large, healthy looking climbers with colossal appetites.

In the general chatter and noisy bonhomie, I began to look more closely at Dij. Although as cheery and jovial as always, there were moments when she seemed to be struggling to keep up the pace of entertaining and, from time to time, she stood quite still, leaning unobtrusively on a chair or the sideboard. I looked more closely at her face and noticed dark shadows under her eyes. In any one else, I would have put it down to all the work for the party, but Dij was used to coping with dozens of hungry people. I watched her in the next half hour and became convinced that she was not well. She had also lost a considerable amount of weight.

At one point, I found myself next to Doctor Mac. 'Have a look at Dij, Doctor, will you? Just watch her, perhaps? I think she is not well.'

After the initial look of surprise, Doctor Mac nodded and I saw him watching Dij during the rest of the evening.

When we said goodnight, Dij was nowhere to be seen. Brian seemed a bit flustered as he apologised and said that she had a headache. Dij? A headache? I said nothing at this stage, just sending best wishes to her via a worried Brian.

On the long trek home, the Land Rover making heavy weather of Brian's track, Nick said, 'What's wrong with Dij? I don't think she's got a headache at all. I saw her bending almost double by the back door, clutching her middle. I asked her what was wrong and she just said that she wanted some air. I don't think that's it – I believe she's ill.'

Next morning, I asked Doctor Mac what he thought of Dij.

'I agree. Loss of weight, tiredness... How old is she?'

'Forty-something.'

'Hmm. Menopause? Heavy blood loss?'

I told him what Nick had seen.

'See if you can get her to come and see me, will you, Nurse?'

But it was not to be! At about eleven o'clock that morning Brian rang (thank goodness for the new phone) to say that Dij was in severe pain and could the doctor go out to Echo House urgently. He thought it might be appendicitis.

I drove the doctor to Echo House in our Land Rover. Dij was pale and obviously in agony. She indicated her right side, and had vomited so, at first, it looked as though Brian was right about the appendicitis. But, after palpating her abdomen, Doctor Mac was not entirely happy with this tentative diagnosis.

'How long have you been having the pain?'

'Some weeks now, but not as severe as this. I thought it was just period pains. I think I have started the menopause, anyway, Doctor.' She was breathless with the effort of speaking.

'We need to get you to hospital. I don't think it *is* appendicitis, but we will treat it as such in case I am wrong. Brian, does your Land Rover have any more springs than Nurse's?' A rueful doctor rubbed his rear with a smile.

'Shouldn't think so. It's about thirty years old.'

'Ours is nearing twenty,' I said. 'What about the helicopter?'

'No! No!' screeched Dij. 'I can't go in a chopper. I just can't!'

'Why Dij? You were a climber; you can't be afraid of heights.'

Brian stepped forward. 'Her parents were killed, some years back, in a helicopter crash. She has had a thing about them ever since, even though we have called it for climbers often enough.'

Doctor tried to soothe and persuade her but all to no avail. If it *was* an inflamed appendix, the juddering of a Land Rover bumping along the track would be dangerous, but we could not *force* her to go in a helicopter and she was adamant. So we gently walked her to our old vehicle. Doctor sat one side and Brian the other while I did my best to avoid the deeper holes and higher bumps, but it must have been a painful journey for Dij. She was brave. Of course, she was brave! This was Dij! At the little island hospital, Doctor Mac examined her more thoroughly, while a bemused Brian sat in a trance. He had never known Dij to be ill and was finding the whole experience mind-numbing.

She was transferred to the mainland hospital for exploratory surgery: the doctor was worried that it was something sinister.

And it was. On opening her up, the surgeons could see that she had advanced cancer of the right ovary, which had spread to the uterus and peritoneum. She was closed up – there was nothing to be done. Dij was terminally ill.

'It's just unbelievable!' I was deeply shocked when Doctor Mac told me the ghastly news. 'She was as busy and healthy as ever just a few weeks ago.'

'She is staying in the hospital in Inverness for a night or two and then Brian is bringing her home. He insists. How he will manage I can't imagine, but there seems to be a side to Brian that none of us suspected.'

'What do you mean? He is certainly a great character and a very hard worker but I didn't think he had *time* to have a deeper side.'

'You will see what I mean. They will need perhaps two or even *three* visits a day, until…' Doctor Mac left the sentence unfinished.

And so I began one of the most arduous, harrowing but inspiring series of visits of, perhaps, my entire working life. Dij had failed significantly in just the few days that she had been in hospital but she tried to do some of the cooking whilst instructing the two local girls in the mysteries of the vast old range. She seemed to be trying to arrange things so that the business could carry on without her. She and Brian had been told that she could not expect to live for more than a few months. Did they really believe that her life was coming to such an early end? Or did they hope against hope that they had longer?

As Dij began to experience more severe pain, the morphine injections had to be administered twice daily. She was too weak to do any cooking now, but sat in a chair by the range, overseeing the preparation and cooking of the evening meals. Brian had tried to get in touch with climbers who had already booked in order to cancel their visits, but many were unavailable (there were no mobile phones or emails then) and so a steady stream of folk arrived as planned. Brian tried to make them comfortable and some of the less sensitive stayed on and climbed their mountains as usual, but others immediately departed with embarrassed condolences or best wishes. Some who had become friends over the years stayed to help with the chores and, rather than departing into the hills each day, chopped wood, fetched peat, cleaned rooms, washed sheets and towels (now blessedly in the washing machine) peeled and washed vegetables and took Brian's Land Rover to collect supplies from the mainland. These big, strong men (and women) were appalled by the grim news and were determined to do what they could to help the folk who had looked after *them* so well for so long.

So now I bumped and slithered through the glens, over the little bridges and up the steep slopes in a sort of horrible dream. The beauty of the hills was tinged with melancholy, a gloom that tore away my professional detachment. Every turn and twist in the track opened up a vista of heather-clad slopes or chattering burns, deep in the rowan-fringed gullies. Ben Criel's lofty summit (often clothed in gauzy mist) loomed over the scene, majestic as always, against a blue-black thunder-ridden sky or the clear, sunny splendour of a perfect day. Or, perhaps, the silvery light of a welcome moon might give an eerie glow to my journey, as it picked out the eyes of the cattle and deer grazing uncomprehendingly on the lush grass in the brief summer night. All this beauty – romantic and timeless – and yet Dij was fading away before my eyes.

Brian stayed with her almost all the time now. The helpers made this possible. When I arrived to wash and tidy her and give her the morphine, Brian, who did not like to see the needle entering her thin body, went off for an hour or so to 'attend to things'. Many times, when I arrived, I found him lying on the bed beside her, holding her and almost crooning to her – just murmuring about nothing in particular. Sometimes, he might be sitting on a chair by the window with her on his lap, talking gently about their climbing days, or about Echo House and how happy they were there, or just gazing with her at the rugged splendour of their surroundings. Dij would respond with smiles or just a few words; she was now too tired for prolonged conversation. Their love for each other was almost palpable and I realised at last, what a complex character Brian had probably always been. We had just never seen that side of him.

It was now four weeks since the terrible diagnosis. Only four weeks!

Doctor Mac visited with me several times a week, sharing my bumpy but efficient transport.

'She will not last anything like the months that the oncology consultant estimated,' he said, gloomily. 'I shall be surprised if she has another week.'

But Dij had other ideas. One day, after Brian had left the room, she seemed to want to talk.

'Mary J, wait a bit. Don't give me the injection yet. I want to talk to you and I might go to sleep instead if I have the morphine.'

'But you are gasping with pain, Dij.'

'Never mind. There are a few things I want to say.' She took a shaky breath. 'Brian and I have not had children – we did not feel the need – we had each other, you see. Neither of us has any relatives. So each is the reason for the other to live, if you see what I mean... And now I have to leave...' Here, she paused and gathered strength. 'I know I haven't many more days. I'd be an idiot not to know. So I want you to promise me something.'

'Of course I will, if it is in my power, Dij.' I was wondering what could be so important that she was willing to delay the morphine and suffer such pain.

'It's midsummer soon. Shortest night. We met in the Cuillins, climbing. On midsummer night. I had broken my ankle. Brian was with some friends. He carried me down the mountain. It really was love at first sight. We have been together ever since that night. I am going to ask him to take me up to Stony Field... you know it?'

I nodded. Stony Field was not a 'field' at all, but an odd, flat slab of rock, perched on Echo hill high above Echo House. It was a long way up.

Dij gasped again but carried on. 'On midsummer night. From there you can see all the way to the Cuillins. On midsummer night. Like the way we met. We go up there every year.' She suddenly seemed to panic. 'When is it, Mary J'?'

'It's tomorrow night.'

'Oh, that's good... I wondered if I might not make it... But tomorrow is good.'

She paused for so long that I prompted her. 'What do you want me to do, Dij?'

'Oh, yes. You will be here to do the night time injection. They will try to stop us... I know they will. They will think it too much for me... So what? I'm dying anyway. But you will tell them to leave us alone... We will come down when we are ready.'

'And Brian? Is he happy with this idea?'

'Oh, he will be. We *have* to have this time together on the hill. within sight of the Cuilllins.' She was beginning to sweat with the pain, her face was deathly pale and her usually fluffy hair was sticking to her head.

'Dij, you must let me give you the morphine now. You are in far too much pain.'

'Yes,' she whispered. 'I've done... But remember.'

'I will. I promise,' I said. I had deep misgivings, but a promise to a dying woman was just about as sacrosanct as anything could get. 'I'll see you in the morning,' I said to the now peaceful Dij.

As I crept away, Brian appeared on the stairs.

'It's alright. I heard every word. I will take the greatest care of her, you know I will.' And, with a shuddering gasp, this six foot five inch giant of a man seemed to fold up as he collapsed onto the top stair. I sat beside him and held him as I would a baby, while all the love and all the hurt came roaring out of him in howls and wails and long, jarring shudders. No tears – just this terrible, terrible, animal-like bellow of pain. Instinctively, I rocked him to and fro, and a ring of climbers at the foot of the stairs gazed in deep concern at their friend, helpless to ease his pain. These men, used to the dangers of the mountains, would have witnessed death, sudden and devastating. But this raw despair and single-minded devotion was something entirely different.

Gradually, he quietened. 'I'm sorry. I shall do it for her,' he vowed. 'I shall do it.' He kept repeating this, like a mantra.

The next evening, I drove to Echo House at about 10pm. I had hoped that she might have changed her mind but she was as determined as ever.

Brian, white and strained, said, 'I'll take her up at about eleven o' clock. I shall sit with her until then – help yourself to a coffee.'

So I left them together and joined four climbing friends to sit in mutual misery round the big table at which they had eaten so many hearty meals. They had heard Dij's plea and were going to follow at a distance – in case there were problems.

'We must not interfere, though,' I reminded them. 'I, too, will follow and keep watch from a little way off, in case she needs anything. We shall have to be very discreet because it will still be light – it is such a clear sky.'

We stayed in the kitchen until we heard Brian's footsteps as he descended the stairs and set off for Stony Field with his precious burden. Then we quietly followed up the steep, boulder-strewn path, keeping some way behind. Even though she had faded to almost nothing, the strain of carrying her so tenderly over the rough ground would be exhausting – but Brian had promised and nothing would stop him!

At last he reached the huge, flat rock which gave the place its name. The sun had dipped behind the far hills and the silvery light of the gloaming showed him sitting on the ground, arranging her on his lap so that she could see the Cuillin hills in the distance as they rose in silhouette against the turquoise sky. In only a thin sweater, he seemed oblivious to the cool wind but had wrapped her in a shawl and a warm blanket and held her closely to protect her.

I settled down in a hollow, where I could just see them. The four climbers stayed a little distance away. None of us knew how long the couple intended to stay there, but so long as they remained, so would we.

Brian was holding and rocking her and I could just hear the murmur of his deep voice as he bent his head over her. I think the sight of that heart-rending tableau will be with me forever. This was not the superficial romantic notion of a flashy pair of drama-seekers, or a mere whim on the part of a sick woman. This was the very merging of two souls or spirits in their own way, in the place that meant so much to them: for the last time here on earth. Did they believe that they would meet again in another place and another time?

I went on watching. An hour went by and then another. I was stiff with cold. But I could just hear that Brian was still murmuring to Dij. This had gone on for too long, I thought. Although swathed in blankets, she would be getting chilled. But I had made a promise, so what should I do? I crept back to the huddle of climbers.

There were only three of them now.

'We were getting worried,' said one called Bob. 'Dave has gone for the doctor... I know... I know... The promise. But there is a limit. Brian is only just about in his right mind and who knows...?

I returned to my spot, wondering what Doctor Mac would think of the whole crazy scheme, as he would probably call it.

I gazed at the couple through the gathering mist of the approaching morning and something about them was different. Brian's head was lower. He was no longer speaking.

I knew! In that moment, I knew! I was trembling and I held my breath as I watched Brian stand up, still cradling Dij in his arms. He lifted his head and howled. It was the same animal howl as before, despair just pouring from him into the hills and mountains that they had loved so much. This time the roar of pain came back again and again, rolling round and round on Echo hill until it gradually faded in to the night – just as Dij had faded this night.

I stood quite still until the roaring ceased and Brian seemed to crumple to the ground, holding the now still, quiet body of his beloved wife.

Then I approached and began to talk to him. I don't know that I actually said anything – just vague murmurings that I hoped might help to bring him out of his torment. He quietened but still clutched Dij.

Doctor Mac was beside me; I had not heard him come. 'Brian, we have to take you and Dij back to the house now. There is a storm brewing.'

'Yes, yes.' Brian seemed to respond to the doctor's quiet authority. 'I shall carry her home.' But his strength had gone and he was stiff with cold.

Bob and Dave helped to lift Brian to his feet and, gently taking Dij from him, Bob carried her down the hill in the early morning light. As Doctor Mac and I followed, I wondered if Dij had known – or even if, somehow, she had decided to die out there on the hill. How do we know whether death can be willed like that? One thing was certain. She had wanted to go to the hill with Brian on midsummer night and see the Cuillins and she would undoubtedly have wanted to die in his arms. She had achieved both this night!

Once inside Echo House, Doctor Mac made Brian sit by the fire while he talked to him. I asked the men to carry Dij to her bedroom so that I could attend to her. Brian made no objection. I think he was exhausted, mentally, emotionally and physically.

Upstairs, I gently unwrapped the blanket and shawl around the cold little body and then stopped in surprise. She was wearing her wedding gown! She had been plump when she was married and was now emaciated, but Brian had dressed her and pinned the dress together so that it did not hang in ugly folds but looked beautiful – as did its wearer. Somehow, although ravaged by the cancer, she looked peaceful and happy. There was another quality to her face that I could not quite place. But gradually, as I gazed at her, I realised what it was. Even in death, she had the serene glow of someone who had been deeply loved.

We buried Dij in the windy little graveyard by the sea, after a brief but difficult service. I was amazed at the number of people present – locals as well as climbing friends. After the committal, Brian, in a strained but controlled voice, thanked everyone for coming, regretted that there would be no funeral breakfast, turned his back and walked away. We heard his ancient Land Rover start up and depart.

Doctor Mac and I visited Echo House together several times in the next few days: we were worried about Brian. But he was never there. Bob and Dave seemed to be trying to keep the place going.

'He's like a hollow man,' said Bob. 'We can't get through to him at all. He won't talk and he spends all his time up there.' He nodded towards Stony Field. Concerned though we were, if Brian would not see us, we could do nothing.

Then one day, the space where the track left the road was devoid of the usual cars. I drove up to the house. It was closed; windows shuttered, door padlocked, livestock gone. The place was as desolate as its owner.

* * *

It was 'van time' again some weeks later.

Starky was weighing apples. 'Have you heard about yon young fellow from Echo House?'

I was suddenly horribly afraid.

'He was killed in a climbing accident in the Cuillin yesterday.'

Starky put six bright red apples into a bag.

'He was an expert climber. They don't understand why he fell.'

23

The School Outing

'WILL YOU PLEASE sit still, Angus?'

I was doing my monthly 'head, hands and feet' inspection at the little junior school and I had started with the reception class.

'I canna sit still, Nurse. You're ticklin' ma feets that bad. Ha, ha, ha.' Angus went off into paroxysms of hysterical laughter. All the other children found this infectious and we soon had uncontrolled hilarity.

Poor Elizabeth, the teacher – the *sole* teacher – was vainly trying to keep the attention of the nine- to eleven-year-olds on the other side of the one and only classroom. They were supposed to be doing geography as she patiently pointed to countries on the wall map.

But they, too, caught the infectious mirth and the whole school was soon laughing with Angus, who was delighted to be the centre of all the fun.

'I'll hold him down for you, Nurse,' volunteered Murdo.

'I'll help.'

'And me.'

Soon a pile of little boys fell on Angus but they were so enthusiastic in their efforts to keep him still that I began to fear for his ability to breathe.

Eventually, I had lines of boys (and it *was boys*, girls are cleaner) waiting at the wash basins to have their dirty fingernails scrubbed and their feet washed. No-one was really filthy but island terrain is wet and muddy, so wellies are worn most of the time causing feet to get smelly. Athlete's foot is a problem, too. Hands that help with the croft work or the fishing are never going to be pristine but fingernails need to be kept short and I sat several wee lads down with nail clippers. The intense concentration on their little faces as they snip-snipped away was most engaging.

Finally, the little ones were finished and sent out to play while I began on the older children. Even on Papavray, in the seventies, some of the girls wore pale pink nail varnish on their chubby, childish fingers. It did not look quite as sophisticated as they fondly imagined.

The head examinations were usually straight forward and I rarely found any 'wee craturs': only when visiting cousins from the teeming schools in Glasgow or other big towns had brought these hitchhiking pests with them.

As I was preparing to leave, Elizabeth took me on one side.

'I haven't told the children yet, but I am trying to organise a proper school outing this year.'

School outings were usually poor affairs as Papavray was so small that the children knew every nook and cranny: nothing was new to them. There were no museums, gardens or castles, other than Duncan's home, so a picnic and a nature walk was about all that could be expected and no-one got excited about that!

Elizabeth continued, 'I want to hire two minibuses. There are fifteen children and I'm sure they will all come, and several mothers will have to come with the tiny tots. Arthur, [her husband] will drive one and I don't drive so I'm having a problem finding a driver for the second...'

I could see where this was going, so I said, 'Yes, of course I will. When is it to be?'

Elizabeth laughed as I pre-empted her request.

'July tenth. I'm booking a tour of Castle Benrigg on Eilean Mor. It is a lovely old place, perched on a rocky isle just off the coast. It has just been restored and opened to the public. They do organised tours; there is a shop and a café. I think the children will like it. The ride alone will be a novelty for some. They will love the rather grim old castle and those who can bring pocket money, can buy things in the little shop. I think we can manage dinner for them all out of funds.'

Elizabeth was so enthusiastic. She loved her job and the children and I was sad to think that she had been unable to have a family of her own.

Gradually, all the plans came together and she thought I would like to be there when she told the children. It took a moment for them to realise that this year's outing was to be very special. Then uproar ensued! There were squeals of delight, clapping of hands and shouted questions.

'How far is it?'

'Is it spooky?'

'Are there any soldiers in the castle?'

'Are we having dinner there?'

'What about a ghost?'

These children from simple backgrounds were delighted to be driven to the next island, to look around a castle, have lunch and be driven home again. They were so easy to please, having no grandiose ideas about sophisticated pursuits or exotic destinations. It was most refreshing.

The great day arrived. When I drew up at the school, having picked up the minibus from Roddy's garage, the playground was already full of screaming, jumping children. And it was only quarter to nine! School days were never like this! I had Andy with me but he soon disappeared into the throng of excited children. Three mothers of little ones were coming with us and two of those had babies as well – so we were quite a crowd. Arthur drew up with the other minibus. Elizabeth looked slightly harassed as she began to tick her lists and control the rush to board the buses with the inevitable jostling to sit at the front. Arthur had insisted that Elizabeth travelled in his bus as he was a little nervous in the presence of so many vociferous youngsters: this was all a far cry from his quiet job as an accountant for the Crofters' Commission. I asked two of the mums to come with me as I needed at least one other adult in my bus.

Eventually, the seething mob of ebullient humanity was seated and we set off. I delighted them by tooting the horn loudly as we passed various crofters, who paused in their work to wave to us. And again, only ten minutes later as we approached the harbour, I tooted to announce our arrival.

On the boat, we drove into the car parking area and then everyone went on deck to savour the views, the sun and the sheer excitement of the day. Even the weather was good to us. A scattering of pellucid clouds in a serene sky was mirrored in an unusually tranquil sea, so clear that sea weed and fish were easily visible. Then to our intense delight, a pod of dolphin swam majestically past.

I was fascinated by one little girl, Amy, who lived by the harbour and had watched the arrivals and departures of the steamer several times daily every summer but until today, had never been on it. She was oddly quiet as she savoured this new experience. Most of the children were jumping up and down and shouting with glee but Amy stood slightly apart, watching the sunlight on the waves, occasionally glancing up at the wheeling gulls and then down again to the bow wave as the ship parted the water. I tried to read her thoughts – I would talk to Elizabeth about her. Was she repressed in some way so that she could not show her emotions or was she just quiet, deep, and maybe prematurely mature for her age? I had a strange feeling about her – that she was somehow different and would be special in some way when she reached adulthood.

I have not kept in touch with many of the islanders over the years but I was intrigued by this little girl and made a point of following her progress. Amy went to university in England, and then became a protestant nun. Later she was one of the first women to be ordained as a priest in the Church of England, in 1994. But of course, we knew nothing of this on the bright day of the school outing when she was just a fascinated little girl, absorbing all the new sights and sounds in her own quiet way.

I was also amused to watch Andy, who was well used to car rides, boat rides, plane rides – all these things since birth – but was now joining in the excitement of the rest of his friends, especially noisy Murdo.

But the boat was soon approaching the little harbour on Eilean Mor and we ushered the children back onto the buses. We drove along narrow roads, scarcely better than our own roads on Papavray but well signposted to Benrigg Castle. Lochans winked in the sunlight as we traversed boggy stretches, burns chattered as we plunged down into chasms and then we were breasting a heather-covered ridge, and there we caught our first view of the castle. I pulled over for a moment so that the children could see what a spectacular position the castle occupied.

''Tis nearly in the sea.'

'We will need to walk over yon wee bridge to get to it.'

'I wonder how they got all the stones over there to build it.'

'It's near bigger than the rock it's on.'

'It doesn't look too spooky.' This was from Murdo, who sounded quite disappointed.

He was right. The imposing castle looked inviting, perched on its tiny island, the granite stones sparkling in the sunshine, and surrounded by the huffing wavelets which splashed gently against the rocky shore. The picturesque little stone bridge had three arches spanning the narrow strip of water separating the island from Eilean Mor, while the high, purple mountains on the distant mainland formed the perfect backdrop to this impressive fortification.

We carried on down the hill to where the road met the sea and ended in a good sized car park.

The castle was on the mainland side of Eilean Mor, which meant that we were out of sight of Papavray and this made the outing seem even more of an adventure. The car park was quite busy with two or three coaches drawn up and people spilling out of them, making for the bridge or just standing about taking photographs.

'All these people!' exclaimed a wide-eyed Angus.

'So many folk; all come to see the castle!' Ailsa stood near me.

'There's millions and millions of them!' This was Murdo, of course.

The children were momentarily quiet, staring at the people, and I suddenly realised that for some of the younger ones, this would be the first crowd that they had ever seen. Nowhere on Papavray would they have seen hundreds of people all together. I had not thought of this.

'Just keep together,' admonished Elizabeth, looking a little taken aback at the number of tourists already here. We gathered everyone together and marshalled them into a crocodile. The mothers who had accompanied their own offspring took charge of an extra child each, but even so, Elizabeth had a head count as we went through the barrier. Once on the little stone bridge, the children surged forwards in excitement.

'I'll bet there's ghosts,' announced Murdo. 'I wonder if people got their heads chopped off here?'

'Ugh! There won't be ghosts will there, Nurse?' (Although out of uniform and only the driver for the day, I was invariably still 'Nurse'.)

'I don't think so and in any case ghosts don't like the daylight, do they?' I did not want to spoil the fun but some of the little girls looked scared.

'I had not thought that there would be so many people here,' said a rather worried Elizabeth. 'Ah. Here is the guide!' A tall man in a kilt, cloak and bonnet smiled at the children and prepared to take us around the castle. He greeted Elizabeth, explaining that, as the castle had only just opened to the public, we were his first school party.

'Is that Rob Roy?' asked young Dougall.

'Nae. Don't be daft, man. He's just nobody dressed up,' explained Martin, informatively.

Luckily our guide smiled at this less-than-flattering description and we were marched into the grand hall. He tried *very* hard to keep the children's interest in the portraits but he had no hope as they had seen into the next room which was full of suits of armour, shields, pikes, cutlasses, knives of all kinds and several life-like sculpted figures of fearsome looking warriors. The boys were in seventh heaven! The girls were more interested in the dresses worn by two figures of women cowering under bushes while a battle raged around them.

'She'll be droppin' that baby. It'll fall from yon tartan cloak.'

'She'll not be too warm in that dress. It's no' got any sleeves.'

'Just look at those feets. They are filthy, just.'

'What particular battle is this?' asked a studious boy of eleven, when the guide had realised the futility of trying to interest everyone in portraits and had wisely moved on. With relief, the man welcomed the question and launched into an explanation of the battle tactics of the time, which were brutal and uncompromising. After many 'oohs' from the boys and 'ughs' from the girls, we moved on into the bedrooms. The huge four poster beds were the subject of much speculation.

'Look! They'll be needin' a step ladder to get in to bed. Why are they so high up?'

I wish I could remember the guide's answer because I don't think I have ever known why four posters are so high off the ground.

There were two realistic figures lying in the bed. Little Ailsa pulled at my sleeve, 'Why have the men got nighties on – not pyjamas?'

Two of the boys were hooting with laughter. 'They've got bonnets on, too. Fancy wearin' your bonnet in bed!' The guide's history lesson did not seem to be going too well!

'They are wearing night caps,' he offered weakly. Then he appeared to brace himself.

'Now I must ask you to walk in twos and be very careful. We are going down to the dungeons and it will be rather dark.' This was the worst thing he could have said. Several of the small girls screamed that they did not want to go while the boys were jubilant and surged forwards in an undisciplined mob.

Elizabeth blew her very effective whistle. 'Children! Behave properly and do as our guide tells you.' She looked at me. 'Would you stay with those who do not wish to go down, Mary J?' I was quite willing as I have no great love of dark places and grim reminders of torture and suffering.

The very young, one of the mums and a number of the girls stayed with me and we found the room given over to costumes of the day. The girls were charmed by the splendid dresses of the aristocracy of that time and the basket cradles for the babies. It was a great relief from the frenetic enthusiasm of the boys for all things warlike or 'spooky'.

After a while, a weary looking guide, a harassed Elizabeth and the group of slightly more thoughtful boys and girls emerged from the dank dungeons. Apparently, the displays had been so graphic that even the most bloodthirsty of our students had been subdued. The horror of the instruments of torture and the terrible methods of inflicting pain and death had quashed all the bravado.

Back in the main hall, Elizabeth thanked the guide, instructed the children to do likewise and then announced that we were going to the café for 'dinner'. Among the enthusiasm that greeted this, I glanced at the retreating figure of the guide as he walked towards a door marked 'staff only'. He was mopping his brow. The poor man had certainly had a baptism of fire!

Part of the café had been set aside for our use, but Elizabeth stopped the children at the door, admonishing them to be quiet as other people were eating in the rest of the room. She then let four or five in at a time, only sending the next lot in when the first were seated. I admired her organisation, which prevented any unseemly rush and pushing.

They sat quietly, eyeing counters laden with hot food which smelt delicious.

Elizabeth sent the children to the counter a table at a time. I stood by to help the younger ones to choose from the rather baffling array of dishes: sausages, beef casserole or shepherd's pie. It took some a long time to choose and again, I realised that I did not know nearly as much about these island children as I had thought. It was apparent that some had never been to a café before and most had not had the luxury of choosing what they ate.

We had healthy children on Papavray. They were adequately fed but most households stuck to traditional meals and the children would have had the meal placed before them and would have eaten without argument or fuss. Unlike today, when we have innumerable sensitivities and allergies, likes and dislikes and often mistaken ideas of what is 'good for you'.

Quietness reigned as they tucked into the first course with gusto. Occasionally someone would glance towards the dessert counter and discuss with a neighbour what they were going to have for pudding.

Suddenly, Andy said, 'Where's Johnny?'

There was silence. Everyone glanced around. No Johnny! Elizabeth paled.

'Toilet, perhaps,' she said. 'Arthur, will you...'

Arthur was already on his way, but was back almost immediately. No Johnny!

'I'll have to stay with the children.' She looked at me. 'Can you...?'

I took one of the mums – Jenny – with me. We tried the ladies toilets in case he had got confused. He was only seven. No luck. I went to the costumes room and the armoury while Jenny looked in the main hall and the bedrooms.

'Have you seen a little boy by himself?' we kept asking as we weaved in and out of the crowds. We asked any members of castle staff that we met, but there were a lot of children running about so it was not going to be easy. Jenny and I met again at the entrance to the dungeons. 'I hope he is not in there. He might be scared,' said Jenny.

'Is he a nervous boy, do you know?' I asked, as we pushed our way through the people queuing to go down the steps. In spite of the excuse me's and the I'm sorry's, we were not popular.

'Could be. He's an outdoor type, really,' puffed Jenny.

Eventually, we descended into the darkness. There were several rooms or 'cells'. We looked in things, behind things under things – no Johnny.

On emerging, we met Arthur who had been searching the staircases and corridors.

'No luck,' he reported.

We were desperately worried by now. Returning to the café, we encountered a pale, tense Elizabeth. The children were devouring steamed puddings or apple tarts by now, completely unconcerned for Johnny's whereabouts. Arthur hurried off to the reception and asked them to put out a call over the tannoy. *Three* calls later – still no Johnny! Jenny and I looked around the tiny rocky foreshore while Arthur went off to the car park in case Johnny had returned to the bus. We met again at the café – no luck.

'I have asked the castle staff to instigate a proper search,' said Arthur. 'We should probably contact the police, too.'

Announcements were made asking everyone in the building to make their way to the main hall to allow an organised search to take place. There were a few grumbles but most realised that the matter was now serious.

It was *very* serious. Somehow, in spite of all the care and having six adults in the party of twenty-four, somewhere we had lost a small boy. How easily these things can happen!

We kept the children in the café while the castle staff searched all the places that we could not have known about or had the right to enter.

The general atmosphere had now changed from a slightly amused interest to a tense concern. Even the children, now replete, were quiet and apprehensive.

The curator was called and decided to involve the police, but our own search continued as the nearest police station was some twenty tortuous miles away.

Elizabeth asked the curator to telephone Cill Donnan post office so that they could tell Johnny's mother. 'I hate to worry her but I feel she should know. His father is at sea.' Elizabeth was white and strained, Arthur had a permanent frown, Jenny was whispering reassurances to some little ones and I was desperately trying to think what else we could do.

A side café door opened to admit an oldish man in waterproof leggings, carrying quantities of fishing gear. He dumped all this on a chair and turned to the counter. He was quite obviously not one of the tourists.

He became aware of the quietness and the strained atmosphere. He looked round and then turned to the counter staff, 'What's wrong?'

'A little boy is missing – everyone is very worried.'

'Oh, dear!' The man appeared to think for a minute. 'Is his name 'Johnny?'

There was a gasp. Elizabeth rushed forward. 'Yes. Oh please, do you know where he is?'

'Yes. There!' He pointed to the small door, which was on the seaward side of the café. In the doorway stood Johnny!

Elizabeth burst into tears. The children rushed at an astonished Johnny. 'Where've you been?'

'Oh, man. We were worried about you.'

'You missed dinner,' observed Murdo, severely.

I took Johnny's hand and led him to a table, indicating to the counter staff to bring him some food. 'Where were you, Johnny?'

The child was totally unaware of the furore that his absence had caused. 'I was with Angus.' He nodded towards the man. 'Fishing.'

'Why did you leave the rest?' I asked.

'I was in the dungeons, but I didn't like them so I came out. You had all gone so I went out and onto the shore.'

We had gone to see the costumes, thinking that those down in the dungeons would stay together.

'Angus was there and he let me fish with him.'

'Didn't you hear or see people looking for you?'

'No.'

Angus said, 'I saw a lot of people poking about, but they were too far away to hear anything. I didn't think young Johnny here was lost. He didn't seem lost to me! He'll make a good fisherman, one day.'

We were in time to stop the curator from ringing Cill Donnan and the police had not even left their station. The members of the public resumed their interrupted tours and we did a lot of apologising to everyone. The children took it all in their stride.

Murdo said scathingly, 'You didna catch any fish, foreby.'

The drive home was quiet as many of the younger ones fell asleep. Johnny, who, at seven, failed entirely to understand the trouble he had caused, was something of a celebrity at the back of the bus.

When we drew up at the school, various parents were waiting to collect their offspring. There was a terrific babble as everyone tried to tell their families about the day.

Elizabeth immediately went to Johnny's mother and told her of his adventure, apologising for losing sight of her son. His mum did not seem too worried about him or by the problems that he had caused, saying, 'Ach, he'd rather be fishin' than anything, I'm thinkin'.'

When they had all gone, I said to a relieved Elizabeth, 'Well. We shall not forget this year's outing in a hurry!'

'How could you doubt it?' she replied. 'They will be talking of it for months, I wouldn't wonder.'

'*But…*' I said.

'What?' she was wide-eyed.

'How will you top this next year?'

She laughed. 'Sufficient unto the day and all that.'

But much was due to happen before the next outing.

24

Miss Amelia Arabella Anstey-Smythe

'SHE'S BACK FROM her cruise, I'm hearin'.' Mary was full of some great news as usual.

'Who?' I asked, without much interest.

'Miss Stephanie Smythe. Her in the big house. Craig Mor, y'mind. She's been away for months. Now she's brought someone home with her.'

'Who?' I asked again. This was more intriguing. Someone new on Papavray was always of interest.

'Some relation of hers,' Mary answered my question. 'Comes from Australia. Somewhere called "Cranberry".'

Was there really a place in Australia called 'Cranberry'? Or did she mean 'Canberra?' Knowing Mary…!

'Weird woman, I'm hearin',' continued my neighbour, as I refilled her teacup. 'Hardly goes out at all; but Mary-Anne saw her one time. Long floppy skirts – I'm thinkin' they'll get gey wet in the grass. And big hats – they'll blow off!'

'Is she here to stay or just on holiday?' I wanted to know. Stephanie's house was large; like a manor house, so there would be plenty of room if some relation had come to live with this solitary woman.

'I'm not knowing.' Mary sounded aggrieved. She liked to know the whole story. 'She's called 'Miss Amelia Arabella Anstey-Smythe!' She was on firmer ground here. 'What sort of a name is that, I'd like to know?'

I knew Miss *Stephanie* Smythe fairly well as a result of my ongoing association with the Laird's children. Duncan and Felicity had five delightful children who were educated at home by a governess while they were young, and then a tutor for a couple of years, before being sent off to boarding school at the age of twelve. Inevitably, there would be a gap; when one teacher left and before another could be appointed. At such times, Felicity begged Stephanie Smythe to step in. She had been a university lecturer, had two degrees, a fellowship and the OBE, but in spite of all these qualifications, she had to be brave, indeed, to tackle the daunting task of trying to beat some knowledge into those resistant little heads. Like their father, the children loved the outdoors, the water, the hills, horses and dogs, frequently accompanying Duncan when he visited the other islands that made up his estate. He was a bluff, happy individual who lived for his wife and his family, and actively encouraged the children to pursue the outdoor life, but often at the expense of their schooling.

So Stephanie filled the gaps and had many heated arguments with the Laird about the children's education. Even so, she managed to cope with Alicia, Victoria, Elizabeth and Duncan junior – a regular little imp – for weeks at a time. Penelope, the oldest, was at a leading public school by the time that I knew them.

My own involvement with these little terrors was all too frequent. Bumps, bruises, cuts, broken bones, mumps, chicken pox, a near drowning and more than one black eye were but a few of the reasons for my close association with them. Doctor Mac declared that he had never known such an accident-prone family, but he enjoyed Duncan's whisky on his numerous visits so he did not complain.

I had encountered Stephanie on many of these occasions and we gradually became friends. She was about fifty, tall and rather 'rangy', much given to knitted stockings, shapeless jumpers and good quality tweeds. With hair scraped back and piercing blue eyes she was a formidable figure.

Stephanie's house, perched on the cliff top at Rachadal, near the recently built Somerled hospital, was huge with turrets and cellars, wide corridors and a baronial-style hall. It was built in about 1850 by a wealthy Victorian forebear who had made his money plant-hunting in the Far East. So why such a person should choose to build a house on the windswept shore of an almost barren island was a mystery. Stephanie inherited on the distaff side, but by then, the bulk of the estate had dwindled away and she now ran the place with only three part-time helpers.

This relative sounded more than a little eccentric and I hoped to see the strange lady soon, but the manner of our eventual meeting was bizarre in the extreme.

It was a Friday afternoon: Nick was coming home from school for the weekend, so at about six pm, I drove over to the pier at Dalhavaig to meet the steamer. Rhuari, told me that there had been some engine trouble (again) and the steamer would be at least an hour late. The shops had closed, the pub had not yet opened and the pier café was putting up its shutters. I knew that I would have been welcome in any house, but it was 'tea' time and I didn't want to disturb anyone. What to do for an hour? The only place that had not been closed for the night was the church.

The door creaked as I entered the cold, stark, gloomy house of God. The smell of dust and damp met me, combined with a faint and welcome aroma of furniture polish. So Anna-Mairi, a devout Free Kirker, had been busy. The good lady did her best to keep the place clean, but it remained a poor tribute to the Almighty.

I sat in the gathering darkness for a while. The building had never been wired for electricity and relied on oil lamps and candles, while Roddy's young son worked the old-fashioned bellows to coax wind into the ancient, asthmatic organ – on the rare occasions that the frivolity of hymn singing was tolerated.

I was suddenly aware of a movement to my right as someone or something flitted down the side aisle. Startled, I was left doubting my eyes. In an empty, gloomy church on a dark evening, it was easy to *imagine* things.

Just then a blast of cold air told me that the main door had been opened. Footsteps advanced up the aisle; it was Stephanie.

'Amelia! Amelia! Are you in here?' she was calling, and as she neared the front of the church, she became aware of me.

'Ah! Mary J!'

I told her about the figure flitting silently around the aisles.

'And where is she now?'

I pointed towards the vestry. The door stood ajar and an uncertain light flickered through the crack. Stephanie put a finger to her lips and we crept forward until we could see the inside of the room. Seated at the desk, attempting to light one candle from another, sat an outlandish figure. I could see long, loose black hair and clothes that appeared to descend from her shoulders with as little shape as an old curtain. Her thin, white hands trembled as she placed the candle on the desk, and were then pressed together as though in prayer.

Stephanie spoke gently, 'Amelia?'

The woman turned quickly and I saw a pale face so thin that the cheekbones appeared sharp beneath the yellowed skin. Candlelight is supposed to be kind, but this face would look ravaged in any light. She looked from my companion to me and I saw burning eyes with the wild look of madness.

Stephanie advanced slowly towards the pathetic figure. 'Amelia, this is my friend, Mary J.'

Miss Amelia rose. She was very tall and her body had a grace and poise that belied the haggard face and wild eyes.

'I am delighted to make your acquaintance.' She graciously inclined her head as she pronounced these stilted words in a deep, but monotonous voice.

Stephanie spoke quietly and gently and, taking Miss Amelia by the arm, led her back into the church and down the aisle. I blew out the candles, shut the vestry door and followed. I was just in time to see the two ladies drive away.

A few days later, Stephanie rang to ask me to 'take tea' with her while Amelia had her afternoon nap. Seated in her spacious drawing room with its view of the sea and the hills beyond, I heard Miss Amelia's sad life story.

The cousins had attended a Surrey boarding school together. Parents and teachers were concerned about Amelia from an early age as she showed signs of extreme eccentricity, gradually becoming irrational and unpredictable. When she was in her teens, her parents moved to Australia, where her father took up a government post. She became more wild and devious as the years past, frequently absconding and she would be found in strange, dark places or wandering in the outback.

When her parents were killed in a plane crash, Amelia was put into a secure mental home run by nuns. She spent about fifteen years there and was happier and calmer than she had ever been. Then disaster struck for Amelia. The home closed! As the only known relative, Stephanie was sent for and had travelled to the Antipodes. There, she discovered that her cousin was not only severely disturbed, but also suffering from cancer and was not expected to live for more than a few months. So Stephanie made the brave decision to bring her back home to Papavray.

I listened to the sad tale with enormous respect and admiration for her, but I could not help wondering whether a cliff-top house on a remote island was an entirely suitable environment for a deranged and very sick lady.

As though reading my thoughts, Stephanie said, 'I know this is not ideal; but she has no-one else. I shall do my best to look after her.'

A few weeks later, Stephanie's altruistic devotion to Miss Amelia nearly cost her her life!

It was purely by chance that I became involved in the drama at Craig Mor. I was driving away from the hospital, when I heard shouting and screaming and the deep-throated bark of a dog, from that direction. Some instinct told me that Miss Amelia was the cause of the commotion, so I changed direction and sped towards the house.

A group of people had gathered where the grounds ended in sheer cliffs dropping to the angry, green sea, some one hundred feet below. Others were running across the grass carrying various bits of rope and chain. It was not hard to guess that someone (Amelia?) had gone over. Just then the island's ancient fire engine lumbered into view and drove near to the edge of the cliff.

Charlie, the roadman, came towards me. ''Tis that Miss Amelia. She climbed down – the Lord only knows how – and now, she's on a ledge away down yonder. They've called the coastguard but they'll be a wee whiley, I shouldn'y wonder.'

I could see Stephanie's tense figure standing near the edge.

'Hurry!' she was shouting. 'She won't hold on to anything. She's just standing there and the wind is going to blow her in. It's catching her skirt.' She noticed my arrival. 'Oh, Mary J, I'm so glad you are here. She'll be so cold and wet when they get her up.'

Peering over the edge, I could see that it was going to be *very* difficult to rescue her, particularly as she was unlikely to cooperate. Meanwhile, the firemen were attaching one end of a rope to the fire engine and dangling the other over the edge.

'What good will that do?' Ally asked. 'She'll no be able to climb up – even supposin' she could understand.'

'I'll go down the rope and get her!' exclaimed Charlie immediately.

'Ach, no. You're too wee. You'd never hold her.'

'Wind's rising to gale,' warned Fergie, who had just arrived.

'I'll go!' Everyone stared at Stephanie. 'I'll go,' she repeated. 'Amelia is my responsibility: it's right that I should go. At least I could hold her until the coastguard arrives.'

There was a shocked silence, and then everyone started to talk at once.

'You'll no' do it!'

'One of us should go!'

'Yon woman down there's daft. She'll no' do as you say. She could take you over the side with her.'

'How'll ye do it, foreby?'

'I insist. I will not allow any of you to take such a risk. Tie me to the rope and lower me over the side.' Stephanie sounded nervous, but determined.

'You will be risking your own life!'

It was no good. 'I can't just do *nothing*. I know the danger, but I cannot just stand and watch.'

The firemen began to loop the rope around her and make it safe, then in a surprisingly sprightly way she wriggled over the grassy cliff-edge and began to descend. Just then, Amelia screamed, startling Stephanie who lost her purchase on the rock face. She fell the last six or seven feet, landing beside Amelia on the ledge.

'Stay still, Stephanie,' I shouted. 'Lean against the rock face if you can. It will be safer there.'

I could see that one leg was at a strange angle and that she was supporting one arm.

'What now?' I asked. 'How long until the coastguards get here?'

Donald shrugged in despair. 'They are supposed to be on their way,' he said.

But fate was kind. Chas (Doctor Charles Spencer, who was standing in for Doctor Mac)) arrived at that moment, having heard the commotion. As he got out of his car, several voices gave him a garbled update and he peered over the cliff edge.

'Miss Smythe,' he called to Stephanie. 'I'm coming down, so stay still.'

Chas was the doctor to the Mountain Rescue Team for several islands, and an obsessive climber, so he always seemed to have a car full of climbing equipment. I ran back to get his medical bag while he collected ropes and harnesses and various bits and pieces from the boot. Once more the fire engine was used for one end of the rope, while Chas stepped effortlessly into the harness and disappeared over the side.

There was only just room on the ledge for the three of them, but he was able to give Stephanie something for the pain. Amelia had begun to scream again.

He looked up. 'I'm going to give the other lady a sedative. We can't possibly get them up the cliff or down to a boat, so you'll have to get the helicopter.'

I was more than familiar with the helicopter, having needed to call it out on several occasions, so off I went into the house to phone.

'Thirty minutes, max,' came the answer. 'Winch job, is it?'

'Yes, it will have to be,' I replied. I returned and relayed the message. Chas replied, 'I shall stay with them.'

The helicopter arrived in less than twenty minutes and hovered above us while the winch man was lowered to the ledge. Amelia was taken up first, and then Stephanie was secured onto a stretcher and lifted to the waiting aircraft, which quickly disappeared into the skies.

Chas climbed back up, wandered back to his car, stowed the climbing and medical equipment, jumped in and continued his rounds as though nothing unusual had happened.

Stephanie recovered well, but Amelia died the following day. I think the escapade on the cliff had been just too much for her fragile body, but probably saved her a lingering and possibly painful death.

25

The Man Who Washed

'WHAT ON EARTH is that bowl of water doing outside the door?'

I had just entered Doctor Mac's room at the surgery to discuss any potential problems for the day. I had been surprised to see a bowl of water on a stand together with a towel and soap outside the door in the little porch.

'Ah well, Nurse. Old Bennie has finally lost his senses altogether, I fear,' answered the precise doctor.

'Bennie?' I queried. I knew most folk on the island but I could not place 'Bennie'.

'The old hermit – or at least recluse – on the moor near the castle. "Old Bennie" is what they call him. I do not even have his full name on my books. He is not a native but wandered here many years ago. He lives in an old caravan tucked away from the world. He found it abandoned by the harbour, took it apart, piece by piece, carried it all up to Dhub Moor and rebuilt it.'

'By himself?' I asked, getting a picture of a large muscleman.

'Yes, by himself. I'm not surprised that you have not met him. Duncan and previously his father seem to have looked after him, giving him food and allowing him to stay on estate land.'

'Does he work for Duncan?'

'Well, officially I suppose so, but I don't think he does much.'

'I look forward to meeting him,' I said.

Doctor Mac looked at me rather wryly. 'Hmm. Well, he has been getting more and more eccentric and now he has decided that he will not enter any house without washing his face, hands and, rather more worryingly, his feet. Hence the bowl.'

I smiled. Having lived in the Middle East, I was reminded of the Muslims removing their shoes before entering the mosque and the five times daily wash before prayers. Could Bennie, too, have lived among Muslims? Was he reverting in his old age? Perhaps he *was* of that faith? This was intriguing.

'So he is here now? What is wrong that he needs to come to the surgery?'

'Duncan told me that the old man was limping badly so I asked him to bring him in. Evidently it took Duncan some time to persuade him into the Land Rover and when they got here he refused to come in without washing. He sat outside until I gave him the bowl of water and now he is waiting quietly.'

Just then there was a hubbub from the waiting room with several raised voices. The door burst open and a dishevelled figure barged in. Bennie! He had obviously got tired of waiting quietly and decided to jump the queue.

'Doctor, sir, I'm here.' He sat himself down in the doctor's chair and, without preamble, lifted his trouser leg.

''Tis here, sir.'

I approached, 'Come and lie on the couch, Bennie.'

Bennie jumped as though shot. He had not noticed me.

'I don't know you,' he said with a frown.

'I'm the nurse.'

He looked doubtful, but obediently climbed on to the couch. I started to take his wellies off.

''Tis not in ma wellies, can y' no see.' And once more the trouser leg was pulled up.

A red, angry area of flesh surrounded a grey, suppurating ulcer some two inches in diameter. I was appalled.

'That must be very painful, Bennie.'

A shrug.

'How long have you had this, Bennie?'

Another shrug.

Doctor touched the angry skin. 'Painful?'

'Aye, some.'

'Bennie, you will need to come here every day for Nurse to clean and dress this.'

'What for?'

Doctor patiently explained about infection and dirt.

'I can wash it. Yes, I can do that,' declared the old man.

'Not really, Bennie. You see it's difficult for anyone to do their own leg, so I will do it for you.' I hoped to calm him.

'Well, I'm no comin' all this way for a bit o' bandage.'

'Shall I come to you, then?'

'No, no, no. Nobody comes to my home. Nobody. 'Tis mine. Mine.' He was quite agitated. He muttered on about 'private' and 'mine'. We were getting nowhere until he nodded and gave a toothless grin.

'There's the box.'

'How do you mean?'

'Ally's post office. The box. 'Tis on the grass by Ally's shop.'

I was beginning to see through the fog.

'You mean the telephone box outside Ally's house. What about it, Bennie?'

Ally's 'shop' was not a proper shop at all – just somewhere where folk had parcels left for them and sometimes the Dalhavaig shop would take groceries and leave them at Ally's house for the scattered few crofters to collect.

Bennie gave me a contemptuous look and didn't answer.

'Do you mean that I should see you in Ally's house – but what about Bella. Would she mind?'

'Do you not understand me, woman. I'm speaking of the box. Ally has put water there for me so I can wash before I go in to get my goods. It's grand just with a wee stool and all.'

'But I can't see to your leg in a telephone box, Bennie!'

'And why not indeed? 'Tis the only way. It's a great wee box – a lovely colour of red and you can see the sunsets from it, too.'

I looked across at Doctor Mac for help and was amused to see the doctor almost doubled up with suppressed mirth. What was I to do with this crazy old man?

The doctor recovered his composure and said, 'I'll give you some anti-biotics too, Bennie. You must take two in the morning and two in the evening.'

'I'm no' likin' pills.'

'No, I know, but they will make your leg better much more quickly.'

Bennie looked puzzled. 'Do I eat them, Sir?'

'Er… yes.'

'Then I'm not understanding how the goodness of them gets to my leg from my mouth.'

Doctor looked taken aback. 'Never mind about that. They will do the job – that's the thing.'

'I shall forget.'

Doctor Mac and I were beaten for the moment. Not so, Bennie.

'I know. Nurse can bring them to the phone box and give me one. Aye. There we go. That's the thing to do.' He was triumphant.

'But what about the dressings, Bennie? We haven't decided where I am to do those.'

'Aye, we have indeed. You are going to do them in the box. Do you not remember, woman? Och indeed, just.'

'Bennie, there is not room in a telephone box for two people and the equipment that I should need or room to actually *do* the job.'

Bennie drew himself up. 'Indeed, there is room. I shall sit on the wee stool and you can leave the door open to give you room to do ma leg. 'Tis the only way.'

Nothing that either of us could say would persuade this stubborn, crazy old man that a phone box was not a fit place for cleaning and dressing a nasty ulcer. We begged, we argued, Doctor became quite firm and I flatly refused at one point.

I was told, 'Well then, we'll no' do it at all and ye canna make me do aught I'm not wantin' to do.'

He was right in that we could not force him to have treatment but at the same time there was no way that we could let him go unattended with such a frightful ulcer.

I drooped as I said, 'So where is this phone box?'

He brightened immediately, ''Tis right by the road, Nurse. Ye canna miss it.'

Then he *really* cheered me by saying, 'All the folk who pass will see that I am having the treatment. It will be grand, just.'

It was definitely *not* grand as, for the next two weeks; I cleaned and dressed that leg kneeling on the concrete floor, with my bottom sticking out of the open door of the phone box while Bennie waved to every passing soul, while happily chewing his tablets.

Against all odds, the ulcer healed well.

26

Johnny's Village

AS THE LAST of the tourists left, Papavray began to belong to us, the 'locals', once more. I once asked one of the crofters if he liked having the 'visitors' as they are called. He said, 'Ach well, it's nice when they come and it's nice when they go.' We soon felt this way, too. The visitors brought a breath of the outside world and much-needed cash into the shaky economy of the island, but its peace and community spirit were severely compromised sometimes by their lack of understanding of any lifestyle other than their own. So, like the crofter, we welcomed the several hundred folk who came to our island each year and did our best to make them feel comfortable in what, to them, was an unusual environment; but we breathed a sigh of relief when they departed.

And now the evenings were darker and the days were colder. Everything was dying back or closing down ready for the long winter ahead. Crofters and incomers alike began to resume their rather cloistered island life, as the summer demands of people, animals and croft work slowed.

And so in the shadowy evenings the ceilidhs began again and here we were, on a wet, blustery night, making our way once more to Fergie's house. Inside, a merry fire was burning and an equally merry group was already sitting before it, and as usual we were afforded the best seats; Andy sharing an armchair with me, while George was ushered to an ancient ottoman, which was unfortunately so low that his knees were beside his ears. Present were Mary, Archie, Roddy, Douggy, Hamish, Behag and old Hughie with his formidable wife, Dolleena.

'Behag! We've no seen you for a wee whiley. Are you well?' asked Fergie hospitably.

Behag grinned and blushed. I had long been of the opinion that she was sweet on Fergie. They were both in their sixties and single. Fergie had lost his wife some ten years ago and Behag had never married, having been 'in service' on the mainland all her life. To be 'in service' was an old-fashioned concept in the South by the seventies, but still very much a way of life in the north of Scotland.

Drinks were passed round and Douggy produced his fiddle. Soon, we were all tapping our feet on the lino-clad floor and 'singing along'. Andy was prevailed upon to recite a poem, learnt at school, and Murdoch improvised on his mouth organ as Hamish' who had a superb voice, sang a Gaelic lament.

Gradually, we came to the part of the evening that I enjoyed the most. The storytelling! Fergie again embarrassed Behag (did he realise?) by asking her to recount a favourite story that her father, Johnny, had told on other occasions.

'Ach, I'm no able – not like m' father could.'

A chorus of protest rose from everyone, although they had probably heard it many times before.

'Ach, well.' Behag had been quietly clearing her throat and I wondered if her reluctance had been entirely genuine.

'It was like this, y'see,' she began. ''Twas in the war – the first one, y'understand, when Father was in France. His platoon was marching through some mountains 'n it was snowin' and blowin' that bad they couldna see where they were going. Well, 'twas rough ground – a lot of boulders and the like, and Father and a couple of others got left behind. The rest went on, not realising that they weren't with them. Ach, they floundered about for a bit and then Father said, "We're lost!" Aye,' Behag nodded and continued, 'Angus agreed with him, but Jake said to carry on – they'd find the others.

'Well, they got into deeper and deeper snow; and the mist was comin' down and it was getting dark. Angus thought they should stay where they were until morning and this time even Jake agreed. They were cold and tired and hungry.'

'Aye, they would be indeed, indeed,' murmured Morag, nodding.

'Well, I just said so,' bridled Behag. Mary handed her a cup of tea to placate her. She continued. 'Aye, well! They found a spot behind a rock and out of the wind and tried to get a bitty warmer, but they were near freezin'.' Here Behag gave Morag a look designed to quell any further remarks. A chastened Morag stayed quiet!

Behag resumed, 'They had something called emergency rations…'

'Iron,' said Mary.

'What?' said Behag with a scowl.

'Iron rations. I've heard of it,' replied Mary with pride.

'Ach, woman, hold your wheisht. You don't know what you're talking about,' ordered Archie.

'Oh, yes, she does!' Surprisingly, Fergie spoke up. We all looked at him in amazement, as he was usually the first to pour contumely on his cousin. 'She's quite right.'

Mary, however, accepted everyone's admiration with the same placid murmur she used when folk laughed at her many mistakes.

'Ay, well. Where was I?' Behag sounded irritable. 'Ah yes, they were trying to get out of the wind and get a bit warmer. After a whiley they fell asleep. I'm thinking that they were lucky to wake up again, as I've heard that folk, caught in snow, should stay awake or they might die. But they *did* wake, foreby, stiff and near frozen they were.'

Behag paused and Morag handed her some dumpling. She continued, her voice a little muffled.

'Angus went to the edge of the cliff they were on and looked around. The snow had stopped, the mist had lifted and the sun was trying to come through. As he peered out over the big lumpy hills, he suddenly shouted, "Come you here!"

'In front and below them, there was a deep glen with a village at the bottom. Father said it was only a huddle of houses. They don't call them "glens" in France y'understand.' Behag was proud to share this knowledge and looked round the rapt circle for approbation.

After a reviving gulp of tea, she continued, 'Jake said it was too dangerous to try to climb down the steep hills but Father said it would be better than freezing to death. Angus said that they ought to get going before the mist closed in again; though Jake worried that there might be Germans in the village. But Father said, "Let's go!" That was Father for you. So they went!

'It took them hours and hours to get to this village because of the snow, and by the time they *did* get there, they were fit to collapse. But there were no Germans there and it hadna been blown up, like most of villages that they had marched through. There wasn't any snow down in the glen either.

'The village was very tiny, Father said: only a few wee houses and some old fashioned looking people busy working in the fields. No-one seemed to notice them, but they saw a church so they made for that.

There was a priest standing in front of the altar. It's all Roman over there, y'see, so the priest was called "Father". They couldn't speak the language much, o'course, but the priest took them to his house. They were that tired, they collapsed onto a seat inside. The Father shouted something and in came a woman in funny long clothes, with some bowls of soup and hunks of homemade bread. Were they thankful for that! Then he fetched some blankets or rugs, or something and they had a good sleep.

'When they woke, there was more food and then the priest told them that his name was "Father Armand" – funny name, that! French, o'course. And the village was called Perrene. Then they were taken outside to a sort o' yard behind the house and there were four donkeys standing there. Father said they were puzzled when the priest got on one and told them to get on the others and follow him. Well, off they went! Up and up and up the hill. It took hours and hours, but eventually they came to the path they had been looking for in the mist the night afore. And they couldn't believe it when there, comin' towards them, were some of their platoon come looking for them. Were they pleased to see them! They jumped off the donkeys and ran to meet them. But then Father thought that they should show a bit of gratitude to the priest and got a couple o' coins out of his pocket. He turned round to offer them to him but he'd gone! Donkeys and all. Not a sign. They were amazed, I'm tellin' you.'

She paused to sneak a look at us, the Macleod family, to observe our reaction. We must have looked impressed, because she continued with a satisfied grunt.

'Their mates looked at them a bit oddly when they started to walk back and peer around the rocks and the like. Jake told them about the priest who'd helped them and that they were wondering where he and the donkeys had gone. Their mates thought they were crazy because they hadn't seen any priest or any donkeys, they said.

'Well, they had to get on to the camp and go before the major or whoever and explain themselves. He said they were a disgrace to the regiment and

I don't know what. They told him about the mist and the village and the priest and so on, but he wouldn't believe them. He sent for the lot who had gone looking for them and they had to say that they hadna seen the village *or* this priest *or* the donkeys. Oh my! What a do Father said that was! The major got out the map of the area and told them to show him where this village was. Well they looked and peered and pointed, but they couldn't find any village at all. The Major thought they had made it all up and they got into awful trouble. They couldn't understand it themselves.

'But they were soon fighting again; so villages and priests and such were a long way from their minds.

'Jake was killed; but Father and Angus went on for another year or more. Then Father lost his leg and was sent home. Angus came home, too, but he died. Father was very upset.' She sighed and shook her head.

She continued, 'Well, there was no work here for a one-legged man and we didna have the croft then, y'see. So he did all sorts of jobs all over the place. Mother used to say that she never knew where he was off to next.

'He'd picked up a bit of the French lingo in the war so he got a job down in England for a while, as a driver's mate in a lorry delivering stuff to France. They didn't have much of anything in France after the war, o' course.'

Behag shifted a little on her seat and we waited for her to start again.

'Father always worried and wondered about that village and the priest and was aye hopin' he might get back there sometime. Aye, well! It turned out that the town he visited most often was "Ay – mens" – not far from the hills where they had been lost. Well, one time when they were there, he decided to try to find the village and thank the priest for helping them that time, back in '16. He'd always been bothered because they had never said thank you, y'see.

'They couldna take the lorry up into the hills; the roads were too steep and narrow. A bit like ours, I suppose. Well, Father got a French taxi driver to take him to find this "Perrene". Well, Frenchie didn't seem to have heard of it, so they drove around for a whiley, with Father trying to remember where it was they got lost. Somehow they found the hill and went down into that deep glen. There was a fairly good road been built by then, y'see.

'The village was there all right but it was all in ruins! And not *wartime* ruins, if y'understand me, but *old* ruins; where it had just gradually fallen down. Father couldn't understand it. He could see the church but that was in ruins too! *And* the priest's house! That had fallen down altogether. No roof – nothing! Then Father looked around and could see that there were no neat fields or tidy walls like before – just heaps of stones and weeds and scrubby trees. And no people! Everywhere was empty'.

Behag looked around to make sure that we believed her.

'Father asked Frenchie what had happened in the village. Frenchie said nothing had happened: it was just that the village hadn't been occupied for about a hundred years. 'Not true,' said Father, and tried to tell him about his adventures and the kind priest.

'Frenchie obviously thought he was mad but, after a moment's thought, he beckoned him to the graveyard. There, they looked at every stone, and the latest burial had been in 1810! And Father Armand's was there too. 1805!' Behag's voice had taken on a sepulchral tone to achieve the sense of drama that the story warranted.

'"But he was alive and helped us in 1916", said Father. Frenchie just shrugged the way they do – the French, y'know.

Well, they went into the nearest town and Father bought a map. He brought it home and I remember him sitting by our lum of an evening with this map on his knee, porin' over it and jabbin' his finger into it. It said very clearly "Perrene – abandoned in 1820 and now derelict". In French, o' course. Then he'd burst out, "But we were *there* in 1916!" None of us ever understood it at all.'

Behag finished triumphantly, but there was a wary look about her challenging gaze as she eyed us all.

'Aye. 'Twas a weird business indeed,' said Archie, from behind his cigarette.

Murdoch nodded, 'Aye, but 'tisn't for us to disbelieve Johnny.'

Behag sat up. 'Indeed, no! Whatever else Father got up to – he was no' a liar.'

Murdoch hastened to smooth ruffled feathers. 'Indeed, he wasna. We canna explain it, was all I meant!'

We all sat in silence for a while, staring unseeingly at the fire. I thought about the weird story. There *was* no explanation! Not in our known world, anyway.

27

Elizabeth, Ina and a Lot of Snow

DRIVING HOME ONE autumn evening after a late afternoon call, I reached the summit of a hill on the side of Ben Criel. I pulled up and could only stare in wonder.

The sun, now low in the sky, was peeping from behind the cotton wool clouds to rim them in liquid gold while distant mist enshrouded islands; mere specks in the endless sea, were pink in the approaching darkness as it fluttered in.

Nearer, the heather-soaked breeze was whispering in the reeds as the shadows of gulls, massing together for the night, crept across the snow that was already softening the stark shoulders of the Ben. A solitary croft house was beacon white against the shadows in the glen and a window winked cheekily in the last rays of the October sun. The scene was so beautiful; timeless but fragile as, in a little while, it would all be hidden: to slumber in the dense darkness of a moonless night.

Reluctantly, I let in the clutch as I remembered two hungry sons and a husband (for once at home) waiting for their supper.

On the steep descent by Loch Annan, I spied the stalwart figure of Big Craig, the roadman, plodding steadfastly homeward with spade and shovel over his shoulder.

I stopped. 'In you get, Craig.'

'Ah, thank you, thank you, Nurse. Aye, 'tis a long trek home.'

Throwing his spade and shovel into the nearby ditch, he clambered in. I often wondered how he remembered which particular ditch he had used on these occasions – they all looked the same to me.

'And the teacher has seen you, then?' This was more in the nature of a statement than a question. What was he talking about?

I looked at him enquiringly.

'You've no seen her, then?'

'No. I've been at old Christina's house.' What was Craig getting at?

'Ach. That Christina woman. She is a right besom, just.'

'What about Mrs Campbell, Craig?'

'Ach, she'll be at your home, I'm thinkin'. Waiting to see you.'

'Right,' I said, as mystified as before.

'She and that nice husband of hers passed me just a whiley back. I'm of the opinion that there is no other body in Dhubaig that she'd be going to see.'

So he had worked it all out and was now wanting to know *why*. Many of the crofters were wily in their curiosity but Craig was so genuine that I knew he would be worried that there was something amiss with the very popular teacher.

'Very quiet man, he is. Yes indeed. Clever too.' He rambled amiably on about this and that until I stopped at the top of his lane.

'Aye then, Nurse. 'Tis going to be a bad morning. Look at yon sky. I'll be about for the hill.' And off he lumbered.

The sky had changed dramatically and now the mist had solidified into low, grey clouds full of waiting menace. Craig thought it would snow in the night – he was often right. He would wait for me to set off in the morning, his cheery bulk beside me in the car giving me confidence on the slippery slopes.

At home, a happy group sat around the fire. I was relieved to see that George had made Elizabeth and Arthur some tea and the boys were now recounting a fishing tale.

I poured myself a cup and joined them, wondering what this was all about. Elizabeth looked slightly on edge and kept glancing directly at me. I got the impression that she wanted to speak to me alone. After a while, I suggested that George should take Arthur into the back room to see if he could get a better picture on our television: he was known to be clever at such things. They all looked a little surprised when I insisted that the boys should 'help' but Elizabeth was quietly smiling, fully understanding my tactics.

'Right. That's got rid of them for a while. Now, Elizabeth, I wonder if you have something to tell me.' I had been watching her. There was a little secret glow about her.

'Mary J. You've guessed!'

I smiled. 'Tell me.'

'After all these years, I think I'm pregnant. But I'm worried in case I am wrong and it is the beginning of the menopause.'

'How old are you, Elizabeth?'

'Thirty-eight.'

'I think it is very unlikely that it is the menopause at such an early age but I understand that you have always thought that you could not have children. On what was that opinion based?'

'Nothing, really. Just that we were married when I was twenty and for years we tried for a baby. When nothing happened, we just became resigned and thought that it was just not to be. Over the last few years, we have not... so much...' she looked down, 'everything is alright,' she added hastily, 'but it doesn't matter quite so much as when we were young. So, we can hardly believe it.'

'How many weeks do you think you are?'

'About twelve, I think. I waited and waited to be sure before saying anything to Arthur and now he's in a lather of worry.' She smiled. 'A very quiet lather, knowing him.'

'Does he want to be present at the birth? It will be in the mainland hospital, of course.'

'Yes, I understand and, yes, he says that he wants to be present for the birth. I don't think he has any idea what it all entails and I'm afraid they will be treating him as well as me.'

I laughed. 'I think you will find that if he faints, he will be pushed aside and left to get on with it. You will be the priority. Now we will get Doctor Mac to examine you, confirm dates and so on. You look well. Any problems?'

'Slight queasiness but otherwise, I feel great.' She certainly looked great, but in view of her age – not old – but this was a *first* baby and after trying to have one for so long with no success, I wanted to be extra cautious. I did so hope that all was well as her joy was wonderful to see.

'What about school later in the pregnancy and then after the birth?'

'I would love to take several months off, maybe more if it is possible. I enjoy the children and teaching but I have been doing the same thing for fifteen years or more and would like time with my own child. We could afford it – Arthur is earning quite well. It might not be possible but if they can get a temporary teacher…'

I thought of Andy's horror at the loss of his beloved teacher – a horror that would be echoed throughout the school. They all loved their 'Mrs Campbell'. In her care, they learnt without really knowing that that was what they were doing – she was so innovative in her techniques and far ahead of her time. She would be missed, but the island folk would be pleased for her. How many times had I heard 'what a shame she has no children of her own, she is so good with them'?

The men came into the room and Arthur looked enquiringly at Elizabeth.

'Yes,' she said. 'I have told her.'

Arthur looked relieved, worried, happy, bemused, all at the same time, while George, guessing the reason, grinned and slapped Arthur on the back.

'Hope you can change nappies,' he said.

Arthur immediately looked scared. 'I wouldn't have a clue,' he said. Arthur was inclined to take everything literally.

'You'll soon learn.' Elizabeth made it sound like a threat.

They left with laughter and good wishes.

'See you at the surgery,' I called.

Big Craig was right. It snowed in the night and we woke to a white world.

'Andy, you can come with me,' I said. 'I think Big Craig might be coming with us.'

'Oh good.' Andy liked Big Craig, who always had a crofting tale to tell or he would identify footprints of animals and birds in the snow or chat about his time at sea.

Sure enough, Big Craig was waiting along the road and climbed in.

'Aye, 'tis a bad do, Nurse. The snow, I mean.' He paused. 'And is the teacher well?'

'Yes, thank you, Craig,' I said without thinking. 'She is very well.'

'Ahh.'

I suddenly (and belatedly) realised what I had done. By confirming that, although the teacher had come to see me, she was fit and well, I had inadvertently started the inevitable rumour that she might be pregnant. After all, they would reason, why should a woman go to see the nurse if she is quite well? I said no more but the damage was probably already done.

Big Craig picked up his shovel and spade from the right ditch and placed them between his legs for the remainder of the journey. We were up and over the top with no trouble, and down to 'the other side'.

I was visiting Ina regularly to check on baby Janet who was still quite delicate.

'Come you in, Nurse. It's cold for October, just.'

Ina looked tired. She was in her late fifties and having to look after a baby long after most women would be putting their feet up a little. Last year, Jaynie, her daughter, had given birth to a baby at the age of only thirteen. The girl rejected the child and Ina cared for her right from the birth – as I knew she would. But the daughter became more and more unreliable and, together with the child's father attempted to abscond by sea, taking the baby with her. They were rescued, but little Janet took a long time to recover from the cold, wet experience. Her father was, in fact, Jaynie's brother, who had escaped from a 'secure' home for mental patients. Jaynie had refused to believe that he was her brother as the family had kept his existence a secret. This attitude was not unusual in the more remote parts of the British Isles until much more recently. Jaynie was eventually sent away to a special school and Ina was coping with a delicate seven-month-old baby, two big sons and her husband. She was exhausted.

'How is Janet?'

'Ach, Nurse, she doesna sleep much at night, and then she sleeps in the day when she should be takin' her food.'

I weighed the child, who was sleeping now. She was not gaining the weight that we had hoped so we decided to gradually change her milk, with an extra feed at about eleven pm. This might help her to sleep at least for part of the night.

'How is Jaynie getting on?'

Ina's face closed. 'No' well, Nurse. She has been sent to a different home now with more discipline. She was a terrible nuisance to the last one. Angus goes to see her but I canna because of the baby. She'll no see the wee child at all, y'see, Nurse.'

I sighed. 'I'm sorry, Ina. Can your sister come for a few days to look after baby and give you a break?'

'No for some time, Nurse. Her man's no well and she'll be busy with him for a whiley yet. But why? I'm managing the wee soul fine.'

'Indeed you are, Ina, but you are exhausted – partly due to the baby, but partly worrying about Jaynie, I expect. And, perhaps Callum…'

'Ach. That one!' Ina turned away. 'I'm disgusted with the two of them and I blame myself… I do, Nurse.'

'None of this is your fault, Ina. You have been the best mother, and grandmother. Callum was probably born with his mental trouble and perhaps Jaynie had had these personality problems for a long time. We just did not spot it; nor did the school. She only seemed a bit slow and unco-operative. That's all. But you are tired, Ina. A few days of rest and relief from the responsibility of the baby would do you good.'

Ina's husband was a good, caring man, an elder of the church, and the two sons still at home were decent boys, but in the island culture of the seventies, men and boys did not look after babies. Even in the more sophis-ticated parts of Britain, babies were women's work until about the sixties. Attitudes have changed a lot in the south but I wondered how long it would be before the islands caught up.

On a whim, I bundled Ina and the baby into the car and took them to the surgery. Doctor Mac would fit them in, I knew. I stayed there to look after wee Janet while the doctor gave Ina a good examination.

He straightened up. 'I think you are severely anaemic Ina, and thorou-ghly exhausted, and your blood pressure is dangerously high. Someone must be found to take the baby, Angus and the boys can look after themselves for a while. I'm going to send you to Callamach House for a week.'

'Oh, no, Doctor. I canna leave them all to fend, nor the wee one.'

Callamach House was a beautiful place on the mainland. Once a stately home, it was now run by a trust for just such cases as Ina's.

Doctor Mac coaxed and cajoled and even spelt out the risk of stroke or heart attack if Ina continued to become more and more run-down.

But Ina insisted that she could cope and she would wait for her sister to be available to come. It was no use and Doctor Mac had to be content with giving her tablets for the blood pressure and anaemia.

I took Ina and Janet home and returned to the surgery to do two dress-ings.

Doctor Mac called me in to his room, 'Elizabeth Campbell has just been in to see me…'

'Isn't it marvellous,' I interrupted. 'After all these years.'

But then I saw the look on the doctor's face as he shook his head.

I was shocked. 'But she was so sure. What is wrong then?'

'Her uterus is distended and very hard to the touch – it could be fibroids or…'

'Oh, Heavens! Carcinoma?'

'Possibly. I have arranged for her to see Mr Bishop, gynaecological consultant in Glasgow. I *think* it is only fibroids. She might have had them for years. That would probably account for her inability to conceive.'

I sighed. 'Does she know?'

'I told her that there is no baby and hinted that, although I think it is fibroids…' He looked at me.

'I'll go and see her.'

Elizabeth was distraught. 'Oh, Mary J! I was sure… I did so want a baby! And now, I might be ill too. Do you think Doctor could be wrong?' She was grasping at straws and I think she knew it.

'Elizabeth, there is no baby. It might be just fibroids, but there is no baby.' I held her as she sobbed.

'Have you told Arthur?'

'Not yet. He is due home in a minute. Oh, Mary J, he'll be so disappointed.'

'Yes, I'm sure he will be, but the main priority now is to follow up on you.'

I stayed until we heard Arthur's step in the porch. I left. It was better for them to face this together and alone.

Elizabeth saw the surgeon in the next few days and the biopsy proved that there was no malignancy present. She had a hysterectomy and, in spite of her deep disappointment about the baby, she made a swift recovery and was home in six days.

'I'm lucky in one way, Mary J,' she said, when I visited. 'It was not malignant.' She sighed. 'But I shall not be able to have babies, ever, so we are gradually coming to terms with that.'

'There is always adoption,' I said, rather tentatively.

'We had thought of that.'

I continued to call on Ina. The house was usually scrubbed until it shone, with baking smells wafting from the door and a bright fire burning in the polished grate. But this time, I was shocked to see dust and muddle, a cold grate and an exhausted-looking Ina slicing a shop loaf. I could hear wee Janet crying in the other room.

'Ina, stop. Sit down and talk to me. Things are not good, I can see.'

I made her a cup of tea, fetched the baby and managed to rock her to sleep. With blessed peace restored, Ina began to speak.

'She is better, I think, and taking a bit more, but she needs so much encouragement to suck her bottle and take anything from a spoon, that I have no time for aught else in the day. I'm tired, Nurse. Too tired to light the fire, too tired to bake…' Ina began to shed bleak, slow tears of utter weariness.

'What about your sister? Any news there?'

She shook her head sadly. 'Her man is worse so it will be a long time before she can be of help. No-one knows when he'll improve – or *if*.'

'If we could get you away to Callamach House, could Angus and the boys manage?'

'We spoke of it and yes, they would do for themselves. But it's the baby.'

I was beginning to toss an idea around in my mind. Would Elizabeth help? She had been considering a break, anyway. Would the baby's needs help to fill her mind and heart? Would the experience of caring for a baby help her and Arthur to consider whether or not to adopt a child? I would have to talk to her and it had to be soon, as Ina was dangerously exhausted and the baby needed some undivided attention and a routine as well as plenty of nourishment.

I talked to Doctor Mac about this idea. Did he think it might be a solution?

'Well, if Elizabeth feels that she can help, I think it would be good for everyone. Yes, it might be a good thing.'

I talked to Elizabeth first and I was relieved at her immediate reaction.

'Oh yes, yes. I'd love to do that. It would stop me from brooding and it would also give us both an idea of what it would be like to adopt a baby.'

Next, I called on Ina. I told her that I had found someone to look after the baby while she had a break. She looked uncertain until I told her who it was.

'But, Nurse, she's the teacher.'

'And so she is good with children. And she has been disappointed about her own baby and might like to consider adopting a baby or a child at some point so it will help her too. She has decided to take some time off, anyway…'

Ina burst into tears of relief and weakness. 'Oh, Nurse. It would be the answer. If I can get myself well…'

'Shall I tell Doctor to book you into Callamach House?'

Ina smiled and nodded.

'I'll get everything organised perhaps for the day after tomorrow,' I said with relief.

As I left the house, I was astonished to see that it had been snowing heavily while I had been inside. Huge flakes were covering the bare trees with shimmering whiteness and my Mini had grown a two-inch hat. But the sun was shining and I revelled in the sparkling surroundings, the 'plops' as snow slid off a corrugated iron roof, the crunch of tramping feet and the bright red of Postie's van.

Anna Vic's muted mutterings wafted to me as she carried her milk bucket home. 'Look here, Nurse,' she called. 'There'll ay be that much snow in the milk that the butter will no turn at all.'

Waving a greeting, I jumped into my car and set off, sliding sideways down the village road. I was already late, having spent a lot of time with Ina, so I was probably going faster than the conditions warranted in order to get to my diabetic patient, now well overdue her injection.

A large lorry appeared around a bend so I moved into a handy passing place. But I was going too fast and on trying to brake, slid inexorably forward and into a ditch, coming to a stop in the cold softness of deep snow.

The lorry slewed to a juddering halt nearby and out jumped four burly men. I recognised them as the road maintenance gang from the mainland. In addition to our own roadmen, this repair gang came to the island from time to time to fill potholes and do a little gentle resurfacing. Why they should come when all the roads were covered in snow and ice was anyone's guess. They were a cheerful lot, their lack of dedication balanced by their sense of humour, while the contents of their pockets were welcomed by the B&Bs and the pubs.

The gaffer strode across to where I sat in my car in the ditch – feeling very stupid.

Peering in at the window, he enquired, 'Taking a short-cut then, Nurse, were you?' He roared with laughter at his own wit.

The rest of the gang approached, guffawing loudly and giving me no time to get out, each man took a corner of the little car and lifted it bodily out of the ditch and onto the road with a very surprised nurse still inside. Joining their laughter, I thanked them, started up and continued my rounds.

But the day's adventures were not over yet. About an hour later, I was 'taking a close look at the bottom of another ditch' (to quote another joker). This time the car, taking on a life of its own, had slid quietly sideways on a slight incline. I was near a group of croft houses and was familiar enough with the island ways to just sit blowing the horn intermittently like a ship's fog horn. In no time at all, two sturdy crofters on an ancient tractor trundled into view.

'Will we gie ye a lift out then, Nurse?' And out I was lifted. This time, in the more traditional way of the locals; with ropes and a tractor, but still with laughter and teasing comments.

Once more, I carried on and had finished my rounds and was on my way home when, rounding a corner, I came on an extraordinary sight. George's Land Rover was out of action, so he had bought a small Vauxhall to tide him over. There was his car, balancing on its underneath (probably the sump) on a small bank beside yet another ditch, with all four wheels off the ground! It was swaying like a see-saw in the wind. George was standing beside it, looking cold and miserable and talking to Fergie, who was gesticulating wildly.

'We canna just pull it off wi' the tractor: 'twould rip her underneath from her, I'm thinkin'. How did you get her up there, George?'

'I didn't. She just got herself up there,' replied a morose George, digging his hands deeper into his pockets.

'Aye, well. She's not going to get herself off there. It will have to be Roddy-the-garage.'

Roddy-the-garage (coalman, undertaker, mechanic, boatmen, shopkeeper) was expensive, but we had no alternative and I drove to the garage leaving George still muttering. '...should have kept the Land Rover a bit longer...' was the last I heard.

'Right, Nurse, I'll be with you in a wee whiley,' said the ever helpful Roddy when I explained. 'But I have to pull Johno out of the harbour first.'

'What?'

'Aye. With his truck. It slid into the harbour.'

'Is Johno alright?'

'Ach. He's fine the now. He jumped out as the truck went in. By! Can that man swear!'

'Where is Johno now and are you sure he's alright?'

'Aye, He's in the pub gettin' dry.' Roddy paused and roared with laughter. 'Only on the outside, y'understand, Nurse. Gettin' dry! Oh, hah, hah'. He wiped his eyes.

'Come to think of it, he'll be too drunk to drive that truck, even supposin' it goes when we get it out. I'm thinkin' I'll come and do George first.'

Guiltily burying any sympathy for Johno, I thankfully drove back to tell George that Roddy would soon be here to 'do' him.

'I'll stay to help,' said Fergie, who seemed oblivious to the cold.

Roddy rattled into sight in his ancient lorry with its equally ancient winch. With him was a huge man whom I had not seen before.

'Angus Mor,' Roddy briefly introduced him. 'He's ma cousin from Glasgow.' More cousins! They all had dozens of them!

Roddy looked at the car. 'How did you get it up there, George?' He laughed loudly and was joined by his cousin. George was a little tired of this sally by now but knew that it would be the joke of the pub and would have to be born with stoicism.

Roddy, Angus Mor and the winch made short work of heaving the car off the ridge. She started first time and, after a swift exchange of money (no complications like invoices here), we were off home in *very* careful tandem. Three ditches between us was quite enough for one day!

Two days later, Ina departed for Callamach house. She had a wonderful holiday and regained her health, strength and sense of purpose. She decided to leave the worry of Jaynie to those who were looking after her, realised that when necessary, Angus could manage by himself and that their two great sons would find that, if they wanted to eat, they had to do something about it themselves.

Elizabeth and Arthur loved having wee Janet, gave her the quiet routine that she needed and their careful feeding made her thrive. Arthur surprised everyone – himself most of all – by taking turns at feeding, changing and waking in the night.

An unlikely friendship grew and blossomed between Ina and the teacher so that Elizabeth frequently took Janet off Ina's hands at the weekends and in the holidays.

Elizabeth and Arthur did not adopt a child after all, but wee Janet had an adoring 'aunt' and 'uncle' who helped Ina and Angus to raise her.

28

Little Boy Lost

ONE EVENING, AS I drew my curtains against the creeping darkness, I could see bobbing lights in the lane below and as I looked, more and more lights appeared. Something was obviously wrong! The torches of just two or three people bringing in cows, shutting chickens up for the night or wending their way home after a day's work was quite normal, but there must have been up to twenty or so lights moving around. This indicated an emergency of some sort.

Grabbing my coat and dragging on my damp wellies, (wellies never seemed to dry thoroughly) I picked up my own torch and hurried towards the agitated lights. As I drew near, Fergie hailed me in stentorian tones.

'You'll be here to help, Nurse.'

'What's it all about, Fergie?' I asked.

'Do you not know? 'Tis wee Timmy has gone missin'.'

I was horrified! Timmy McInnes was only three years old. A strong, healthy, lovable child, he was nevertheless, a constant worry to his mother, Shona, as his well-developed taste for adventure led him into all sorts of trouble.

'How long has he been gone and where was he last seen?' I puffed as I tried to keep up with Fergie's long strides.

'Ach, he gave her the slip while she was milking the cow in the byre. 'Twould be about four of the clock, foreby. He has only a wee jumper on, too – no coat.'

'Do we have any idea where to look? And where are we going at such a pace, Fergie?'

'I've a mind to look on the shore,' he paused, 'before the tide comes in.'

'Oh my God! The shore!' We both began to run as the full horror of the situation sank in.

Many others had the same idea and were searching about among the boulders, calling and flashing their torches. Shona was running to and fro, quite frantic with worry. She raced towards me.

'Oh, Nurse! I'm that glad you're here. Where is he? What will I do? I only took my eyes from him to milk Dollach. I did, Nurse! That was all.'

She swayed as she wailed, blaming herself. But we all knew what a little monster Timmy could be. I put my arm round her shivering shoulders.

'Can you think of *anywhere* or *anyone* that he might have talked about or shown some sort of interest in recently? Or perhaps somewhere that you have told him *not* to go?'

'No, no. I canna think. He'd been playing near the byre when I went to milk the cow, and when I came out he'd gone. I looked in the house, all over the croft – nothing. So I ran to get everybody.'

'Where is Jacky? Does he know?'

'He's away at the fishin'. On yon Klondiker that was here a week gone. He's not had work for a whiley so he tried would *they* have him.'

Archie shouted to everyone to say that some of the men were going up 'the hill' and we were to carry on searching the shore and nearby rocks. Of course, there were many hills around Dhubaig, but we all knew which one Archie meant: the steep, heather-clad, boulder-strewn area behind Shona's croft, where the pastureland gave way to the open moor. On this moonless night, the windswept miles of high ground were only slightly less danger-ous than the shore to a small child. The uneven surface was littered with deep holes full of peaty water and the wind would be biting.

Mary and I decided to search through the various crofts, looking in byres and chicken runs and anywhere else we could think of. We had been over two crofts, when Mary suddenly stopped.

'Hush,' she whispered.

Hardly breathing, we listened. We could hear the voices of the men on the hill and the sigh of the wind, but between these sounds, there was another that was only just this side of silence.

'Timmy, Timmy. Where are you?' We yelled again and again. Then we listened. Not a sound!

'Where did it come from, do you think, Mary?'

'I'm not knowin', but I'm thinkin' he must be in the village somewhere, or we'd no be hearing anything at all.' She paused. 'That's if it *was* Timmy and not just the call of an animal or the squeak of a byre door... The Lord help us!' she added somewhere between prayer and despair.

Just then old Dolleena came bustling up.

'Did you hear yon...?' She paused for breath: she was not built for rushing about looking for small boys.

'Did you hear aught?' she repeated.

'Aye,' said Mary, 'But I don't know where 'twas comin' from.'

'I think it was from the Kirk.' Dolleena was already puffing her way up the muddy path, which led to a miserable tin hut, which stood on the outskirts of Dhubaig. She was referring to the squalid building which had once been a place of worship for Free Kirk folk, its doors having closed some years ago. Its roof was full of holes and the only visitors now were mice and birds. Could he be in that? What a grim, filthy place for a little boy! But I supposed that it was marginally warmer and safer than the open hillside.

We toiled up the steep lane, calling as we went, but there was no repeat of that faint sound that we had heard. Had we heard *anything*? I was beginning to think that we had imagined it. As we came out onto the open moor, we could feel that the wind was strengthening. This would make the search more difficult, as voices would be carried away, and a little three-year-old's cries might be drowned altogether. Drowned! Terrible thought! What was happening on the shore, I wondered?

We approached the ramshackle building. It was in a worse state of repair than I remembered. Sheets of corrugated iron lay about, rattling as the wind caught them, and we could see the skeletal remains of the roof against the mottled sky. The door had gone altogether (it probably adorned someone's byre now). There were creaking and whistling noises as we flashed our torches into all the wet, filthy corners and under the rotten pews.

'All I can hear is the wind,' I murmured. 'There are so many holes.'

Dolleena suddenly jumped as though shot. 'Holes! Holes!' she shouted. Mary and I looked at her in astonishment.

'Of course! I know where he'll be. Yes! Yes, I know.' She began to run back down the path at a spanking pace for one so plump. Mary and I raced after her, not knowing in the least where we were going, but Dolleena had obviously had some sort of inspiration and I prayed that she really *did* know where Timmy would be.

Back down in the village, we seemed to be going towards the Pritchard's croft house.

'But they aren't there,' puffed Mary to Dolleena's back 'It will be bolted and barred like I don't know what.'

'Aye, I know,' panted Dolleena, 'Those folk are gey queer. Always locking doors!'

The Pritchards were absent owners and we had only seen them about twice in three years, so it was perhaps not unreasonable to lock the door during these protracted absences. But it was a habit that was considered very odd.

Over the low croft wall we tumbled and round to the back of the old house. There, low down in the wall, between the granite stones, was a little hole about a foot in diameter. It looked as though something (water perhaps?) had caused the collapse of some of the corner stones.

'Here!' shouted Dolleena. She bent down and called through the gap, 'Timmy? Timmy? Are you in there?'

To our immense relief, a little voice answered, ''Es. I's here. I can't get out.' The sound of sobs reached us.

Dolleena straightened up. 'I'll stay and talk to him to keep him from gettin' feart. He must have got in through this hole and now he canna get himself out again. When you said something about "holes", I suddenly remembered seeing him near that hole in the back wall this afternoon, and I know fine the place is near falling down. Run you both, and tell everyone that we have found him. The men will get him out.'

Mary and I hurried away as Dolleena calmly sat herself down on the wet ground by the hole and began to chat to Timmy.

Very soon Shona arrived, weak and wobbly with relief, and a small army of men marched up to the Pritchard's house. Fergie had thought to bring a hefty-looking crowbar to prise the heavy old door open. Shona went inside and returned carrying a cold, tearful, but unscathed Timmy. Dolleena stood grinning from ear to ear, rightly pleased with herself.

The next day, there was much activity at the Pritchard's house, as the men mended the door and the hole in the wall. Dolleena was watching and turned to me as I slowed down in passing. She was indignant.

'See, Nurse. If yon folk had not locked the door, the wee fellow could have got out no bother. Aye, the Pritchards are a weird lot, indeed!'

29

From the Deep to the Sky

OVER THE YEARS, I have often wondered just how much of Barney Scott's life story was real and how much sheer fantasy.

He was a very English Englishman – tweedy, well-spoken – and he arrived on Papavray with a flourish. One day no-one had heard of him, the next, he had appeared with a young wife, a baby son, two fishing boats, bought a cottage by the harbour and was very much among us. He quickly made himself known in the pub where he regaled the locals with tales of his adventures.

Archie was sceptical. 'He's no had time in his life to do all these things.'

'He's no' tellin' the truth,' added Mary severely. 'I'm thinkin' 'tis all fractions.'

What did she mean this time? We looked at her.

'Well. 'Tis like books. Not true.'

'Oh. Fiction!'

'Aye,' she murmured. 'That's what I said.'

But I think at least a 'fraction' of Barney's tales were true. He was older than he looked, being about fifty, had been born into inherited wealth and so had had the time and the money to indulge his many hobbies. He had climbed in the Himalayas with Chris Bonnington, explored jungles and deserts and dived around the world with teams of naturalists taught by the great Jacques Cousteau.

Did we believe all this? Having travelled a bit ourselves and met such people before, we could see that it was all possible for someone with his personality and background.

I came to know the family because of the wife and little son. Penny, only twenty-one, lived in the shadow of her larger-than-life husband and was the scattiest young mum I had ever met. She had no idea about child care, cooking or looking after a home. She muddled through her days, learning nothing as she went, so yesterday's mistakes were repeated again today, tomorrow and every day. Barney was vaguely aware of this and did some of the cooking but child care was a closed book to him. He had had nannies and maids when young!

So Jimmy's welfare was a concern. He was undoubtedly loved but his nappies were often not changed for many hours and frequently fell off, having been inadequately pinned, he was in the same pullover for weeks, he spent all his time barefoot in a cold, damp cottage, was never bathed and had usually not been washed when I called in late morning. It was a miracle that he was a healthy, happy child!

I visited twice daily for many weeks, teaching Penny how to care for him, what to feed him and even how to wash his clothes. Evidently, her mother, a formidable lady whom I met later, had looked after the child before the family moved to Papavray while Penny completed her Art degree at Manchester University.

All this meant that I was often in the cottage and I wondered where all that Scott wealth had gone. There was precious little sign of it in their haphazard lifestyle and grubby surroundings.

I was there when a boat engine was brought into the living room and dumped in all its oily glory on the carpet. Another day saw Jimmy sitting beside Barney, who was holding forth to a visitor. Jimmy upset his cup of milk over the sofa. Barney's reaction was to simply move to a dry seat and continue his conversation without a pause. The fact that Jimmy and the sofa were wet through escaped his notice.

Nick had always been fascinated by the sea and the underwater world and quickly got to know Barney, offering to help land the catches and make himself useful in the boat. Soon he was accompanying Barney and Doug, the mate, on their trips, watching and learning various aspects of seamanship.

This went on at weekends and in the holidays for some time and then

Nick asked us if he could learn to dive. At that point we ascertained that Barney *was* a qualified diver and that he worked for a company based in Ullapool with a contract to supply scallops to the restaurants of the south. He came to see us and said that he was happy to teach Nick in return for his help on the boat. We were most concerned about safety, of course, but he assured us that rules were strictly adhered to – no unaccompanied diving: you always had a 'buddy' diving with you and you never strayed far from the boat where a careful watch was kept on the divers. With this, we had to be content and gave our consent. All seemed to be fine so far as we could tell.

The only way to get a wet suit in those days was to make your own from patterns supplied by the companies making neoprene, the fabric. A huge parcel arrived from Aberdeen and much cutting and gluing kept us busy for some time, but finally, we had a fully kitted-out Nick who made his first dive (a shallow one) with Barney during the summer holidays.

But fishing goes on all year round and one black evening in November with snow on the hills, rain in the glens and a bitterly cold wind blowing in from the Atlantic, we sat waiting for Barney to bring Nick the seven or eight miles home. They were usually in long before dark so we were already concerned when instead of the cheery 'Hi' as Nick breezed in, full of the day's events, there was a scrabbling at the door and a muffled call 'Mum. Dad.'

I rushed to open the door and in staggered Nick, still in his wet suit. He was shivering uncontrollably as I urged him into the warm living room.

'Couldn't get out of this... too cold... hands...' came the croaking voice from between chattering teeth.

It took George and me nearly half an hour to extricate him from all the clinging neoprene. He was so cold that he could not help himself or stay rigid for us to pull the wetsuit off. Gradually, he emerged, almost navy blue with cold. I have rarely seen a living person that colour! Rubbed down with warm towels, wrapped in a blanket with a hot drink inside him, he began to look like Nicholas once more and was able to tell us what had happened.

Apparently, the engine of the small open boat had failed while the three of them were still a long way from the shore so they had taken it in turn to row – not easy in the cumbersome wetsuits of the time. Warm while rowing, but very cold while resting, they had taken about two hours to reach the shore. Doug immediately made for the pub and, because it was so late, Barney brought Nick straight home rather than changing in his harbour-side cottage. This was a very bad idea because the van had no heater!

However, Nick recovered well with no permanent ill-effects and the adventure grew in the telling.

Nick was not happy with Doug, who was a coarse man much given to swearing and excessive drinking. He was often not fit to dive, but just about able to man the boat. Unfortunately, on Papavray, together with most of the Western Isles, there were many drunken skippers and mates on the fishing vessels so we were thankful that Barney was virtually teetotal and was always in charge of the dive, only allowing Doug in the water if he was sober.

But, as we know, the best laid plans...

Nick had been diving for about a year now and was very useful to Barney: able to undertake the deeper dives to the sandy sea bed. Doug was getting more and more unreliable and rarely dived but still accompanied them to man the boat, often with a bottle of whisky beside him, leaving Barney and Nick to dive together.

But one day, Doug being sober and Barney having a severe cold that was making breathing difficult, Doug was preparing to dive.

Many years have passed since the incident that day, so I asked Nick to recall the event from his own perspective. This is what happened in his own words.

* * *

'It was a Saturday morning when I embarked on Barney's fishing boat. Doug was supposed to be the back-up diver as he was unusually sober. We sailed for about two hours to the dive site which, today, was over a sandy sea bed at the bottom of a steep reef near the mainland coast.

'Doug and I had kitted up and completed all the usual safety checks – testing air supply and so on, when Barney announced that we were over the site. I entered the water backwards from the low part of the gunwale, gave the thumbs up and swam a few yards away to be clear of the props before duck diving beneath the swell. I thought I heard a splash as Doug, too, entered the water.

'I always enjoyed this moment of the dive when everything suddenly became tranquil as, apart from the faint hum of the engine, the world that I had entered was silent and all embracing. I began my descent. Slowly the colour faded and the light became diffused as the depth increased. About a fathom above the sea bed, the details of the sandy expanse below me came into focus.

'My first realisation that something was wrong was at this stage. I was still descending when I found that inhaling was becoming difficult – rather like trying to breathe with a pillow over your face. A few seconds later, I found that there was no air at all coming through. I remember looking at my contents gauge – it read over three quarters full so, thinking that the demand valve must be stuck, I exhaled sharply to clear it. This had no effect and as I attempted to take another breath, there was no response from the apparatus. By this time I had exhaled almost all the air in my lungs. As I looked up towards the faint light about eighty feet above, I think I had already started to strike out for the surface.

'The physics of diving are that as you descend, the air that you are breathing has to be pressurised to match breathing at normal atmospheric pressure and the deeper you dive, the higher the air pressure that you require as the weight of the water above presses on your body. For every thirty feet that you descend, the pressure increases by one atmosphere (14.77 psi). On ascent, the reverse is the case and to compensate for this, you must exhale throughout an emergency ascent or risk the residual air in your lungs expanding as you rise towards the surface, possibly to such a degree that it causes ruptured lungs.

'I recall a sudden and biting pain in my chest just before breaking the surface. The pain increased sharply as I took my first breath of fresh air. I remember looking towards the boat and seeing that Barney had spotted me. Then everything went black.

'Evidently, Barney brought the boat round and he and Doug hauled me over the side, while radioing the coastguard for assistance. (Apparently, Doug had not dived at all as he had been violently sick when he hit the water.)

'The next thing I remember was looking down from a great height on the ever-diminishing boat with faces staring up at me. I thought that I was already dead. Then I became aware of a throbbing, whirring noise above me and I realised that I was suspended beneath a helicopter. I must have passed out again – perhaps with relief at knowing that I was still alive! I came round briefly to hear a voice saying, "hang in there, Nick, we land in five minutes," and then I passed out once more. I returned to a semblance of consciousness while being pushed at speed on a wheeled trolley along a brightly lit passageway with doors crashing open before us. I was rushed into an even brighter room where a hazy, white-coated person peered at me.

'I finally came round properly in the recompression chamber: the pain had gone and I felt a great deal better. I believe I was in the chamber for about four hours.

'I remained in Aberdeen Royal Infirmary for several days being cared for and bossed about by some very strict Royal Navy nurses. The doctor told me that I had ruptured my left lung, which had collapsed, filling the left chest cavity with air. The swift and efficient rescue and recompression treatment had ensured a quick recovery, but I remember a lot of very painful coughing for some time.

'Had Doug dived as he should have done, I would have been able to take a breath from his apparatus, alternating with him, using the air from his tank for both of us. This is called "buddy breathing". But he had not dived as planned, so I was alone.

'Sadly, I was told never to dive again.'

* * *

So ended a career before it began! Although sorry for Nick's dashed hopes, I was so relieved at the positive outcome of a dangerous accident that I could only be glad that his flirtations with a watery eternity were at an end.

30

007 in a Morris Minor

IT HAD BEEN an odd week, I reflected, as I arranged some very business-like cups and saucers on a tray for the visitor due this afternoon. George had been working on the island for two or three weeks now so life had assumed a pleasant, gentle normality which was a nice change from the often frenetic dashes for the plane or the long trek south by road when the company that he used to work for got in touch. They seemed to forget that he was not actually employed by them any longer and called on him in various crises. He was usually only too pleased to accept the challenge and the adventure but, occasionally even *he* felt that time spent at home was beneficial. Then he had time to appreciate the peace and beauty of the island and the slower pace of life which, after all, was why we were here.

But yesterday, the phone had rung and a very stern voice had asked to speak to George.

'Am I speaking to the George MacLeod who works for Control Gear and Engineering 'CA?'

'Well, I am not actually employed by them any longer but I do work for them from time to time. Who is this?'

'I am not at liberty to discuss anything on the phone but I represent MI6. One of my colleagues will call on you tomorrow afternoon. We would like a little information from you.'

'Oh. Um. Yes, of course.' George was flummoxed. This was not what one expected on a remote Hebridean island!

It was arranged that the 'colleague' would call at about half past three, and we were to keep the matter quiet. What a hope on Papavray!

Yesterday evening, we had puzzled over what it could be. I was inclined to be nervous. George had worked for a California-based company, but had been sent to some countries with dubious reputations for human rights observance and several communist regimes. I wondered if George had 'witnessed' something or other. I was always wryly amused by the fact that a company from the most overtly capitalist nation in the world seemed to be in such demand in communist countries.

Andy had to be told that someone was coming because he would be home from school while the visitor was here. His eyes were enormous with excitement as we explained that it was someone from MI6.

'It's just like James Bond,' he said. 'Will he have a gun? Will he be in an Aston Martin like in the films?'

'I hope not,' I said. 'Papavray would never get over it.'

'He might want to talk to Dad in private so we will have to push off somewhere,' I said. Our house was open-plan with no really private room.

'Does he want to know about that country where you gave the man who was following you the slip by jumping off buses?'

'Well, if it is, Andy, he is jolly late because that was a year ago now.'

'Tell us all about it again, Dad.'

So George began to reminisce.

*   *   *

He had worked in three different communist-held towns in the Eastern Block where the American company was involved in installing computerised control systems in factories. (Computers were in their infancy in the seventies.)

On their first visit, George and an American colleague, Hank, flew in to the capital of the area on an international airline arriving at seven in the morning local time. They were met and swept out of the airport in a large car with darkened windows, straight to a meeting. No quiet coffee to recover from the trip, no gentle introduction to the country. No – they were taken directly to a meeting like no other!

A long, shiny table was surrounded by large, earnest men in badly made suits and several female interpreters, who were the only people to speak English, other than George and Hank. Down the length of the table stood bottle after bottle of vodka and many of the assembled company were drinking heavily already. It was not even nine am!

George and Hank were pressed to partake and their refusal was clearly resented until the interpreter explained that they were not used to drinking so early in the day or at a meeting. This was greeted with much mirth and little understanding but as the meeting was discussing the job that they were to do, they said they needed a clear head. This seemed to be an alien idea and caused more laughter.

When the meeting broke up, the two were taken for a meal. They had a while to look at the shops, which were pitifully empty, and at some of the architecture left by a more affluent age before communism swept away a lot of the beautiful buildings.

They were then hustled off to the railway station and onto a hissing steam train of outdated design which rattled off across vast, snow-covered plains. They slept until the train pulled in to a station in the darkness of the Arctic winter night. They were met by a dour giant of a man, muffled in smelly furs. He pointed to a car, once more with blacked out windows, which looked as ancient as the train and, taking their cases from them, flung them into the boot, jumped into the driving seat and took off at an alarming rate, horn blaring continuously. Of course, George and Hank knew that in going to a communist country, they would be subject to all manner of rules and restrictions but this extreme treatment was worrying. Were they being protected from something, or suspected of something? Neither spoke the language (or languages – there were many dialects) and here, there was no interpreter so they could not ask the driver for any information. They had the feeling that in any case, he would not tell them anything.

Although he drove at break neck speed, his eyes seemed to be on them in the mirror more than on the road. Happily, there was no traffic at all and they were to find that there were very few cars in any of the three towns that they were to work in – the regime was too strict and the general public too poor.

At last, the car stopped before a shabby, but once-ornate building which appeared to be in darkness. The driver opened the car door, grunted, wagging his head towards the door of the hotel, as it turned out to be. They went to retrieve their cases but were pushed aside while the giant lifted them and strode into a dimly lit hall. Here, he held out his hand, and they realised that he wanted the keys to open the cases. They stood by while he rifled through their possessions, grunted with apparent satisfaction, stuffed everything back in and marched off with them up the stairs. Hank and George followed. It was obvious that the stairs and the corridors had not been cleaned in a long time. They passed bits of food, dust, discarded clothes and an empty vodka bottle. The giant opened a door and almost pushed the two men inside.

Where were the two well-appointed single rooms that had been promised? By the dim light in the centre of the one room, they could see two wooden beds, old and chipped. There was a faded rug on the linoleum floor, two arm chairs and a table, while a curtain was drawn across a corner to form a wardrobe. But the linen looked clean and there were two large, new towels on the end of the beds. The giant grunted again and led them along a corridor to the bathroom, which they could smell well before they reached it. This too was primitive but had a shower of sorts and a washbasin as well as a disgustingly stained toilet without a seat.

Back in their room, they tried to indicate to the giant that they were hungry so where was the restaurant? With a shake of the head, and the word, 'Nya', the man pointed to his watch. It was past midnight so presumably the restaurant was closed. They would remain hungry, it seemed.

With that, the giant left the room, banging the door behind him. It was bitterly cold and there was no heating but there seemed to be plenty of blankets on the beds – all rather elderly and topped by old-fashioned eiderdowns. So, tired from their journey and resigned to their hunger, they undressed and climbed into the lumpy beds.

Before it was light, there was a pounding on the door and a shout. They assumed that they were being given the local version of an alarm call. Downstairs, the restaurant was vast and bare, but already full of men eating what looked like salami and grey bread. At least there was tea to drink – they almost thought that there would be more vodka. How different this was from the sophisticated town of yesterday!

Almost everyone in the town seemed to be employed at the factory that George and Hank were to computerise. The crowd, made up of many different nationalities clumped along the rough road, the scene reminding George of the men of the northern mining towns of England back in the thirties. The two immersed themselves in their work and at the end of the day, ate in the canteen and returned to their dingy hotel.

During the night, George woke to hear some very colourful language, interspersed with loud thumps. He opened his eyes to see Hank chasing round the room whacking the floor with his shoe.

'What *are* you doing?'

'Killing this bugger – I hope.'

A huge brown rat was scuttling round the room, pursued by Hank. Just then, there was a sickening 'squish' as Hank finally killed it. He calmly opened the window, dropped the body out and went back to bed. But that was not the end. Several more nights were disturbed in the same way. When they complained (with difficulty) they were told, with a shrug, that it was not at all unusual. It seemed that they just had to put up with it.

There was little to do in the town. There was a market and a few shops which were poorly stocked. Such things as fruit, cakes, even meat and milk were only available occasionally, so everyone took to carrying a string bag, in case they happened to see something which they would have to buy there and then, because it would be gone tomorrow! These became known as 'in case' bags and George and Hank soon took to carrying them.

'Is that the town where you had a secret policeman following you all the time, Dad?'

Andy was enthralled by the rats, but eager to get to the fun bit.

'No, that was in the next town. That town was so-called 'closed' and up to a point, it was. We were taken in and out of the place by train under cover of darkness, only allowed to walk about in a small area of a few streets and not allowed outside the town at all. But there were some nice old buildings and a few churches – hardly used – and a few up-market shops for foreign workers like me so, as I was by myself on this job, I enjoyed wandering into these places. A secret policeman was assigned to me...'

'Did he have a gun, Dad?'

'Oh yes. They all had guns. I sometimes wondered if they knew how to fire them or, indeed, if they even had bullets in them.'

'Wow!' said Andy.

'Well, this guy followed me everywhere – to the shops, to the nice old buildings, to the factory, to the scruffy little park and so on, so I decided to have a bit of fun. I used to get on a bus, wait until I saw him get on and then just as it started up, I would jump off again, leaving him stuck on the bus behind the automatic doors. Then I'd walk alongside the bus and wave. He would get off at the next stop and plod along behind me wherever I went. He was rather fat and I often walked and walked and walked just to tease him. Eventually, we came to a kind of understanding. He was always waiting in the hotel foyer when I came down in the morning ready to follow me when I left. It was a lot of nonsense really because he knew that I knew that he was always watching me. So, in the end, I would tell him (in sign language) where I was going. He had more sense of humour than many, because he'd laugh and put his thumb up.

Andy laughed. 'I wish I could have seen his face when you jumped off the bus!'

* * *

As I was putting out some cakes and biscuits in readiness (no cocktails here – shaken or stirred) Andy came in.

'I'm home in time. And I haven't told a soul, I promise.'

Half an hour went by, then another and then the sound of a very ordinary car engine was heard and a small Morris Minor began slowly to descend our track.

Andy's face was a picture. 'This can't be him!'

But it was. The elderly car drew up by the gate and an equally elderly man emerged.

Poor Andy! The man was short, arthritic and wore thick glasses – not the dashing James Bond type of Andy's dreams.

We greeted Mr Downs – not even an interesting name – and invited him to have some tea. In a broad northern English accent, he accepted.

He and George sat by the fire and, when I brought the tea, with Andy helping, we were invited to join them. Mr Downs seemed reluctant to begin but after a lot of 'humming' he began.

'I believe you have recently been to...' (He mentioned one of the communist countries.)

'That's right. I was there helping to install computerised control gear in a factory making trucks. But it was not recently. It was a year ago!'

Mr Downs seemed rather embarrassed. 'Oh. Ah. Yes.' But he offered no explanation for the immense delay.

'Can you describe the work, the factory, the towns for me?'

This was going to take some time. The American company had contracts for many computer-based projects at a time when computers were very new and many less well-developed countries and those under oppressive regimes had no experts of their own.

Andy tried to ignore his disappointment in Mr Downs and his Morris Minor because the fact that MI6 wanted George's opinion on things was exciting in itself. And then suddenly, he became a part of it.

'Have you any photos of the factory?' Mr Downs asked, taking notes.

'Well, no,' said George. 'We were not allowed to take photos – in fact we were not allowed a camera at all. I was followed by their secret police everywhere I went.'

'Dad! I have that booklet that you brought home, showing the lorries – not the factory or anything. Just the lorries.'

Mr Downs looked at Andy with surprise. 'Can you fetch it for me to see?'

The booklet was an attempt on the part of the regime concerned to impress its people and merely showed pictures of rather old-fashioned looking lorries, but Mr Downs seemed very interested.

So the interview went on. Nothing new to us was revealed as Mr Downs was there to *gather* information rather than impart any.

Right from the first call from MI6, I had been shaking my head in disbelief. There were so many things that were so unbelievably amateur about all this. Being discussed was a visit that took place a year ago! Here was a government department relying for some information on a booklet given to a child! Questions were being asked about the location of the factories that were obviously already well known to the American company concerned and an employee (George) was asked for photos. Surely Western agents had had a year in which to take any number of pictures that might be of interest.

This was the time of the so-called 'Cold War', so there was skulduggery on both sides. Yet the information that Mr Downs was gathering was a year old! Some of the towns that George had worked in were supposed to be 'closed cities' – in other words no foreigners were allowed in, so it was assumed that all sorts of secret and possibly sinister 'goings-on' were being kept hidden. Hmm! We knew about eight or ten people from the West who were working in – or *had* been working in – these places.

Yes, George was followed everywhere and not allowed past the town perimeters and the trains taking him to these towns travelled at night and many of these factories were underground, but none of this was unusual in such secretive countries. There must have been dozens of trained agents at work in the Eastern Block, so why George?

Mr Downs stayed for about two hours, filling page after page of his notebook with neat writing and asking often very simple questions. He seemed to me like someone who had never been abroad and was unsophisticatedly interested in the most ordinary things.

After he had gone, we discussed his visit endlessly and realised that if the British Intelligence Service was generally as pathetic and out of date as on this occasion then we, the public, had much to fear. Hopefully, this was an isolated incident but we were amazed and appalled and completely unbelieving about the sheer naivety of MI6.

We were told to discuss the visit with no-one. We would not have been inclined to do so anyway as we were embarrassed by what we felt was the stupidity of the whole thing. We also knew that the locals would have been intrigued by a visit to the island by MI6 and it would have got in the local paper. But of course we allowed Andy to tell Nick, who was mightily unimpressed when told about the Morris Minor!

We never heard from MI6 again. It was as if none of it had happened at all. Andy never saw his book of trucks again. I wonder what they did with it?

31

Home!

I SEEMED TO have been packing forever.

'And how long are you away?' Mary was watching with interest. She was going to look after the cats and the chickens and keep the Rayburn stoked.

'Just the week,' I said.

'You'll no wear all those clothes in just a week, foreby. I'm thinkin' you'll be puttin' one on top of the other. And how will you all get in that wee Mini? It will be a gey squash!'

She was right. It was going to be a frightful squash in the Mini for the long journey, but the Land Rover had developed some alarming rattles and groans (in addition to the usual noises) and George spoke darkly of 'big ends' and 'gaskets'. The one and only garage would have to order parts, which would take weeks to arrive, no doubt. So the Mini, it had to be!

But I was looking forward to the break: to the sophisticated lifestyle of the capital, the shopping, a theatre trip and a real English Christmas. But I knew that the one week would be enough; and that I'd be happy to return to the island with its island ways, island people and slower pace of life.

There was a knock at the door.

'Come in, Roddy.'

'Now, how did you know it was me?'

'Your knock is different from everyone else, Roddy.'

'And how is that, then?' Roddy was nothing if not persistent.

'You start softly and get louder by the third knock,' I said. I had noticed this strange habit, which made the knock sound like a drum beat. 'What can I do for you?'

Roddy produced a rather soggy parcel, wrapped in newspaper.

'I have a wee bit venison for my cousin in London and I was wonderin' if you would take it to him.'

After ascertaining this cousin's address, I realised that the task would be impossible.

'I'm sorry, Roddy, but he lives much too far away. We will be on the opposite side of London.'

'And is that a long way, then?'

'Yes, Roddy. London is a very big place.'

'Is it, indeed?' Roddy seemed unconvinced. I realised that if I were ever to get the car packed, I would have to explain a little more clearly.

'London is about ten times the size of Papavray, perhaps more.'

'Is it, indeed? London is that big?' Roddy was amazed, but still hovered.

'Yes, Roddy, it is.'

'Well, well.' He paused, pondering. 'Then it will be bigger than Inverness, I'm thinkin'.'

'Indeed, it is, Roddy.'

'Well, well.'

He wandered off with his soggy bundle, muttering to himself, 'I'd best be having my wee bit venison for my own tea, then.'

'Silly old bodach!' said Mary with good-natured contempt. Mary had never ventured farther than Mallaig, but felt that her study of all the glossy magazines that her cousin in Cheltenham sent her qualified her to feel superior. She was another one with far-flung cousins: they all seemed to have dozens of them!

Nick was travelling south with us, but staying for an extra week with relations and returning, by air. Heathrow to Glasgow and Glasgow to Papavray on the 'new' plane. George too would not be returning with Andy and me as he was off on Boxing Day to South Africa on another contract.

The Christmas trip south was a great success! Shopping (Oxford Street style), theatre, meetings and greetings, 'catching up' gossip and Christmas fun with the family filled our days.

But all too soon, the dogs were stowed in the back and Andy and I were climbing into the car for the journey home. A very sleepy group waved from their porch: it was only four am. When travelling back to Papavray from the south of England, I always tried to get through Birmingham and the Manchester area before the 'rush hour'. It is so much easier now with all the motorways, bypassing or flying over these towns.

As we left the city, the weather was cold and clear. Andy and both dogs slept peacefully until, by mid-morning, we crossed the border into Scotland. We were making very good time, but as we approached Glasgow, I noticed a white covering on the far hills and the sky, heavy with more snow, seemed to be hovering only just above our heads.

We skirted Loch Lomond: the nearby fields wore the same white mantle, while the verges of the road gradually disappeared under a snowy blanket... I was regretting the fact that we had not had room in the over-crowded car for the usual spade and shovel; my travel companions during the winter months.

Deeper and deeper into the Highlands, we drove. The snow ploughs were already busy; so that, for the most part, the surfaces were fairly clear, but the growing walls of snow beside the road, told their own tale, while the gap between them rapidly became narrower. Progress was slow now, as the road was only cleared to the width of one vehicle, meaning long hold-ups.

But abruptly, we came out of the snow. We were skirting a large loch and, while the surrounding hills were still white and sparkling in the welcome winter sunshine, the wide, newly built road was clear, and I hoped to make up some time before tackling the more remote stretches of our journey.

Suddenly, we were spinning! Black ice! I wrestled with the steering, trying to come out of the spin. The loch was perilously near on the left but somehow we spun towards the right, waltzing across the road. I realised that we were heading for a very deep, rocky, purpose-built ditch – but there seemed to be nothing that I could do to stop us. We slipped, bumped and bounded over a stone edge and plunged down into this gully, head-first. A young tree, growing in the bottom, stopped our progress with a bone-jarring thump!

Andy, who had not so much as squeaked, was unhurt; I was also unhurt. I looked towards the back of the car. It was an estate car and we had a grille to keep the dogs in the rear. Two very puzzled looking animals were sitting on the grille! I realised that we were wedged in this gully almost vertically, nose down.

I opened my door and struggled out among the stones and boulders. We were so far down, that the back of the car was lower than the road surface. Thinking of the danger posed by other vehicles on the icy road surface, I told Andy to stay in the car. So far down in the ditch, he would be safer than standing beside the road. I climbed up and waited for a vehicle to round the far bend. I intended to flag one down to ask for help.

I was lucky! The first vehicle to appear was a Land Rover. The driver, obviously used to these conditions, slowed carefully, and gently pulled to a slightly sideways halt.

'Trouble?' was the succinct question, asked by a weather-beaten face peering from the open window. I explained and pointed to where, from his elevated position, he could just see the back of the car.

'Ach! We'll have ye out o' there in no time at all. Much damage?'

'Nothing obvious, bar a few dents. But I don't know if she will start. I had my feet off the pedals, so she stalled on impact.'

'Aye, so she would, so she would.' This man of few words was already heaving a sturdy rope from the Land Rover.

'Get the wee boy out and stand well away.'

Andy joined me and pointed, 'Look, he's got a winch on the front.'

Only then, did I realise that this was about the best vehicle I could possibly have stopped! It belonged to the Forestry Commission, and was well equipped for pulling anything and everything out of trouble.

Our friend, ever resourceful, was winding the rope from the Land Rover round a tree on the opposite side of the road, stretching it back to the tow hitch on my car. A splendid idea, I thought. Then I went hot and cold with apprehension, for the rope was across a major highway, on an icy road, round a bend!

'Um… what if something comes…?' I stuttered.

'Ach, never you mind about that. Just get yourselves away over behind yon rocks.'

Unconvinced and terrified for everyone's safety, we nevertheless did as we were told and got ourselves behind yon rocks.

Leaping in to the Land Rover, our friend started the winch. At first, there was a whine and nothing seemed to be happening but then, slowly, the car, with two miserable canine faces peering out of the rear window, made its slow and jerky way up out of the ditch and onto the road. The driver leapt out, undid the rope from around the tree, wound it back into his vehicle, which he then eased over to the verge, beside our car.

At that moment, an enormous articulated lorry came round the bend far too quickly, hit the ice, nearly jack-knifed, was righted and carried on with a cheery wave from the driver. As we watched, I found that I was holding my breath. If that lorry had been two minutes earlier, we might all have been killed!

Shakily, I approached the driver of the Land Rover, who was in my car by now, trying the engine.

'That was a bit close,' I said.

He looked up, 'Oh aye,' he said vaguely. 'Daft Donald always goes too fast. But no' mind.' He was completely unimpressed by what I had looked on as a brush with certain death!

'Well, there y'ar. She's goin'. There's a wee garage round your next bend. You'd best be getting her underneath looked at.'

'Yes, yes, I will. Thank you so very much for your help. We might have been there a long time, if you had not come along and been so kind.' I think I was gabbling a bit. One shock after another was taking its toll.

'Ach, no, no. 'Tis nothin'. Mind you how you go. Where is it you are goin'?'

I told him.

'Ach. I know it well.' He frowned. 'I'm no sure she'll get so far. She's a wee bit bumped about. See and get the wee garage to look at her.'

I assured him that I would, and tried to thank him again.

'Wheisht you. I told you, 'tis nothin'.' And with a wave, he had gone.

I got into the driver's seat with trepidation, but the car responded to my very gentle pressure on the accelerator, and we moved slowly forwards. No sliding, no spinning! I seemed to have control, so we drove to the 'wee garage'. The mechanic peered under the car and affirmed that it had had a 'wee bit bump or two' but that it would be 'fine, just'.

I filled up with petrol (this was the last petrol station that we would pass) and we were on our way. A little farther on, I let the poor dogs out. They were rather subdued, but unhurt, while Andy seemed to have enjoyed the whole episode!

Gradually, we drove out of the area with black ice and back into the snow. The ploughs had been out here, too, so the roads were passable with care and as I began to regain my nerve and confidence we made reasonable time. But I knew that we would have to rouse the steamer and ferry crews, as we would now be *very* late and finding anywhere to stay the night in the Highlands in midwinter was virtually impossible back in the seventies.

We were now in the remote Glen Slachan and it had been dark for some time. Andy was happily munching a sandwich and chatting between mouthfuls, when the car headlights began to flicker. They went out and then came on again. This happened several times, and then they came on and stayed on, but they were so dim that I could only see a few feet in front of the bonnet. Then the heating stuttered and failed.

'Put your coat on, Andy, before you get really cold.' I knew that this state of affairs could become dangerous: there were no other vehicles on the road now and it was very, *very* cold without the heating. I carried on – it was the only thing to do – but the car went more and more slowly, until the lights went out altogether and the engine failed. I had enough momentum to drift into a handy lay-by, which was mercifully free of snow.

'What now, Mum?' Andy had no real idea of the danger that we were in. Because of the lack of space in the Mini on the way south, we had not brought the usual emergency blankets.

'There is nothing we can do except try to keep warm,' I said. 'It is very unlikely that anyone will pass. The best thing, I think, is to get the dogs onto the back seat, put all the luggage into the rear and then we, too, will sit on the back seat and cuddle up to the dogs to keep warm. Dogs have a higher temperature than humans, so we will be alright.' I hoped! Many folk have owed their lives to dogs in this way – but it was *very* cold.

I was just about to put this plan into action, when, to my utter amazement, some headlights appeared behind us. As it neared, the vehicle slowed and pulled in to the lay-by behind us. Although thankful in one way, I was mindful of the fact that we were in a dark, remote glen and therefore very vulnerable.

A youthful figure emerged and loped towards me.

'What's the trouble? You are not having a picnic, are you?' This was delivered in a jocular English voice.

I tried to emulate the jollity. 'No. We are going to leave that until daylight.' Then I explained about the ditch and what had happened to the lights and engine.

'Ah. Yes. I think you have trouble with your alternator... or perhaps...'

Just then, incredibly, another set of headlights appeared. This car slowed and pulled in behind the first. A huge man eased himself out of the driving seat and approached.

'Howdy, Little Lady! What have we here, then?' A deep Texan voice boomed through the darkness.

Before I could answer, the first of my 'knights in shining armour' launched himself into a complicated opinion of what was wrong and a technical sounding conversation rumbled to and fro.

I was sitting in the car with the window open, in order to hear what the verdict was, when the first young man handed me an oily looking 'something' saying, 'Pop this on the back seat.' Then the American pushed something else in through the window, 'You sure won't need this for a while.' After a few minutes, various other bits of the engine were deemed unnecessary, and passed in through the window. I began to think we would have more in the car than under the bonnet. (Or, perhaps – 'hood'?)

They slammed the lid down and both leaned in to the car. 'Start your engine, Little Lady.'

To my surprise, there was an instant response.

'Now! You will be alright if you keep going. Don't switch off, whatever you do, because you will not get it started again.'

'Yes, yes. I understand. But I have to go on the ferry and the steamer – the little winter one – to Papavray...'

"Papavray? Gee! That's where my Momma's Momma came from!'

The other young man was unimpressed. 'Never mind all that. Just remember not to turn the engine off. Those boats will have to put up with it. If you explain, it will be OK...'

But the Texan was not so easily put off and demanded to know where on Papavray we lived and so on, so I told him to call if ever he got there. Being an American, he *would* get there, I knew. But it was so cold that our teeth were chattering.

'Can I put the heating on?' I asked.

There was a combined howl, 'No, no, no! There is not enough power.'

'Off you go now.' The first young man was keen for us to get on our way, and once more, I was thanking kind people for their help. We were just pulling away, when our Texan poked his head in the window to instruct Andy to 'mind, look after your Momma, now'.

At last, we drew away. We had an uneventful – if extremely cold – fifty miles or so, and as we approached the ferry, the first of the two crossings, I was puzzled to see that the crew were still on board because it was long past the time of the last normal sailing for the day.

I drove onto the ramp, with my window open, to say that I must not turn the engine off, and why.

'Well, well. And here you are, then, Nurse. And the wee boy, I see. Ally Mac didna tell us about the engine, foreby.'

I was completely at sea (in more ways than one) wondering how everyone knew about our adventure, but eventually, it emerged that 'Ally Mac' was the name of the Land Rover driver, who had deemed it wise to ring his cousin (another one with cousins) on the ferry to look out for me. From his description, they immediately knew who he meant, but of course he had not known of the engine problem. They had had a very long wait, and once again, I was thanking everyone for such help.

'I'm thinkin' the wee steamer will be about ready for you by the time you get there. I rang them when I saw your lights comin'.' They would have been pretty sure that mine would be the only lights at this time of night so they had even alerted the steamer for the crossing to Papavray!

Eventually, I drove over the familiar island roads towards Dhubaig, with the feeling that nothing was real any more. We were living in a fairytale! The amount of help and kindness that we had experienced this day was truly 'awesome' – as our Texan would probably say.

As we rounded the last bend into the village, the engine started to splutter. Would our luck hold to get us home? As we descended the steep track to our house, the lights went out and the engine coughed and died. We free-wheeled the last few yards and we were home!

We fed the dogs, had some soup, stoked the Rayburn and, thankfully climbed the stairs.

It was three am! The New Year would begin in a few hours' time. What would that bring, I wondered? And all the following years – what of those?

* * *

The next few years passed in much the same way as the last three or four. The boys grew, Nick left for pastures new, Andy, now thirteen, was ready to start at the senior school, patients came and many often sadly went as our population aged, and Papavray remained as beautiful and challenging as ever.

Then, suddenly, everything changed. Far, far away in sunny California, plans were being hatched, visas arranged, contracts drawn up and our lives were about to change yet again.

32

Californian Sunshine!

GEORGE, ANDY AND I woke at four am.

We were jet-lagged after the thirteen-hour flight so we were *really* awake with no hope of further sleep at all.

George blinked across the motel room, which we were all sharing.

'Let's go and have some breakfast,' he said.

'It's four in the morning,' offered an astonished Andy.

'That's OK. This is California.' George seemed in high spirits in spite of the lack of sleep.

We dressed. I had a problem remembering to put on just a tee shirt and jeans although it was only four am. Where were the emergency calls on Papavray when I was woken at four am by the phone and bundled myself into layers of clothes before braving a sub-zero world and lashing rain?

Two bleary-eyed dogs, Pip and Squeak, peered at us from their make-shift bed in the door way of the en-suite. They seemed to be very reluctant to wake. It was likely to be the after effects of the sedative that they had been given before being caged and loaded into the live animal hold in the plane on which we had all travelled. This hold was pressurised and heated, so they had been comfortable. They seemed to take the whole thing in their stride but had been *very* pleased to see us at the airport in LA.

I took them round to a scrubby patch of grass at the rear of the motel, gave them a drink and they seemed only too happy to go back to sleep. No problem for them, apparently.

The enormous 'Ford Country Squire' which George had bought on his previous visit to see his new employer, was standing outside the door of the motel room.

It was huge! And it was an automatic! Such cars were still rare in the UK and I was intrigued by its sophistication. It seemed to think for itself.

In we got and set off on the 'wrong' side of the road. I could tell that George was having to concentrate very hard to remember this at road junctions. I too would have to be careful and I felt apprehensive. As it turned out, it all seemed quite logical and there was so much space on the city roads that one had time to think. Not so the Interstate Highways, encountered later, which were crowded and an altogether frightening experience with sixteen-year-olds racing each other in 'Ford Firebirds' and the California Highway Patrol (a formidable lot, bristling with firearms) chasing them as they weaved in and out of the traffic.

Near the motel there was a 'diner' – a restaurant to us – called 'Big Bob's'.

'Big Bob?' Andy hooted when he saw the name. 'Who is Bob and why is he so big?'

We were unused to the rather brash names that we were now encountering. We were accustomed to 'Ye Olde Tea Shoppe' in England and the something 'Arms' or 'Hotel' in Scotland where they spurned fancy names.

Breakfast was another surprise. The diner was at least half full (four am?) as we found a seat by the window.

Why was I asked if I wanted my eggs 'over easy'? And what was the alternative? And how come we ate pancakes with syrup at four am? And where was the longed-for cup of tea? I asked the trim waitress for a pot of tea and George and Andy requested coffee with which Americans are so familiar and which seems to be drunk incessantly and in vast quantities.

My tea arrived, weak, without milk, iced, sugarless and in a glass with an umbrella balanced in it! Oh dear! That was the last time I asked for tea in a diner. The food, however, was good: filling and tasty.

George had to meet his new boss and some colleagues at eight am (the Americans start early) so Andy and I were free to wander. At first we seemed to be the only people walking as cars whizzed by and the 'trash collectors' emptied bins. There was so much space: space beside the roads, space between diners, space between office blocks and shops. Conditioned as we were to the use of every bit of land in British towns, leaving no gaps between buildings, we found this very refreshing. We had a sense of airiness. Later we realised that this 'air' was heavily polluted and hung over Los Angeles like a pall for much of the time.

The road signs seemed unintelligible even to us as pedestrians. What was a 'PEDXING'? Why were there *two* red lights in the same place at junctions but restraining different lanes? And when I came to drive, how would I know which to obey? And where were the roundabouts with which the UK keeps it traffic moving? California and most of the States move their traffic by means of batteries of traffic lights swinging in the wind on wires above one's head. I could see that we had a lot to learn but a good breakfast had helped us to be positive and excited at being in a new country.

We ambled along the 'sidewalk' (*not* the pavement-that was the road surface it seemed) crossed at the PEDXING and entered a large shopping mall.

There might have been one or two such malls in the UK at that time but, coming from the wild north, we had not seen such a thing so the vast, shiny expanse of marble floor, the glass roof and the brilliant lighting were yet another startling contrast.

'Whatever would Fergie think of this? Or Archie?' wondered Andy as he gazed around. Goods offered for sale were another source of amusement to him.

'Who on earth would wear those?' He laughed as we passed a sort of open shop selling Bermuda shorts of every gaudy hue. Andy was beginning to be a little more particular about clothes. He was older and the island wear had been very much designed for the weather rather than the appearance. Later, he was surprised to find that the American school clothes were of man-made fibres. The UK had tried these and, apart from the very cheapest of wear, had reverted to using natural fibres which we felt were superior in quality and appearance. But now we had to conform, of course, or go without.

We pottered about for some time and then decided to have coffee – *not* tea – and a burger. Such things were unknown on the islands but Andy had seen them in London. He thought the enormous American version was much better and began to feel that this strange place was going to be fine after all.

Feeling sleepy at the wrong time of the day, Andy and I returned to the motel. I had hoped to take the dogs for a walk but there seemed to be a conspiracy against dogs and their owners. 'No Canines Here'. 'Owners are warned against exercising their canines here'. 'Fouling by canines is liable to prosecution'. Why could they not say 'dogs'?

We eventually found a scrubby area beside a dried up 'drain' – perhaps 'brook' or 'gully' to us. It was many feet deep and about forty feet wide. Here we 'exercised our canines' undisturbed. On our return to the motel, we were severely admonished for having our canines in the motel at all. No-one had told us that this was not allowed. Apparently, they 'constituted a health risk'.

I thought of the collies on Papavray, who wandered in and out of the croft kitchens at will, shared the warmth of the fireside or Rayburn and, in the case of our two, often slept in the bedrooms. And what about Louis the Lamb, who walked on the coffee table and the new-born lambs, housed and fed in cardboard boxes beside the Agas or Rayburns in the croft house kitchens?

George returned from his meeting to tell us that the first few months of his new contract would be spent not in California but in Nevada.

Andy was hazy about American geography. 'Where is Nevada?'

'Oh, it's the next state to the north and east,' said George nonchalantly, as though we were talking about the next street.

'I will be working near a little town called 'Hawthorne'. It is by Lake Walker, in the desert. It is to do with defusing and exploding old bombs.'

'Wow!' said Andy, impressed. 'Which war are they from?'

'World War Two, Korean War and Vietnam. Some are very old and unstable so it is all done by robots controlled by computers. That is what I will be doing.'

Robots were still quite new, except in science fiction, and George was looking forward to the challenge. I was not so sure!

It was only May so Andy would have the summer vacation (holidays) in Nevada before returning to California to begin school in Mission Viejo at the start of the fall (autumn) semester (term). If George's job in Nevada overran the summer, Andy and I would return, with George joining us later as his next assignment was in San Clemente.

'So when do we go to Nevada?' I wondered, trying to absorb all this information through a sort of fog of tiredness and confusion.

'Now.'

I looked at him. 'And how far is it to Hawthorne?'

'About seven or eight hundred miles, I think.' He paused and at last seemed to be taking in the difficulties. 'We will find somewhere for the night.'

'Do you know the way?'

'Um... No.'

'Map?'

'Oh. Right.'

After a brief snooze we set off with a map, two dogs and just the few clothes that we had been able to bring within our baggage allowance on the flight. Our furniture and possessions were in a container on a ship in mid Atlantic. We had only the vaguest of ideas of what might await us in Hawthorne. Our accommodation was provided by the company. What was it like? Were we near this Lake Walker? Was the place really a desert? And so on. I decided to stop thinking about it and just drive. It was unbearably hot and the air-conditioning was either not working or we had failed to understand its controls.

We headed north, hugging the Pacific coast of California and passing through many of the towns, familiar by name as a result of films made on location. Then we turned inland and started up the steep side of the Santa Monica and San Gabriel mountains which form the backdrop to LA and the coastal strip. These are not high but they trap the smog created by the millions of car exhausts and hold it in a brown, foul-smelling and eye-watering blanket over LA and surroundings.

This is the State where the car is undoubtedly king. You *need* a car to live in the coastal area of California. The whole way of life is built around the car – the distance from residential areas to shops, schools, medical and leisure facilities and work means that everyone needs a car: families often had several.

Driving up the six-lane highway into these mountains, I reflected that many crofters in the islands could not afford even one old banger and walked for miles if they were physically able.

It was already getting dark as we left San Bernadino behind and far below us. The lights were already coming on in the streets, outlining the strict grid system of roads and avenues. Almost all Californian cities were laid out in this way and it was probably very convenient and logical but I did not find it attractive at all. To me, it looked boring and too far removed from the familiar random and picturesque assortment of streets, alleys, and buildings in Britain. I also found myself uncomfortable, perhaps embarrassed by the uninhibited use of vast quantities of electricity. A strange feeling for one who was, after all, just a visitor but we had been hearing so much about the fact that the world's resources were under strain that this scene seemed reckless. I stopped worrying. At least it was cooler now.

We drove on to the high, flat Mojave Desert where we bowled along for miles seeing nothing but the occasional tall cactus which loomed, human-like, out of the gloom as tumble-weed rolled across the road in the draught of every passing vehicle. There were few cars but huge articulated trucks, towing at least two trailers roared out of the night, blaring their horns. In case we had not seen them? How could we miss them? Their every outline was lit with multi-coloured lights and their metalwork gleamed in our headlights. They were magnificent! Truckers in the USA take great pride in the appearance of their trucks, washing, polishing and generally maintaining their splendid appearance. Do they have some sort of federal competition, I wondered?

Not for these men (and women) the small, grubby lorries of the UK. In fact, the Americans are inclined to laugh at the very word 'lorry'. I don't know why it is so funny but I soon stopped calling these monsters of the highway 'lorries'.

At the aptly named 'Four Corners', where four roads and a railway met, we found a motel. We smuggled the dogs in very quietly, praying that they would not bark. We were so tired that in spite of the rattling of the long, long freight trains that moved so slowly through the junction and the swish of the trucks, we slept.

Next morning, we set off very early, travelling along the eastern side of the mighty Sierra Nevada mountains. For some miles the road ran beside the LA aqueduct. Southern California is so short of water that several such aqueducts were built to carry the precious resource from lakes and reservoirs in North California to the orange groves, vineyards and the thousands and thousands of swimming pools of the south. This one was as wide as a road, the water in it about eight feet deep and flowing at quite a rate. I was full of admiration for the brilliance of the concept and the precision of the construction.

'Imagine *not* having enough rain,' murmured Andy, obviously thinking of the Hebrides.

On we went, passing a small scattered community with the iconic name of 'Lone Pine'.

'It's like living in the Wild West,' said Andy and was happy to see a Stetson or two among the baseball caps of the residents of Lone Pine.

After some lunch and the purchase of some *dark* sun glasses, we came to Mono Lake: a salt lake formed about a million years ago. There is no outlet from the lake, so the water gradually becomes more and more salty. When we passed it that day, the water level was very low and we heard later that this was the subject of a bitter dispute between the locals and LA which had taken water from it into the aqueducts. In the 1990s, this practice was stopped and the lake is filling again.

When we saw it, the lake was an eerie-looking, dead place with tall pillars of salt standing in the remaining water like the stumps of submerged trees and no sign of wildlife. Now that the levels are normal again, the wildlife is back. A happy end to a very long dispute.

We skirted the lake and set off east along an unbelievable twenty-seven miles of dead straight road into Nevada. No notice proclaimed the boundary with California, no fence or frontier post – only a sudden change in the road surface told us that we had passed from one great state to another. A line in the road with a perfect tarmac surface on the Californian side: well-kept and smooth and a rough, broken surface with ill-defined edges on the Nevada side. And that was all. I almost felt at home. Bad roads were a very real feature of Papavray.

We had passed through several ugly towns of scarcely more than one long street festooned with advertising hoardings on every building. Coca Cola signs, burger signs, beer, tyres, truck rentals and more! 'Flags' waved in the breeze in a horrid attempt to lure folk into the rather seedy looking premises lining the road. We were very aware that we were now in Nevada when we saw arrows pointing the way to numerous casinos.

Now we drove into Hawthorne and it was exactly the same with even taller hoardings and a few side streets. My heart fell. Among it all a tiny notice told us that we were at four thousand six hundred feet. It was so warm that I had not noticed the gradual rise.

We had to meet a colleague of George's at 'El Capitan' – the largest and gaudiest casino in Hawthorne. Over an impressive lunch (casinos do not expect to make a profit on food, I was told) we were shown the way to a little cluster of homes about four miles away at Walker Lake.

We turned off where we could see a block of about eight apartments, a few houses, a restaurant, a boating centre and several wooden jetties. Andy was ecstatic! He had always loved water and boats and this looked just 'great'.

Our apartment was on the second floor, approached up an outside metal staircase to a balcony overlooking the lake. We were home!

Unpacked, dogs walked, everyone fed, I stood at peace on the balcony and gazed in wonder and delight. The lake, about twelve miles long and five wide, lay sleeping below, shining palely in the bright moonlight. Surrounding all sides were dry, barren but beautiful mountains, outlined against a deep blue sky alive with stars. Turning slightly I could see, behind the apartments and so near that it seemed to rise from the roadway was Mount Grant standing proudly at eleven thousand feet. It had a dusting of snow on its peak.

Now I felt at home. Mountains, the lake and snow!

33

Nevada

I WOKE IN the night. I was cold. Thinking that the night would be warm like the day, I had only a sheet over me. Hastily, I located the duvet and snuggled down, remembering belatedly that we were in a desert, high maybe, but far from the ocean and therefore subject to extremes of temperature with hot dry days and bitterly cold nights and hot, dry summers and icy winters.

By seven in the morning, the sun was up and the apartment was uncomfortably warm. There was a cooling system called a 'Swamp Cooler', a large, ugly affair on the roof. This seemed to be the poor relation of the air-conditioning that we would enjoy later in California.

George went off to explode his bombs. Andy appeared in bathing trunks and not much else and we took the dogs down the wide, gravel approach to the lake. Our two 'canines' plunged into the green water with glee and Andy followed more gingerly: the water was still cool from the cold night but he was soon striking out between the boats moored near the jetties.

I sat nearby and could now see that the mountains across the water were higher than I had supposed in the darkness and were part of a red-brown range stretching east and south of the lake. I believe them to be part of the Monte Christo Range.

Andy came back. 'There were some boys here last night,' he observed. 'Perhaps at the weekend...?' He was missing his island companions but he was a gregarious boy and would soon make friends, crossing whatever barriers might arise. And I felt instinctively that there would *be* barriers.

There was another man living nearby who worked at the Hawthorne Army Munitions Plant and who had given George a lift so I had the car to get supplies. *We* go shopping, the Americans generally, and certainly the Nevadans, *get supplies*.

Andy and I went into Hawthorne. Although very ugly, the town had some good shops with a smattering of Native American craft work and paintings. I was told that there was an Indian reservation at the north end of Walker Lake but, disappointingly, we rarely saw any Native Americans.

It seemed that they were kept very strictly to their own land and this seemed a gross injustice to me but I soon discovered that this opinion is not one to be voiced in certain circles in Nevada.

We began to get to know other residents in the apartments. What a diverse group! In one, there was a tall, bronzed, muscled young man living with his equally bronzed and determined wife. His father, also bronzed and tall, picked him up each morning in a huge, red truck. They went off to their nearby silver mine which had closed in the 1930s as being 'worked out', but new technology meant that there were now ways of extracting the silver from the rocks and these two hard-working, hard-drinking men were sure that they were going to make a fortune.

Two girls, whom I took to be in their twenties but who turned out to be sixteen and seventeen, worked in El Capitano, departing in the evening wearing high heels and make-up but helping in the silver mine in the day. When did they sleep, I wondered?

A young couple, devout Baptists, lived below and to the right. During our time there, Babs gave birth to her second child. They had no health insurance and the cost of maternity care was such that she had had no antenatal care at all and only went in to the local(ish) hospital when her waters broke and she was well advanced in labour. She was back again in less than two hours, driven home by the Pastor of their church. Her husband could not afford to lose even a few hours work. This was rough, tough Nevada, not the easy living of California.

That evening, however, all the residents of the apartments were invited in to their home to sit in a circle on the floor holding hands, to thank God for Bab's safe delivery and God's gift of a baby. From my perspective, I certainly felt that He must have been smiling on her and the baby. The whole scenario seemed unbelievably desperate.

In the apartment below us were a very odd couple and their nine-year-old son, Jason. Being Jewish, they did not attend the celebrations; in fact they seemed unwilling to even talk to Babs and her husband, Harley, a tall, thin man who wore a lungi most of the time and no shoes.

Jason's mother was a New York lady with an accent to match. (I was apparently an 'English Poyson'). Jason was at school in Hawthorne. His stepfather was a very angry individual, who shouted at our dogs for no reason except that they were there, who grumbled at all the residents for a variety of imagined slights and was generally disliked and ignored. He had a 'sidearm' and a rifle, both of which he carried everywhere, even down to the restaurant by the lake if they were eating there in the evening. When Jason announced that he had saved up enough money for a bicycle and mentioned the figure, his stepfather remarked, 'What a waste of money. You could buy a good gun for that.'

Being unused to the gun culture of the States – very obvious in Nevada – we were uncomfortable with his general attitude, wondering if he was perhaps dangerous. Eventually his wife told us that he was a Vietnam War veteran who still had nightmares and whose insecurities stemmed from some horrendous experience that he had endured but would not speak about. We all tried hard to be friendly and to find something to like in him, but were rebuffed at every turn. We were very sorry for him but we gave up – what else could we do?

Two other girls lived at the end of the block. Sheila was about seventeen and her sister, Amy, about twenty. There was some sad reason for the sisters living there, away from their parents, but I did not understand this at the time. They worked together in the restaurant at El Capitan and Amy seemed very protective of her sister. They loved swimming in the lake but by the time they got home, it was dark. No long, northern twilight here: darkness fell suddenly at around seven and, apart from our little group of lights, the twelves miles of the lake and its surroundings were completely dark. Except for the moon and stars. Delightful!

One evening there was a knock on the apartment door and the sisters stood there in their swimsuits.

'Come swimming,' they invited. Andy was out. Were they asking me? Two young girls asking a fifty-year-old grandmother to swim with them?

'Me?' I asked.

'Of course! It's quite warm. We always dive off the jetty. See you there.'

Dive off the jetty? In the dark? Into dark green water of unknown depth?

Suddenly, I felt almost flattered to be asked to join two young girls in their swim. I was being asked just as myself with no reference to age or foreign-ness.

'I'll be there,' I said.

I changed rapidly and ran down to the jetty – no longer the dignified Nurse Macleod.

They dived into the blackness. Heart in mouth, I followed, shutting my eyes long before I hit the water. It was still warm from the heat of the day and we swam about, treading water sometimes to chat and get to know each other. What I did not let them know was that I had always had a dread of *dark water*! Only later did I see, hanging in their webs from the underside of the jetty, dozens of 'Brown Recluses'. I am more scared of spiders than of dark water and these enormous creatures were just inches from our feet as we joyfully ran along the boards. They are about three inches across (taking the leg length into account) and have the unpleasant habit of biting folk. Although the bite usually has no generalised effect on the body, the flesh around the bite rots away to leave deep and lasting scars, sometimes an inch in diameter. Once I knew about these monsters, I began to notice such scars on the bare arms and legs of some of those around us.

We swam most evenings after that until the lake 'turned over'. Like the Recluses, this phenomenon was a total surprise. In high summer when the sustained heat gets to a certain point, the plant life from the bottom of the lake rises to the surface, sending the cleaner water down. This process happens in many of the hot desert lakes. The resultant smelly mess of algae and other plants make the lake impossible to swim in and very difficult even to launch a boat, and this state of affairs lasts for several days or even a week until the whole disgusting, slimy matter sinks again. Clever people have tried to explain this to me but I still have only the vaguest notion of why it happens.

But long before the lake 'turned over', George and I had a 'conference'. Here we were beside a lake for the long hot summer and boating was free with no charge to launch, no licence needed or restriction of any kind – so why did we not have a boat? Andy was ecstatic when we decided to fill this gap in our lives. Enquiries were made, a few telephone numbers rung: someone was selling his boat business and there were bargains to be had.

Next weekend, we set off for Topaz Lake. Topaz and its lake are on the border of California and Nevada in the mountains to the north and west of Hawthorne. The fact that it was about two hundred miles away did not seem important.

We looked at several boats including a pretty, comfortable potterer. This took my eye but was instantly dismissed as 'useless' by Andy and George who wanted something fast. Andy wanted to water-ski.

We bought a sixteen foot fibreglass boat and a seventy hp Evinrude outboard engine and some water skis (later found to be far too heavy and had to be replaced) and some special propellers to cope with the four thousand feet altitude of Walker Lake. We intended to ski on the six thousand feet Lake Tahoe at some point, too. A trailer came with the boat: we had a hitch fitted there and then and set off back through the now darkening mountain roads.

Next morning, we reversed the trailer into the lake. As with all boating, there always seems to be help on hand coupled with much advice, delivered on this occasion through puffs of an enormous cigar rolled from side to side in the mouth of a huge young man, who seemed delighted to push the boat in, start the engine, adjust this and that and generally take us under his wing.

After a while, we got the hang of it, loaded the dogs into the boat and Andy jumped over the side, prepared to ski. In his first few attempts, he failed to 'get up' at all but in less than half an hour was skiing well and enjoying himself enormously. Watching him, I decided that if a fifty-year-old grandmother could swim nightly in inky black water, she could surely learn to water-ski. So I did!

34

Storms and Speed

ONE HOT EVENING we stood on the balcony watching in wonder and amazement as no fewer than *five* thunder storms roared, rumbled and rattled through the mountains around the lake.

The air was still: no wind at all and I could feel the crackling charges in the atmosphere as the pink and orange lightning snaked through the mountains, momentarily illuminating the red rocks against the dark sky. Now and again a jagged fork of white light would hit the water and the brilliance of the flash bounce before disappearing into the depths. The spectacle was truly magnificent.

Trying to watch all the storms at once, we stood in wonder, awe, respect even, for the strength of nature's rage. The tumult made speech impossible so each had his own thoughts and I reflected how such spectacles had inspired writers and composers for hundreds of years. 'The Hebrides Overture', 'Fingal's Cave', 'The Flying Dutchman' all mirror the savagery of storms. I was reminded, too, of the thunder storms in the Western Isles where the noise bounced off the solid rock faces, like the sound of an explosion and rumbled away in the gullies. I was just thinking that this was easier to watch as there was no wind or rain, when suddenly a hot blustery wind sprang up, blowing into our faces and buffeting our bodies. One moment, we had been quietly watching the dramatic scene and the next, we were clutching the balcony rail for support while doors and windows crashed back and forth behind us.

'Storm's coming this way,' shouted a neighbour. 'Get off the balcony!' The balcony was metal and not the best place to stand among lightning strikes. We continued to watch the storms across the lake from inside, but Mount Grant was behind the apartments so we could only *hear* the fury as it hit that great mountain. And what a noise! One almost felt the need to duck or cover one's head as the exploding claps of thunder seemed only inches above us. And still there was no rain!

In all our wanderings, I have not experienced a storm like that one with five different locations, experiencing lightning and thunder at the same time while the ferocity of the wind and the roar of the onslaught on Mount Grant, so close behind us, was fearsome in its savagery.

During the next week, we witnessed more electrical storms – as the Americans call them. They are correct, of course, but for me the technical term detracts from the awesome splendour of nature's anger and the romance of the spectacle.

One day, Andy was swimming quite far out in the lake when lightning hit with speed and ferocity, striking the water and appearing to create sparks. Horrified, I rushed down towards the lake, yelling to him to come out of the water. Swimming swiftly, he made the shore and we both raced back to the apartments, but I wondered just how safe we were on that metal staircase!

Storms held off, however, to allow a lot of water-skiing and even I became quite proficient. The first thing I learnt was how to fall over without the intense agony of plunging into the water at speed straight onto one's lower back. Falling sideways was a much better option until I managed to stay up. I was very proud of myself as I had had no idea that I was capable of mastering anything quite so physical. Some five years later, I surprised myself even further by learning to windsurf. And what fun that was!

Andy, of course, outstripped us both and became proficient almost at once, making 'Rooster tails' of the spray, slalom-skiing and doing various other tricks.

One day he was wandering about among the boating fraternity as usual when two burly fellows approached him. They were paramedics from California at Walker Lake for the weekend. Andy had been admiring their fast, shining speed boat with an enormous engine. They needed a 'spotter', they said and he was delighted to oblige. The rules on water-skiing require a spotter to be present in the boat if there is only the helmsman and the skier so that a fallen skier, who could be injured or severely winded, is picked up as soon as possible. Off they went at a ferocious speed with one or the other man skiing behind and Andy spotting. There was little to 'spot' as these fellows were so adept that they did not fall off at all. As the morning wore on, Andy's private hopes were fulfilled as the paramedics invited him to ski behind this magnificent boat. The speed achieved far out passed anything that our quite fast but rather more modest seventy hp engine could produce.

As the following weekend approached, we became aware of much activity at the waterfront. Seating was set out (just benches), bunting was strung between lamp posts ('light poles' – I think) and extra staff were taken on for the restaurant. Then large luxuriant RVs (motor homes to us) started to arrive, many trailing large, fast speedboats bearing romantic or quirky names and competition numbers in brilliant colours. Soon we had a bay full of these fantastic craft and a small town of RVs. on the open land beside the lake. Everyone was in good spirits and Andy mingled happily with these enthusiasts, admiring their boats. A sure way to their hearts!

Everyone was here for practice runs or heats for the 'Hundred Mile Marathon' due to take place later in the summer. Walker Lake was virtually straight for its twelve mile length so most suitable for racing, the one hundred miles being achieved by racing to and fro. The serious boating was to take place the next morning, so there was a party spirit in the evening with BBQs, and general meeting and greeting and the inspection and admiration for the 'tunnel hulls' the 'mono hulls' and many other types of boats in the various classes. Andy can probably reel off their names to this day but I just thought they were all fantastic craft as I have always loved speed, especially on water.

But among all the jollity there was concern for one of their main competitors – tipped to win in fact – who had not arrived.

Apart from its ability to 'turn over', Walker Lake had another unpleasant habit. In the summer months, the lake would be glasslike until about lunch time when the heat reached a point which caused the wind to swing round to the south and strengthen, churning the surface and making it unsuitable – even dangerous – for high-speed boating. All the boats had to compete in the few hours of the morning for this reason.

It was about ten thirty am, when the missing competitor, with wife and two children arrived, having had a breakdown on the way. He started to launch his boat but everyone was telling him that it was too late: that the water would be too choppy in just a few minutes. *They* had all done their 'runs' by then – and very impressive they were. But he took no notice. They pressed the point home but he was stubborn. He knew that he had a good chance of winning in the final races and wanted to be sure of taking part in the heats.

Despairingly, everyone watched. His wife and children stood on the jetty with the competitors and a crowd of onlookers that had materialized, no doubt sensing drama. He launched and roared off to the starting point at the Southern end of the lake. Then he began his run, accelerating and quickly gaining speed. By the time he was opposite the bay, he looked invincible and he was still gaining speed. As predicted, the water was now choppy with small waves forming here and there.

He hit such a patch. The bow rose. There was a gasp from the crowd. The boat righted itself and there was a sigh of relief. But it rose again on the next wave, righted again, hit a third, rose, turned bow down and plunged at a terrifying speed deep into the water. The boat just simply broke up! People watched in horror – it had all taken only seconds – then the man's helmet appeared, not far out but a little way along the shore line.

Everyone set off along the edge of the water, but two workmen were building a house near the accident and immediately plunged in, striking out towards the man. We could see them from our balcony, dragging the inert man shoreward through the water. They pulled him out and the paramedics were there in an instant, giving CPR. But he did not respond: he had been so badly injured as the boat broke up that he was already dead when he was taken from the water.

A horrible silence fell on the previously vociferous crowd and then there was a thin scream. The man's wife had been told the dreadful news and presumably the children too. What a terrible day! I cannot imagine what it must have felt like to stand and watch a husband and father killed in this way.

Someone took the family home and there was a subdued meeting of the remaining competitors to decide what to do about the practice runs due the following day. After much soul searching, they decided still to hold the event. Many had come hundreds of miles and without the second practice day, no-one would qualify for the finals. But they held a short silence before the races started as a mark of respect. I am sure that tragedy is remembered on Walker Lake to this day but perhaps the most sobering thought of all is that no one was surprised!

Present among the competitors was Lee Taylor, an ambitious man who was practising for his attempt to beat the world water-speed record in his fantastic boat which eclipsed all the other boats, fast though they were.

We watched from the shore almost in disbelief at the incredible velocity that this craft achieved. The hull looked like the fuselage of an aircraft and was designed purely for speed over 'short' distances and so carried only enough fuel for the proposed 'run' in order to keep the weight down. Several men launched this monster and then it was towed by two ordinary speed boats to the end of the lake ready to start the run.

Lee started and accelerated at a phenomenal rate so that by the time he passed us – roughly half way up the lake – the two speedboats following him were left way behind although they were travelling at their maximum speed. As he reached the end of the lake, the speed boats caught up and towed him back to the bay. I do not know what speed was achieved that day but we heard that he was confident and would attempt the actual record later on Lake Tahoe. It had to be Tahoe as he was being sponsored by one of the casinos bordering the Nevada side of that high lake. The enthusiasts on Walker Lake seemed to think that it was not particularly suitable-something to do with the winds swirling among the surrounding mountains, I understood. Later that year, we heard of another tragedy.

The actual attempt at the record was called off at the last moment, as the weather conditions were too volatile. But thousands of well-wishers had gathered on the shoreline and Lee decided to do the 'run' for their benefit although it would not be the official record attempt. As before, he was towed into position and accelerated. He had reached two hundred and seventy miles an hour when the wind hit and the bow rose and then dived. The fuel tanks, located behind him, broke loose, slipped forward and crushed him. Once more a dead man was pulled from the water.

Understandably, we were rather depressed by the Walker Lake tragedy and, when everyone had gone, the place seemed empty and ghostlike. Someone mentioned that there was a rodeo the next weekend so we decided to go. We had all seen such things in cowboy films but I wondered if this one might be just a publicity stunt and not the real thing at all. I need not have worried.

Yerington, a hundred miles or so to the north (no-one thinks anything of travelling hundreds of miles for a day out), was a small township? village? group of ranches? – I don't know what it was, but it seemed to be very scattered but with a large permanent venue for the rodeos. These took place frequently and were *real*: owing nothing to tourism but concentrating on the competitive nature of the cattle ranchers of the area.

But to us, and particularly Andy, this was like something out of the films and we had to keep reminding ourselves that it *was* real.

We sat on tiered benches of sun-bleached wood and were very glad of our hats and sunglasses as no-one seemed to have heard of *shade*. Some of the stunt riders were unbelievably skilled, standing, hanging off the horse's flank, hand-standing, *head*-standing, etc, and all with no saddle and at incredible speed. There was some bull riding which was probably not quite as dangerous as it looked but the bulls did *not* appear to enjoy it, snorting horribly all the time. And they were enormous.

Some very skilled young folk then had a competition lassoing calves. Although they were undoubtedly very clever and practised, I hated to see the animals brought to the ground with such a bone-jarring thump. They must have been badly winded and bruised and I considered that it bordered on cruelty. But I suppose commercial cattle ranchers have to catch the animals somehow. One can only hope, naively perhaps, that the animals are well fed and watered and well looked after for their short lives. But, says my cynical side, probably only because a well fed animal will fetch a good price at the market.

I wonder if ranchers talk interminably about the price of cattle at the last sale just as the crofters do about the price of sheep at *their* last sale.

35

A Grasshopper and a Black Widow

BASKING IN THE hot sunshine, I sat on a rock gazing over the water to the far mountains and thought that, apart from the hot sunshine, I could have been sitting on a rock on Papavray, gazing across water at far mountains. I began to consider the parallels as well as the contrasts between the 'old life' and this rather amazing new one, which puzzled me sometimes. Puzzled and confused me because I seemed to be an entirely different person.

I was no longer the dignified Nurse Macleod whose advice was listened to and help accepted with a kind of respectful gratitude. Here, I was just another person, responsible only for looking after George, Andy and the dogs. I had no employment and no status. This did not worry me nor did I think that it diminished me in any way as I felt that I was on a semi-permanent holiday. I was relaxed but baffled. I was not usually given to self-analysis so even these musings were out of character.

Physically, I was 'playing' in the sun rather than battling through wind and rain to attend patients. I was water-skiing, walking in the hills – just enjoying free time and new experiences. I also felt younger! (This alone was surprising as I had undergone major surgery and follow-up treatment only a year ago). The evening swimming with the girls had boosted my ego. I had overcome my fear of dark water (but not of spiders – yet). I had achieved a level of proficiency in water-skiing that amazed me. I was different!

The parallels were there among the contrasts. Papavray had been 'behind the times', like Nevada was by American standards. The island community had been small and intimate – we had been known by all because of our jobs and the boys and the fact that we were incomers. Here, it was a small community, down to earth as the crofters were with a similar view of life, work and leisure. We were the only Brits. Here, objects of interest, curiosity and a certain surprised respect, and everyone was friendly towards us. But although very happy here, there was nothing that I could offer in return – only pleasant chat, offers of help which were never needed and an attempt to understand the way of life – relaxed, unambitious, expecting little. That was like the crofters, too, and I liked that attitude. I realised that I was never going to really get to know people well as we would only be here for a few months.

George was contented. He was interested in the work, had regular hours, enjoyed the water sports and liked the space and freedom of Nevada. I loved that aspect of this state, later to be contrasted with the sophistication, the rules and regulations of California with its traffic, its smog and its fast pace of life. Both states, however, had seemingly unlimited sunshine.

Practically, there was little to worry about. George was well paid and we were housed in company accommodation, our only bills were for food and petrol (for boat and car) and this was very cheap compared with the UK, so this too added to the delightful feeling of being on holiday. But one peculiarity to do with finances was a real difficulty to us. We had come from a culture where, apart from a possible mortgage, one tried not to accumulate debts of any sort. In America, everyone seemed to live on credit and their credit worthiness or rating was based on their ability to pay the various interests in full and on time. Obviously, we had taken with us no debts so we had no proof that we were in a position to pay them off. In other words we had no proof of credit worthiness, so we were refused American Express cards or any other sort of credit card. We could not be trusted. We had no proof of our financial position, no proof that we were 'good payers'.

The result of this extraordinary situation was that, in order to buy two cars and a boat, we had to withdraw vast amounts of money in order to pay for these commodities in *cash*. After long months of arguing and referring American banks to our UK bank, we were grudgingly allowed an American Express card. Two days later another arrived. No one knew why. Even then there was a certain amount of disbelief. How could anyone *not* owe any money? This concept was beyond their ken. I think they eventually decided that it was because we were Brits and therefore bound to be slightly odd.

Andy, untroubled by such things, was certainly enjoying his extended summer holiday (vacation?) in the sun-drenched freedom of the waterside. He was at just the right age for all this physical activity and mingled with all the locals and the sailing fraternity no matter what their age. That was another thing. If you were younger or older than the locals – perhaps by a long way – they did not seem to notice.

Andy and Jason were chatting one day when Jason mentioned the CAP (Civil Air Patrol) rather like our Air Force Cadets and suggested that Andy went along to one of the meetings. An ex-US Air Force officer welcomed Andy into the group of only about five boys and he began to enjoy the various activities. Sometime before he joined, a trip in a small aircraft from a local airstrip had been planned. The Cessna aircraft would only take three boys and they had already been booked, the officer told Andy, but he could go to the airfield any way to have a look around.

Quite resigned, Andy wandered around the airstrip after the lucky boys took off.

'You look kinda lonely, youngster.' A large man, dressed like a cowboy addressed Andy, who explained why he had been left behind.

'Aw, Gee! We can't have that,' declared the grey-haired cowboy. 'Come ee here.'

Andy followed, as the big man strode towards a hanger. Throwing the doors back, he began to heave a tarpaulin off a small plane.

'Give me a hand here. We'll see about leaving you behind, young fella.' He paused to take a breath. 'I was a flier in World War Two. Picked this beauty up afterwards.'

Andy could scarcely believe his eyes. There in all its understated glory, was a 'Grasshopper' Reconnaissance plane with USAAF in letters and the insignia of the star still on the khaki-coloured fuselage!

'Fancy a ride, young 'un?'

'Oh, yes, *please*.'

They pushed the iconic plane out onto the runway. The 'cowboy' pilot climbed in, handing Andy in behind him, started the engine, taxied around and lined the plane up for take-off.

They climbed into the sky, the pilot pointing out all the places of interest and telling Andy tales of his wartime exploits and explaining how the controls functioned. They roamed about the heavens for some thirty minutes. Andy was ecstatic, asking questions about the plane and the pilot's war service. They eventually came in to the airstrip to find three boys scowling with envy. *They* had only had the proscribed ten minutes flight with virtually no input from their pilot. Andy tells me now – thirty years later – that those boys did not speak to him for the rest of the afternoon. He was the outsider, but had had by far the best flight and some personal attention from the pilot.

An interesting point to his CAP membership is that he should not have been enrolled at all. He was not an American citizen! The CAP was American for Americans but no-one had thought to ask and we did not know that there was such a requirement.

Andy's next adventure is chiselled into my memory alongside the 'Block and Tackle' incident on Papavray some years before.

The two big, cigar-chewing silver-mine owners saw Andy wandering about at the waterfront one day and asked if he would care to earn a little pocket money. They were constructing a 'bed' of sand (a huge area about the size of a football pitch) onto which they would tip the shale that had been removed from the mine forty years earlier. At the time, it had been thought that the mine was worked out but new technology now meant that the remaining silver could be released from the abandoned shale. The men would pour cyanide on to the shale to tease the silver out of its rocky home and into their pockets, so to speak. Creating this bed was labour-intensive and unskilled and they would be glad of his help. Sensing a new experience as well as a little cash, Andy was happy to go off to work with them about twice a week. As he was only thirteen, I suspected that employing him was illegal. But, then again, this was Nevada.

It was hot out there on the open desert, so frequent breaks were needed. Andy sat on a pile of stones, eating, drinking and chatting. Sweat was running down his back and his tee shirt was wet. As he rose to start work again, he brushed his hand round his neck and face. All was well as he shovelled sand onto the 'bed' and the miners brought him home as usual, bidding him a raucous 'Goodnight, Kid. See ya tomorrow.'

Andy seemed tired and went off to bed early. He enjoyed the sense of earning some money and found the two men to be good companions but working in the hot sun in the shadeless desert *was* tiring.

I had a little difficulty rousing him the next morning but he pottered off to the bathroom as usual. When he emerged and I looked at him properly, I could see that he looked pale.

'My eyes are funny, Mum,' he reported. 'I feel really weird. I don't want any breakfast.'

He sat, almost collapsed, onto the settee. 'Everything is blurred – I can't see.'

Too much sun, I thought, and not wearing sunglasses, perhaps.

Just then, Jake, one of the men shouted from the big red truck outside, 'You comin', Kid?'

I called down to him. 'He's not well. I don't know what's wrong.'

Jake loped up the outside stairs. 'You sound worried, Ma'am. What's up, Kid? You crocked up?'

'Can't see properly. Feel sick. Back of my neck is sore.'

Jake looked at me. 'Mind if I have a look, Ma'am? Used to these parts, y'see. All manner of bugs…'

He carefully lifted Andy's head forward and peered at the back of his neck. 'Spider bite, Ma'am. I'd get him to a physic…'

I was getting my car keys. 'Where… who?' I realised that I had no idea where the nearest doctor might be.

Jake looked at Andy again, picked him up and strode down the steps to the car. He put him in, where he slumped against the back of the seat with his eyes closed. His face was sheet-white.

'Best go straight to the Air Base – just up the highway to Hawthorne.' He shut the door. 'I'd shift a bit,' he advised.

I certainly 'shifted'. With no traffic and a straight road, we quickly reached the heavily guarded gates of the USAAF Base.

Wondering if I might have trouble getting past the gun-encrusted, uniformed giant at the gate, I drew up and lowered the window.

He was shouting, 'Hey. You can't come in here, lady.'

Suddenly inspired, I shouted back, 'Spider bite,' and nodded towards Andy's inert figure.

The change was instant!

'Right, Ma'am – surgery – second building on the right… I'll call them…'

Others had rushed to open the gate and I roared in to pull up at the second building on the right.

In that short time, two men in white coats had been mustered to lift Andy gently but at speed onto a trolley. They ran with him into the treatment room where two doctors stood beside the examination table and, just as Andy was lifted onto it, he fainted. He came round as I was telling them what I knew of where Andy had been the day before, the circumstances and what the miner had said that he thought it might be.

'Did you feel a bite anywhere?' Andy was asked.

'No – just a tickle – I think,' he murmured woozily.

'Where?'

Andy indicated the back of his neck and then closed his eyes as though that small effort had been too much for him.

He was gently turned over and his neck thoroughly examined.

'Just here,' said Doctor Number One, pointing to the marks that Jake must have seen.

'Hmm. Brown Recluse? Black Widow?'

Doctor Number Two peered and poked a bit. 'Bit near the…' Then they dropped their voices and I heard 'nerve' and 'carotid' and then just a lot of 'hmmms'.

Doctor Number One was pondering, 'Marks too small for Brown Recluse. I'd say Black Widow.'

I was holding Andy's hand. He must have felt grim because he made no objection to this embarrassing maternal gesture.

The doctors looked at each other and at me. 'The Widow could not have emptied her entire sac, or he would have been ill right away and perhaps much worse.'

'What now?' I asked, very frightened.

'We can give an antidote, but he will not be feeling well for a while. He will need to be watched carefully and to rest. No more shovelling sand in the sun. He has been lucky. He must have brushed that Widow off in time or he would have been in real danger. Oh! And no swimming in Walker Lake until the bite is completely healed.'

Doctor Number Two looked surprised. 'What is wrong with Walker Lake?' he asked.

Doctor Number One replied, 'You can walk on it.'

'What?'

'When it turns over – about now.'

Doctor Number Two still looked puzzled, but Doctor Number One gave the antidote and we were off. I did not wait to hear about the disgusting plant life shortly to be heaved up from the depths of the lake. The doctor obviously thought that it was a health hazard.

Andy did not look any better in spite of the antidote and I had hoped for some assistance getting him up the outside stair, but there was no-one about. With my help, he managed it, but the effort was too great and, as soon as he flopped onto his bed, he fainted again.

For the next few weeks, Andy was really ill. He was weak, tired and had no interest in anything. He could not eat and had to use a straw to take liquids as the inside of his mouth ulcerated. The bite itself healed – it was very small – but the toxin had done its damage to his entire body. I did not dare to think how ill he might have been if that wretched Black Widow had emptied the whole contents of her sac into him.

Gradually, he regained strength, looked better – if thinner – and began to wander about at the waterfront but it was a while until he water-skied again. The doctor had been right: the lake had 'turned over' and was only now becoming fit to use again.

36

Back to California

WE WERE ALL enjoying the relaxed atmosphere of Nevada so much that we were reluctant to confront the fact that George's work in Hawthorne was almost at an end and that we would have to start looking for a house in California. His contract with the company was for several years so we intended to buy a property and settle Andy in school. The company was based in San Clemente and George's work would be in that area so a home somewhere nearby was a sensible option.

George was not due any 'vacation time' so I would have to drive down to San Clemente and go house hunting. We had arranged for John and Joanna to come for a holiday, so I timed the two trips together – the house hunting and LA airport to fetch them.

Andy and I set off with two confused dogs – they had only just got used to Walker Lake – completed the 'marathon', found a motel and the next day began the round of the realtors (estate agents to us). We looked at many beautiful homes, some on one level, some on two, some with a sizeable yard (garden), some with none. We found two that took our eye and I began to learn about the complications of the finance attached to house buying.

Back in the UK, we had no mortgage, totally owning our home. The various realtors found this unnatural and I was told that I must choose somewhere with finance on it. I gradually understood that home loans (mortgages) in California stay with the property when there is a sale: the buyer does not arrange his own, so you 'inherit' the existing home loan.

'You must get a house with a good loan on it,' I was told and found all this advice difficult to comprehend until it was made clear that when we came to sell, no American would be keen on a home without a substantial loan in place. No-one buys for cash so everyone *needs* a loan. I only just made sense of it all but needed to get on with actually locating somewhere to live.

Then we found a home with a swimming pool and a jacuzzi. As soon as Andy saw it, I knew that it would be ours! It was the best option at the right price anyway with, of course, 'a good loan'. I knew George would love it, which was just as well as I was going to have to buy this home in Mission Viejo without him having a sight of it.

I set things in motion and the following day, set off for the airport to fetch John, Joanna, Josh and six-month-old Maxim.

We spent the night at the motel, showed the family the house the next morning and then started for Nevada. Once off California highways, John took over the driving. None of us was sure if his UK licence was legal in the 'Sunshine State' but knew that Nevada would be relaxed about this as with everything else.

Back at Walker Lake, the family settled down to enjoy the sun, the water, the space and relaxed life style. John took to water-skiing immediately and the youngsters liked paddling about at the edge of the lake.

Among the various excursions was a trip to Bodie, a ghost town which had thrived during the gold rush and had now been preserved in a semi-derelict state for the benefit of tourists. Josh, old enough at three, to enjoy everything, including Disneyland and Magic Mountain later in California, talked interminably about Bodie for years, whilst scarcely mentioning the more exciting amusement parks. Now, thirty years later, with a family of his own, he loves remote areas, old things and historic places. So perhaps his young fascination for Bodie is not so surprising after all.

We were in the apartment one afternoon. Joanna was knitting, the boys were playing on the floor, John was snoozing and Andy was sketching. All was quiet and peaceful. Suddenly all the cups and saucers on the dresser (hutch) started to rattle, knives and forks on the table, laid for dinner, danced on the shiny surface while the chairs on which we sat took on a life of their own.

Joanna looked a question with a scared gasp.

In unison, Andy and I said, 'It's only an earthquake.'

How stupid that seems as I write it. Indeed, after a momentary disbelieving gaze in our direction, John and Joanna began to laugh. With relief, perhaps? We had become so accustomed to earth tremors that we just did not bother about them. One could not *do* anything or take cover anyway: there was never any time and no warning, so all the advice so confidently broadcast was of little use.

There is a huge fault at the meeting of two tectonic plates. It runs through California and Nevada and when these two monsters meet and one grinds over the top of the other, earthquakes large and small can happen. Disasters are *not* rare but everyone has to live with that threat so they live as though it were just not there. It was amazing to see how folk simply ignored this sword of Damocles hanging over them.

The next morning, George happened to be the first in at the Army Munitions Plant. He entered the building where all the computers were housed and had begun to settle at his desk when he heard a rattling sound. At first, he took no notice, thinking it was the wind blowing some papers around. Then he realised what it might be. A rattlesnake!

With the hairs on his neck prickling, he looked behind his chair. There, not six feet away, with its head raised threateningly, was a sizeable rattlesnake which did not appear to be pleased with life. Perhaps the earthquake of the day before had disturbed him and he was prepared to vent his displeasure upon the first piece of flesh that presented itself. George beat a hasty retreat and waited outside until one of the local engineers arrived.

'Hi. What's with you, then?' The engineer noticed George's tense expression.

Cocking a thumb, George said, 'In there. Snake.'

'Ah! Rattler, is it?'

He picked up a stick, grabbed a sack and edged gingerly through the door. With expertise probably born of long experience, he 'hooked' the snake and dropped him neatly into the bag. He strode off into the desert for some distance and let the creature go.

Nervously, George said, 'Won't it come back in?'

'Might do. Poor little sod's frightened by the quake, I guess.' And with this less than comforting opinion, that burly individual nonchalantly ambled off to start work.

The same afternoon, Babs (of baby fame) came panting up the staircase. (She was not built for rushing about.) Catching her breath, she told us of her adventure earlier in the day. She had been to help the Pastor in the church and when he was driving her home, she felt a movement in her rather tight jeans. She discreetly felt around and could tell by the slight lump on her thigh that it was a scorpion. A scorpion! What a predicament! If she did not remove it at once, she would be stung, but to do so meant removing her jeans very carefully and completely, in a car with the Pastor of her church? Dare she wait? It would take only five minutes to get home. Then it moved again!

Babs screamed and the Pastor nearly drove off the road.

'Scorpion in my jeans,' she gasped.

'What? Oh, umm. Ahh.' The Pastor might have been used to delivering long sermons, but he was certainly lost for words now.

'Yes. I'll pull over then you can umm... yes.'

So beside the road in full view, with the Pastor politely looking the other way, Babs had to remove her jeans altogether, rolling the scorpion in them as she rolled them down her legs. Then she jumped on the folded garment to kill the intruder. So there was Babs, a well-endowed woman, clad only in pants and bra, leaping up and down beside the road for what appeared to be no reason at all to a passing truck driver. This escapade earned her several appreciative blasts on his dual horns. She was breathless with laughter as she told us that the Pastor was more embarrassed than she was.

Just before we left Nevada, George obtained permission to show Andy round the Army Munitions Plant. We teased George about 'Going off to explode his bombs', but he was actually writing the programmes for the computers which were to control the robots that were doing the work. A building had been cleverly designed in a cross, the outer 'wings' made of very flimsy materials while the central 'pod', where the men worked, had walls of concrete three feet thick. The four outer areas contained the mortars and shells and the robots which were being programmed to empty the devices of the explosive, but if something went wrong and the 'bomb' exploded, the blast would destroy only the outer wing with the blast going outwards to be dissipated in the open desert while the men were safe in the heavily protected 'pod'. Andy was most impressed by such technology. I'm sure it would now be considered outdated.

So one early morning, we set off for California with everyone crammed into the car and all the luggage in the boat on the trailer. We were all going to stay in a rented apartment while the Escrow (solicitors? property agents?) people finalised the purchase of our house. While there, we maintained the holiday spirit by visiting all the tourist attractions such as the theme and amusement parks. Everyone bathed in the blue Pacific and we had a trip to San Diego for some excellent boating. Finally, we waved John and Joanna off at LAX. It was a pity that they had to go before we moved in to the house.

Andy began school. Predictably the buildings were almost lavish and the campus extensive. The school, the scholars, the timetable and the curriculum were all so different that he was quite daunted and confused for a while and not at all happy during the first semester. Home, however with its swimming pool and jacuzzi were a great success and he did not lack for friends as everyone found his accent – part English, part Scottish – most attractive – especially the girls who said that they 'luuuurved' it.

I found that it was not easy to exercise our 'canines' as rough open ground was some way off but, at weekends, if not boating, we walked in the 'wilderness' – the area behind the Coastal Plain and towards the San Gabriel mountains. We attached bells to the dogs' collars to frighten snakes away.

Surprisingly, Nick had married at about eighteen and now came for a holiday with his wife and one-year-old daughter, Natasha. Nick was fascinated by the sheer size of everything – especially the cars. Smaller Japanese built cars were only just appearing on the market and many Americans found it difficult to relinquish the feeling of space and safety that a big car delivered. George had another Ford (a Fairmont) but my huge Ford Squire was the family car and Nick's firm favourite, although it was deemed to look like a 'wardrobe on wheels'.

The nearest lake for water-skiing was Lake Elsinore – a strange body of water about eight miles long which was inclined to overflow one year, flooding the surrounding homes and almost dry up the next. At least it didn't 'turn over'! Nick was quick to learn and we spent happy times at Elsinore. I often wondered if it had been given its romantic name by a Dane or perhaps a Shakespeare enthusiast, but was never able to find out.

One afternoon, Nick was playing with Natasha, who could not quite walk and so grabbed the furniture for support. Suddenly, just as she reached for the small television on a side table, everything started to rattle and shake and Nick only just caught the TV as it slid towards the child. The water in the swimming pool was washing from side to side, spilling over the edges and onto the patio and there was a roaring sound. I have always been amazed that so few reports of earthquakes mention the noise. I have now been in a few minor 'quakes and I am well aware of the noise but I have never understood what causes it. Nick had hoped that there would be an earthquake during his visit – he was not disappointed!

George found that, far from working nearby, he was expected to go to all manner of places, some in other states – Texas, Michigan and others. I was amused to know that there really *was* a town called *Kallamazoo*. I had only heard the name in connection with a song about a cat called Kalamazoo.

At about this time, I started to think about a nursing post but only got as far as consulting the paper and noting the whereabouts of hospitals when Elizabeth and Paul arrived for a holiday with us. George had some accumulated time off and it was the end of a semester at Andy's school so we bought a large tent, a portable barbeque, loaded the boat (on its trailer) with all this camping equipment and personal belongings and set off, dogs as well, for a trip to Yosemite National Park.

On the way, we needed to stay in what is called a 'primitive' camp site at Bass Lake, a beautiful, wooded spot in the hills about three thousand feet above sea level. Here, one washed in the lake, but with special environmentally friendly soap (purchased for a vastly inflated price at a nearby 'store'). The toilet arrangements were as bad as anything that I had encountered in Papavray, amounting to a smelly wooden hut containing a chemical loo.

By this time, I was well aware that Black Widow spiders are partial to sitting *in* loos because they like moisture! Elizabeth and I envied the men who did not need to get too near the loo to relieve their bladders and, already standing, were well placed for a hasty retreat should one of these beasties appear. *We* on the other hand…! We decided to tramp off deep into the woods, trusting the back of a tree rather than the wooden hut.

We carried on to Yosemite. What a fantastic area it is! Wild and empty, with high mountains, deep valleys and wonderful view points. There were not many visitors as the weather was cool by Californian standards and at over ten thousand feet there was a chance of snow. In the winter months, the Park is closed to visitors, most of the roads being impassable.

At one of the view points, I stood alone for a moment, and savoured the eerie feeling of looking into the past. The flat bottomed valley far below was green with trees and a gentle river which flowed through on its meandering course, all surrounded and protected by the sheer sides of two thousand feet high rocks rising straight from the lush green fields. A tribe of Indians had lived in this valley hundreds of years ago, safe from other marauding tribes, pitching their tents and lighting their fires, watching the smoke gather between the high pinnacles, or hang in the tree tops and finally drift away on the breeze. They had left behind an indefinable atmosphere: an *old* atmosphere, full of history and legend. It is thought that 'Yosemite' is named after that tribe – 'Yo-se-mat-ey'. I felt a part of the ancient scene as I used to do in the Hebrides when watching the sea or the clouds drifting through the mountains. A moment of nostalgia overcame me and I wanted to capture and keep it. But family and dogs claimed me and we drove off to find a camp site.

We set off early the next day and were rewarded by seeing a young bear crossing the road just a few feet in front of the car. He stopped in surprise, scrutinised us for a moment, and then carried on. He was probably used to having the road to himself at that time of the day.

We were making for Lake Tahoe and intended to camp there for about a week. The sites there proved to be well organised with quite large, private areas for each 'rig' whether it was a car and tent like ours or one of the many enormous RVs. There were wooden seats, a barbeque and a fire pit with a supply of wood, replenished daily. There was good hot water in the shower blocks and slip ways for launching boats. This was camping Californian style!

The surface of the lake was at six thousand two hundred feet above sea level and the rim a little more. At first, I felt the slight breathlessness that the thin air causes but soon became used to it. No one else seemed to notice it at all. Maybe they were too intent on enjoying themselves. Even with our high altitude propellers, the engine took a while to reach a good speed for skiing. The water was quite cold as it was composed of snow water from the surrounding mountains but this seemed not to deter anyone and the holiday was filled with laughter.

Andy eventually settled into his school, but was much more interested in the outdoor life, sport, physical activities in general and a new love – karate. He had joined a karate studio and seemed to have a natural ability. He started, as everyone does, as a white belt but quickly passed through the various colours until he eventually reached the coveted black belt status. On the way he became the first student in the studio to win a trophy and this was to be followed by many more huge ornate affairs that festooned his room. When, in later years, he attended a boarding school in England, his prowess at karate was a great attribute and ego booster as the Californian teaching had left large gaps in his education which meant that he was far behind others of his age. But at least he was able to entertain the staff and pupils alike, giving exhibitions and earning points for his house. The American way of teaching seemed very fragmented and inadequate compared with the strict regime of an English public school.

Continuing my quest for work, I was horrified to find that UK nurse training to State qualification was not recognised in California so I would not be able to work as a trained nurse. I was told that I could retrain under Californian mandate, but that would take three years. George's contract might be finished by then. It was an unexpected dilemma and a huge setback. While in Nevada with its relaxed way of life, I had been happy to be unemployed, knowing that we would not be there for very long. But now, I was ready to be useful again. This state if limbo continued with no resolution for some months and then disaster struck.

37

The End of an Era

THE COMPANY FOR whom George was working had gone bankrupt!

There had been no warning, no hint that anything was wrong but when George arrived at the office this particular morning, he was confronted by the managing director and his assistant.

'Sittee down,' he was instructed.

'I'm done! Finished.' The dramatic announcement was lost on George for a moment.

'I have overdeveloped, overspent, taken on work that did not pay… Oh! Just everything.'

Then George realised what Harry meant. And what it meant to us, as a family. Suddenly, here we were in a foreign country, with no work and therefore no visa. The regulations applying to 'aliens' working in the US meant that if such a person had no employer (as from this minute, in George's case) he had no right to a visa and if he had no visa, he was unlikely to get work. Very much a 'catch-22' situation.

George had been employed by the company *before* we came to the States so arrived with a visa and a job in place. That visa did not cover me, as his wife, for work – I would have had to apply separately but now there would be no chance at all as the main breadwinner now had no employment.

George came home early to break the devastating news. He was pale and worried.

'What are we to do? I have a month's salary to come. They assured me that it is safe. But after that…?

We had two cars, two boats (we had brought a sailing dingy from the UK) and a home loan (mortgage). Andy had been in school now for about a year and felt settled. He was not a good pupil but had made many friends. We, too, had met neighbours, enjoyed barbeques with them and got to know two of George's work colleagues quite well.

All this – everything in our lives – was suddenly in jeopardy!

'We will have to sell up and go back to the UK,' muttered George morosely. He enjoyed the Californian lifestyle, his job and the weather. I loved the weather and our home with its swimming pool and the feeling of space. The materialistic approach to life was not quite so much to my liking, but I had thought that I would get used to it, perhaps even embrace it.

'I suppose I will get work there,' George continued without enthusiasm and I remembered that he had not truly worked *in* the UK for years as he had always been off on contracts abroad for this, as of today, defunct company.

We had sold our home on Papavray. To leave a house empty and unheated in the damp atmosphere of the islands, perhaps for years, had not seemed a sensible option. My job had been filled in a different way in the changing world of the NHS. More than a few of my old patients were now dead, or 'passed on' or 'passed over' as the islanders would say and the island itself was changing. For the better, I felt, as galleries and cafes started up and the planning rules were relaxed, allowing croft owners to build one extra house on their land. At last the population drain was halted. I felt nostalgic about the island and its inhabitants, but now I was no longer a part of it. My life had moved on.

I think we were in shock for a few days, not able to formulate any plans. Andy was appalled at the thought that he might have to leave his school, his karate, his swimming, boating, water-skiing and his girlfriends. There were several pretty girls who came and went, swam in the pool, joined us for meals, but they changed so often that I was always afraid that I would address them by the name of someone else. I adopted a ruse that I had used when Elizabeth had been about the same age. I always addressed all new friends as 'dear' at first.

So what now? We knew that George's month's salary would soon evaporate and would not be replaced. And yet, we seemed to be trapped in a Micawber-like frame of mind, hoping that something would turn up. It just did not seem possible that there was *nothing* out there for George.

We began to sell our possessions. We had some favourite antique furniture and a few unusual articles from other lands. It would have been hard for the crofters to recognise their 'Nurse Macleod' in the person taking the box of goods into an antiques shop. We sold two rare Japanese dishes, a real Russian samovar, a lovely old Davenport and many more precious things. The proceeds would keep us for a month.

We were about to sell the boats as well when Mr Micawber was proved correct – at least in our case, and something *did* 'turn up'.

A Californian colleague who had worked for the company for many years came to see George, telling us that he had found a job with a major engineering company in Pasadena. He confessed that he had suspected that all was not well and had put 'feelers' out *before* the company went bankrupt and had landed a good position. He had recommended George to the manager and an interview had been arranged.

George got the job! What a relief!

Andy relaxed, George was content and I... well, I felt that it was all too good to be true. And we know what they say – it usually is! But I tried to dismiss these doubts and began to think about retraining. I had to be sure that it was what I wanted as it would cost a considerable amount and, I suppose, we had had such a shock that I was reluctant to commit our replenished funds to a project that might not work out. It was many years since my UK training: I had been a district (country) nurse in a gentle, behind-the-times area in the Hebrides and I realised that I would be very out-of-date even in my native country, let alone in California with its modern technology, faster life style and its emphasis on youth. So I might be too old now anyway. I let things drift.

At about this time Argentina invaded the Falklands. Little was made of it in California – it was all so far away, but there happened to be two Argentinian boys at Andy's school, one in his class. Andy and this lad very sensibly shook hands, saying that it was not personal in any way and would make no difference to their friendship. The other boy confronted Andy, dubbing him 'an aggressor', 'filthy British enemy' and much more. Luckily, no-one took much notice of his ranting, but Andy was careful to avoid him. How differently these two Argentinians dealt with the situation. If only nations could shake hands!

We resumed our confident boating, swimming, dog (sorry – canine) walking in the hills and as a family, we had good times but I was not convinced that our future lay here and I was reluctant to form any really close ties only to have to walk away from these friendly generous people one day.

Winter came again. Down near the coast where we lived, the temperature rarely dropped below seventy degrees but when the thermometer plunged to that apparently magical level, out came the fur coats. We felt it to be very pleasantly warm. But then again the ladies in fur had not known a Hebridean winter.

Less than one hundred miles away, up in the San Bernadino mountains, lay the winter playground of Big Bear Valley with its lake, lying at six thousand feet above sea level and the surrounding peaks topping nine thousand. In the summer the water sports were the main attraction but ski shops and ski lifts suddenly appeared like magic the minute that snow was forecast. Andy swiftly added snow skiing to his list of achievements. There was no snow skiing for George and me – far too cold – so we drank coffee in the ski restaurants and watched the world go up and down. It was a fascinating fact that, had we wished, we could have been skiing at about nine thousand feet in the morning at Big Bear and swimming in the ocean at San Clemente in the afternoon: the temperatures were so diverse and the road to Big Bear rose dramatically from the flat coastal plain into these mountains through steep and dangerous terrain.

Then, quite suddenly, the gentle, easy living that we were enjoying began to change yet again. I had a feeling of déjà view. Apparently overlooked in George's contract was a phrase requiring him to be available for work overseas if necessary.

'Would you be prepared to travel?' he was asked.

'Yes, of course'.

'And to stay for months at a time?'

'Well, um… yes, if I have to.'

I think the bankruptcy scare had made George ready to comply with almost any requirement that guaranteed his continuing employment.

So off he went. To Saudi Arabia!

At first Andy and I stayed in California, but eventually plans were made to return to the UK and put Andy into a public school as a boarder. Predictably, he did not like this at first but it proved to be an excellent education and he soon adapted. I would join George in Saudi and Andy would fly out for school holidays (which he *did* like). Life was changing irrevocably once again.

And the canines? Unfortunately, Pip had died while we were in California but Squeak came with us, becoming a much-travelled dog; one day, at the end of all our wanderings, he would fly back to the UK to resume a more normal doggy way of life in the English countryside.

So I watched from the plane as California with its sunshine, its friendly people and its easy, but somehow frenetic, lifestyle faded into the dusk.

Epilogue

CALIFORNIA AND NEVADA were fascinating episodes in my life, giving me an insight into lives lived entirely differently from those that I knew so well on Papavray.

In California, there was the need to strive to be always young and beautiful, to climb the career ladder as fast as possible. The near obsession with all things material was baffling to me and I contrasted these attitudes with the stoic acceptance of the status quo in the Hebrides, however harsh that might be. I saw the incessant purchasing of anything newly on the market and thought of the old, worn furniture and out-dated possessions of the crofters of Papavray, unnoticed and unimportant.

And yet, in this materialistic, fast-paced society, there was an unrestrained welcome for us: an instant familiarity. The invitation to share a barbeque after the briefest of meetings, the interest in us that was transparent and unembarrassed and I compared this with the equally welcoming but quiet attitude of the islanders and their gently probing questions.

I suppose the greatest and most obvious contrast between those precious islands and this big land of tall, blond people was the weather. Oh, the sunshine and the warmth! To be able to swim in the blue water of the warm Pacific, to lie on a beach in the sun with no thought of wind or rain was like a storybook existence to one who had been used to such things as answering night calls in snow, gales and bitter cold.

Life in Nevada was less focused on the need to possess 'the latest' or 'the best', to be always striving to climb the financial ladder or follow fashion. People were content with less and seemed somehow more real because of it, while the space and freedom of that state reminded me of Papavray and its inhabitants. So there were parallels as well as contrasts.

But even warm weather and easy living could not keep us in California or Nevada and, after only three years, we left for Saudi Arabia and continued to wander the globe.

Both these States, however, have taken their place in my heart and my memory and I often think of them and their people with warmth. I look back sometimes and dream of all the different countries, contrasting cultures and remarkable people that I have encountered and wonder, rather forlornly, if I really *belong* anywhere.

Then I remember those misty, mysterious islands which will always call me back. *They* will never let me go.

Although I might wander the world in my remaining years, I shall always feel the threads that bind me to the Hebrides. Kind, comfortable threads which, like gossamer, are hardly there at all but are oh so strong!

Compelling, embracing. How could I live without that memory of the purple mountains, the silver sea, snow and sunshine, starlit skies and scudding clouds, fierce storms and the lilting tongues of island people?

In the heat of deserts or among the roar of city traffic – wherever I might roam – I can fly in my imagination to 'my island' where, once more, I can feel the welcome of the unique and friendly people. I can absorb the peace and the raw beauty of moorland flowers and barren, rugged hills. I can stand on the shore, feeling the spray from the restless waves as they pound against dark cliffs or I may sit beside a chattering burn in the glen or on a rocky promontory where I can bare my soul to the splendour of a fearsome, fiery sunset.

I'll never *want* to be free from the call of those windswept isles, those little worlds surrounded and protected by the tumultuous ocean. We will perish, as all mortals must, but they will endure for ever: timeless and eternal.

Glossary

Ben, Beinn or Bheinn	A mountain.
Besom	An unpleasant and irritating woman.
Bodach	An old man. Not necessarily derogatory.
Burn	Small stream, often fast- flowing and stony.
Caillach	An old woman (often wife). Not necessarily derogatory.
Cairn	Mound of stones etc., often as a memorial.
Ceilidh	1. A neighbourly meeting together in each other's homes for food, drink and entertainment (amateur but often very accomplished). 2. Large, organised dances arranged for the tourists.
Clootie Dumpling	A pudding, made in a cloth (the 'cloot'), and boiled. It contains flour, suet, dried fruit, oats and sugar and. sometimes other fruit. Very occasionally it might be savoury.
Hogmanay	New Year: 31 December, from midnight on (often for several days).
Loch	Lake. Can be freshwater inland loch or sea loch.
Lum	Chimney: – 'sitting by our lum'.
Peat	Decomposed vegetable matter, laid down thousands of years ago, mainly in acidic soils. Scotland and Ireland. It is dug and dried for fuel (or gardens).
Peat Hag	An area of a peat bog which has been delineated for rental.
Sheiling	Rough shelter for use by crofters on the high summer grazing for cattle and sheep. (Now largely obsolete).
Strupak (strupach)	Tea and a bite (and a gossip).

Some other books published by **LUATH** PRESS

Heads on Pillows: Behind the Scenes at a Highland B&B

Joan Campbell

ISBN: 978-1-906307-71-4 £9.99 PBK

With so many people looking to leave the rat-race and start their own bed and breakfast in the country, *Heads on Pillows* give readers a personal glimpse into the unique world of B&Bs, where owners open up their own homes for guests to enjoy. This book offers witty anecdotes, personal experiences and helpful hints to anyone who aspires to enter the trade, from an award-winning B&B owner. From its modest beginnings as a single room B&B to the first five star Bed and Breakfast in the northern counties of Scotland, follow the story of the Sheiling and its owner. Part autobiography and part 'how to' guide *Heads on Pillows* is both informative and entertaining. This true account charts the growth and the development of the Scottish tourist trade, especially in the Highlands where the Sheiling is located, and offers through the experience of over 30 years an unparalleled insight into the Bed and Breakfast trade that is so enticing to so many. Foreword by Peter Lederer, Chairman of VisitScotland and managing director of the famous Gleneagles hotel.

A Problem Like Maria: A Women's Eye View of Life as an MP

Maria Fyfe

ISBN: 978-1-910021-04-0 £14.99 PBK

A Labour Whip once revealed that in their office they sang songs about certain backbenchers. In the case of the Member for Maryhill, their choice was 'How Do You Solve A Problem Like Maria?' A frank account of fourteen years in Westminster from the rebellious Maria Fyfe – the only female Labour MP in Scotland when she was first elected. Fyfe recounts some of the most significant moments of her political career, from the frustrating and infuriating, to the rewarding and worthwhile.

A significant aim of writing this book was to set the record straight on that period in our UK Parliament. Another aim was to encourage interest in a political life when widespread cynicism discourages good people from thinking about it.
MARIA FYFE

Covering some of the most turbulent years of British and Scottish political history, *A Problem Like Maria* takes the female's perspective of life as an MP in the male-dominated Westminster. This book reaches the parts of politics some people hope you never reach.

Women of Scotland

David R. Ross

ISBN: 978-1-906817-57-2 £9.99 PBK

In a mix of historical fact and folklore, 'biker-historian' David R. Ross journeys across Scotland to tell the stories of some of Scotland's finest women. From the legend of Scotia over 3,000 years ago to the Bruce women, Black Agnes and the real Lady Macbeth, through Kay Matheson – who helped liberate the Stone of Destiny from Westminster Abbey – and Wendy Wood in the 20th century, these proud and passionate women shaped the Scotland of today. Leading his readers to the sites where the past meets the present, this is a captivating insight into some remarkable tales of the Scottish people that have previously been neglected, a celebration of and tribute to the Women of Scotland.

Often in my daily life I find that it is the women of Scotland that have the true patriot souls their menfolk sometimes lack. Scotland means something to so many of them, and Caledonia burns deep within their collective memory. I hope that both Scots men and women are inspired or moved by some of the stories told here. Women of Scotland, it is you who will bear and nurture our future generations. Instill in them a pride in their blood that will inspire the generations yet to come, so that our land will regain its place, and remain strong and free, defiant and proud, for the Scots yet unborn.

DAVID R. ROSS

Days Like This: A Portrait of Scotland Through the Extraordinary Stories of Its People

ISBN: 978-1-906307-97-4 £6.99 PBK

Days Like This is an anthology of selected true stories showcasing the ordinary genius of Scotland's people. The book also features stories by celebrity curators Irvine Welsh, Roddy Woomble, Hardeep Singh Kohli, Siobhan Redmond, Jamie Andrew, and Evelyn Glennie. The stories are the result of a project run by Scottish Book Trust in partnership with BBC Radio Scotland, which gave people across Scotland the chance to write about a special day in their life. The project gathered hundreds of extraordinary tales, from born-and-bred Scots to newly arrived immigrants with the best ones broadcast on BBC radio Scotland.

Details of these and other books published by Luath Press ca at: **www.luath.co.uk**

Luath Press Limited

committed to publishing well written books worth reading

LUATH PRESS takes its name from Robert Burns, whose little collie Luath (*Gael.*, swift or nimble) tripped up Jean Armour at a wedding and gave him the chance to speak to the woman who was to be his wife and the abiding love of his life. Burns called one of 'The Twa Dogs' Luath after Cuchullin's hunting dog in Ossian's *Fingal*. Luath Press was established in 1981 in the heart of Burns country, and now resides a few steps up the road from Burns' first lodgings on Edinburgh's Royal Mile.

Luath offers you distinctive writing with a hint of unexpected pleasures.

Most bookshops in the UK, the US, Canada, Australia, New Zealand and parts of Europe either carry our books in stock or can order them for you. To order direct from us, please send a £sterling cheque, postal order, international money order or your credit card details (number, address of cardholder and expiry date) to us at the address below. Please add post and packing as follows: UK – £1.00 per delivery address; overseas surface mail – £2.50 per delivery address; overseas airmail – £3.50 for the first book to each delivery address, plus £1.00 for each additional book by airmail to the same address. If your order is a gift, we will happily enclose your card or message at no extra charge.

ILLUSTRATION: IAN KELLAS

Luath Press Limited
543/2 Castlehill
The Royal Mile
Edinburgh EH1 2ND
Scotland

Telephone: 0131 225 4326 (24 hours)
email: sales@luath.co.uk
Website: www.luath.co.uk